# ADVANCE PRAISE FOR *RED FLAGS*

"Is a radical, democratic, and emancipatory socialism possible in these grim times? Yes, says David Camfield. In *Red Flags*, he invites us to settle for nothing less than a liberated future beyond capitalism, oppression, and ecological disaster. This thoughtful and hopeful book is essential reading for everyone who wants to change the world."

— DAVID McNALLY, Cullen Distinguished Professor, University of Houston and author of *Blood and Money: War, Slavery, Finance and Empire*

"*Red Flags* is a much-needed reckoning with a fraught history. Camfield insists on assessing states that practised 'Actually Existing Socialism' not just from what advocates and detractors have said about them but by adopting a radical critique of authoritarian politics to understand the societies that lived under AES. The conflation of communism — a radically pro-democracy worldview — with AES continues to limit the anti-capitalist imagination today, as many self-declared leftists take it upon themselves to 'defend' AES societies from attacks from the right instead of critiquing authoritarian 'left' politics and moving beyond them once and for all."

— ELIA AYOUB, co-founder of *From The Periphery* and founder of *The Fire These Times* and Hauntologies.net

"Thank goodness someone had the clarity of mind to write this book. We are especially lucky that it was David Camfield, who combines his knowledge of world history with a fiery, unwavering commitment to working-class democracy. He is fair to proponents of 'Actually Existing Socialism' without blunting his argument that their politics have disastrously distorted the meaning of communism. This short, readable book answers urgent questions on the path to human emancipation."

— SAIMA DESAI, former editor of *Briarpatch Magazine*

"I grew up under a Stalinist regime in the West Bengal of the 1970s and '80s. I witnessed the courting of big business and the eviction of people from their land by the regime in the name of 'development.' We were encouraged to read Marx, but never encouraged to apply Marx to our reality. This dissonance between theory and practice also marked my observation of the regimes of the USSR and Eastern Europe. While capitalist states did not always justify their repression, so-called socialist states justified present repression in the name of a bright communist future. I found it difficult to hold on to a theory, Marxism, that could so easily accommodate repression. I only wish I had read *Red Flags* in my teens; it would have assured me not only of the emancipatory potential of Marxism but also its incompatibility with both capitalist state and market."

—TITHI BHATTACHARYA, associate professor, Purdue University and editor of *Social Reproduction Theory*

"*Red Flags* explains the attraction and influence of the ideas of the rulers of the former Eastern bloc and China, and why they are inadequate in the struggle for human liberation."

—IAN ALLINSON, author of *Workers Can Win: A Guide to Organising At Work*

# RED FLAGS

# RED FLAGS

A RECKONING WITH COMMUNISM
FOR THE FUTURE OF THE LEFT

## DAVID CAMFIELD

FERNWOOD PUBLISHING
HALIFAX & WINNIPEG

Copyright 2025 © David Camfield

All rights reserved. No part of this book may be reproduced or transmitted in any form by any means without permission in writing from the publisher, except by a reviewer, who may quote brief passages in a review.

Copyediting: Jenn Harris
Development editing: Tanya Andrusieczko
Cover design: Amanda Priebe
Text design: Brenda Conroy
Printed and bound in the UK

Published by Fernwood Publishing
Halifax and Winnipeg
2970 Oxford Street, Halifax, Nova Scotia, B3L 2W4
www.fernwoodpublishing.ca

Fernwood Publishing Company Limited gratefully acknowledges the financial support of the Government of Canada through the Canada Book Fund and the Canada Council for the Arts. We acknowledge the Province of Manitoba for support through the Manitoba Publishers Marketing Assistance Program and the Book Publishing Tax Credit. We acknowledge the Nova Scotia Department of Communities, Culture and Heritage for support through the Publishers Assistance Fund.

This book has been published with the help of a grant from the Federation for the Humanities and Social Sciences, through the Awards to Scholarly Publications Program, using funds provided by the Social Sciences and Humanities Research Council of Canada.

Library and Archives Canada Cataloguing in Publication
Title: Red flags : a reckoning with Communism for the future of the Left / David Camfield.
Names: Camfield, David, author
Description: Includes bibliographical references and index.
Identifiers: Canadiana 20240534654 | ISBN 9781773637327 (softcover)
Subjects: LCSH: Communism—History—20th century. | LCSH: Communism—Forecasting. | LCSH: Socialism—Forecasting.
Classification: LCC HX44 .C36 2025 | DDC 335.4309/04—dc23

# CONTENTS

Acknowledgements ................................................................................ x
A Note on Terminology and Format ................................................... xii
Some Acronyms and Abbreviations ................................................... xiii

1   Thinking about "Actually Existing Socialism" in a World on Fire ......... 1
    Anti-Communism ............................................................................ 2
    Questioning Anti-Communism ....................................................... 5
    The Approach of This Book ........................................................... 10

2   The Russian Revolution: From 1917 to the "Great Break" ................. 22
    From the Fall of the Empire to Working-Class Rule ...................... 22
    From Working-Class Rule to Bolshevik Leadership Rule .............. 25
    From Communist Leadership Rule to a New Ruling Class ........... 30

3   The USSR 1928–91 ............................................................................. 38
    How the Great Break Was Made .................................................... 38
    What Was Built ............................................................................... 40
    The Costs of Class Society ............................................................. 42
    The USSR and Global Struggles ..................................................... 45
    What Kind of Society? .................................................................... 49

4   China 1949–Present ............................................................................ 54
    The Path to AES and How AES Went to Market ........................... 54
    Achievements of AES in China ...................................................... 59
    The Costs of Class Society ............................................................. 61
    China and Global Struggles ........................................................... 67
    What Kind of Society? .................................................................... 69

5   Cuba 1959–Present ............................................................................. 73
    The Cuban Road to AES ................................................................. 73
    Achievements of AES in Cuba ....................................................... 78
    The Costs of Class Society ............................................................. 79
    Cuba and Global Struggles ............................................................ 81
    What Kind of Society? .................................................................... 82

| 6 | So, What Kind of Societies Were They? | 85 |
|---|---|---|
| | Objections and Responses | 86 |
| | *"That's Anti-Communist" or "Purity Fetishism"* | 86 |
| | *The Productive Forces Objection* | 89 |
| | *Distorted But Still in Transition* | 90 |
| | *The State Property Objection* | 91 |
| | *"At Least It Was Better Than Capitalism"* | 93 |
| | What Mode of Production? | 93 |
| | The Historical Significance of Stalinism | 97 |
| 7 | Why Does It Matter Today? | 99 |
| | Stalinism versus Human Emancipation | 99 |
| | Marxism-Leninism: A Ruling-Class Ideology | 101 |
| | Strategy for Revolution? | 104 |
| | Fighting for Reforms | 109 |
| | To the Left of the Marxist-Leninist Mainstream | 111 |
| | Campism and Credulity | 113 |
| | Democracy in Movements | 115 |
| 8 | An Alternative Tradition | 118 |
| | Swimming against Strong Currents | 118 |
| | Three Ancestors: Marx, Engels, Morris | 122 |
| | Luxemburg's Liberatory Politics | 123 |
| | Pro-Bolshevik Anti-Stalinists | 125 |
| | James, Dunayevskaya, and Castoriadis | 128 |
| | Anti-Bolshevik Anti-Stalinists | 129 |
| | Anarchist Communism | 130 |
| | Resources for a New Communism | 131 |
| 9 | What Can We Hope For? | 133 |
| | Current Conditions for Communists | 133 |
| | Is There Any Hope for Communism? | 135 |
| | From Possibility to Politics | 140 |
| **Further Reading** | | 144 |
| **Endnotes** | | 145 |
| **Index** | | 176 |

"Men fight and lose the battle, and the thing that they fought for comes about in spite of their defeat, and when it comes turns out not to be what they meant, and other men have to fight for what they meant under another name."

— William Morris, *A Dream of John Ball* (1886)

# ACKNOWLEDGEMENTS

I thank the following people for responding to questions or providing other assistance over the course of my work on this project, which ended up being quite different than what I first imagined: Gregor Benton, Ian Birchall, Sebastian Budgen, Steve D'Arcy, Andy Durgan, Sam Farber, Aleksei Gusev, Mike Haynes, John-Paul Himka, Ian Horst, Aaron Jaffe, Alex de Jong, Dovid Katz, Liz Kessler, Kole Kilibarda, Stathis Kouvelakis, Raghu Krishnan, Zachary Levenson, Olena Lyubchenko, Patrick McGuire, Owen Miller, Jeff Noonan, Charlie Post, Barnaby Raine, Alan Wald, Jeff Webber, Steve Wright, and others I am undoubtedly forgetting, for which I apologize (the starkly gendered slant of this list in part reflects the gendering of certain areas of specialized knowledge, to which I hope this book facilitates access, especially for people who are not cis men). Over gelato, Sean Carleton helped me come up with the title when I was stuck. Halle Rempel provided some initial research assistance. Olivia Mager helped with the formatting of notes. At the University of Manitoba Libraries, Cody Fullerton helped locate data. Stasia Meseman's skilful physiotherapy enables me to keep writing. Monique Woroniak's companionship and love during the writing of this book made a real difference.

Thanks to Charlie Post for reading a draft of the book, to Sam Farber and Kevin Lin for reading drafts of chapters on Cuba and China respectively, and to the two anonymous reviewers for the Scholarly Book Awards of the Federation for Humanities and Social Sciences. Ian Allinson not only endorsed the book but sent me some comments and corrections.

This book has been published with the help of a grant from the Federation for the Humanities and Social Sciences, through the Awards to Scholarly Publications Program, using funds provided by the Social Sciences and Humanities Research Council of Canada.

At Fernwood Publishing, Tanya Andrusieczko was an enthusiastic supporter of my project from the first time we discussed it. Her detailed and insightful comments on drafts have made this a much better book, as did the Fernwood editorial team's suggestion that the project expand to discuss what is now Chapter 8. Working with Art Bouman, Anumeha Gokhale, Lauren Jeanneau, and Beverley Rach at Fernwood has been a very positive experience. Thanks to Jenn Harris for expert copyediting. Thanks to Brenda Conroy for text design.

# A NOTE ON TERMINOLOGY AND FORMAT

In this book I use "communism" (with a lower-case *c*) to refer to a classless and stateless society of freedom in which people democratically organize production to meet their needs and flourish. I also use it to name politics whose ultimate goal is the creation of such a society.

I occasionally use "Communist," capitalized, to refer to societies ruled by parties that were officially committed to Marxism-Leninism. These parties often used "Communist" in their names. I usually refer to these societies in a generic way as so-called "actually existing socialist," abbreviated simply as AES. AES was originally a term used in many Marxist-Leninist states to officially characterize these societies. I use AES in a strictly neutral sense, without endorsing the implication that these societies were moving towards communism. Sometimes I use "Communist," capitalized, to refer to politics that seek to create societies structured along the lines first developed in the USSR from 1928 on. The relationship between Communism and communism is central to what this book is about.

Within quotations, letters, and words within square brackets are my own insertions or changes. All use of italics for emphasis within quotations is from the original.

# SOME ACRONYMS AND ABBREVIATIONS

| | |
|---|---|
| AES | "Actually Existing Socialism" |
| CCP | Chinese Communist Party |
| Comintern | Communist International |
| CP | Communist Party |
| CPGB | Communist Party of Great Britain |
| CPSU | Communist Party of the Soviet Union |
| CPUSA | Communist Party of the United States of America |
| ML | Marxist-Leninist |
| NCM | New Communist Movement |
| NKVD | People's Commissariat of Internal Affairs (internal security and secret police force in the USSR) |
| PRC | People's Republic of China |
| US | United States of America |
| USSR | Union of Soviet Socialist Republics |

#### CHAPTER 1

# THINKING ABOUT "ACTUALLY EXISTING SOCIALISM" IN A WORLD ON FIRE

**CAPITALISM HAS AN IMAGE PROBLEM.** In a 2022 poll, younger people in Australia, Canada, the United States, and the United Kingdom were less likely to endorse capitalism as an ideal economic system than people over thirty-four. The results worried the authors who reported on the polling for their very right-wing funder, the Fraser Institute; "tepid" is the word they chose to describe support for capitalism among people aged eighteen to thirty-four. Worse from their perspective was that "all four countries recorded at least 4 out of 10 respondents between 18 and 34 years of age indicating agreement or strong agreement that socialism is the ideal economic system for their country."[1] Similarly, in the US a large 2022 survey reported that 57 percent of people had a positive view of capitalism, down from 65 percent in 2019. Among people aged eighteen to twenty-nine, only 40 percent said they saw capitalism in that light.[2]

We should not put too much weight on surveys, but these and similar opinion polls register a growing popular understanding that the way society is organized today has many serious problems. Steadily rising rents and house prices; homelessness; the growing cost of food and other necessities; insecure employment; wages whose buying power is shrinking due to inflation; the loss or deteriorating quality of public services — all are making life harder for many people in even the richest countries. The effects of climate change are often palpable: spells of extremely hot weather, smoke from forest fires that drifts great distances and makes breathing difficult, droughts, floods, storms, and more. Yet in spite of what's happening and all the talk about climate change, little is actually being done in most places to reduce the greenhouse gas emissions that governments claim to be committed to be lowering. The same goes for action to address other aspects of the global ecological crisis, such as the loss of biodiversity (species extinction) and access to safe water and air.[3] Right-wing political forces, including fascist and other far-right tendencies, are gaining ground internationally.[4] The US and its allies are enabling Israel's genocidal violence in Palestine.[5] Growing tensions between the rulers of the countries of the US-led "West" and those of China and Russia raise fears of war. The term "polycrisis" has emerged as a way of naming the entangled and mutually reinforcing nature of today's crises.[6] These conditions corrode hope for a better future. Is it any wonder that more people are experiencing so much mental distress? Is it any surprise that enthusiasm for capitalism is fading?

## ANTI-COMMUNISM

Many of capitalism's champions no longer project the confident optimism that they displayed between the collapse of Communism in Eastern Europe and the USSR at the end of the 1980s and the Great Recession of 2007–09. Yet defenders of the current social order can still marshal an array of arguments to support the idea that, whatever its flaws, there is no alternative to it (other than perhaps the collapse of civilization). One way they defend capitalism is with anti-communism. Under this banner the US state and its allies and proxies went to great lengths during the second half of the last century to "eliminate leftists or accused leftists" in the Global South. The number of people they killed in campaigns of "intentional mass murder" numbered over one million. This figure "does not include deaths from regular war, collateral damage from military engagements, or unintentional deaths (starvation, disease) caused by anticommunist governments."[7] Under the banner of anti-communism, the US and other Western states also used repressive measures against leftists within their countries.[8] Anti-communism is the ideology expressed in a US congressional resolution passed in 2023 proclaiming that "Congress denounces socialism in all its forms, and opposes the implementation of socialist policies in the United States of America." This denunciation is backed by dubious assertions, including:

> socialist ideology necessitates a concentration of power that has time and time again collapsed into Communist regimes, totalitarian rule, and brutal dictatorships ... socialism has repeatedly led to famine and mass murders, and the killing of over

100,000,000 people worldwide ... many of the greatest crimes in history were committed by socialist ideologues, including Vladimir Lenin, Joseph Stalin, Mao Zedong, Fidel Castro, Pol Pot, Kim Jong Il, Kim Jong Un, Daniel Ortega, Hugo Chavez, and Nicolás Maduro.⁹

While the resolution left socialism undefined, it is clearly a licence to stigmatize even social reforms (I use the term reform to refer to changes within a social order, whether minor or major) like public health care, price controls, and public housing. The implication is that these are steps towards Communist tyranny because they "interfere" with markets. Even though China today is very different from China under Mao, anti-communism can also be harnessed to motivate support for the US, Canadian, and Australian governments in their increasingly aggressive rivalry with the state led by the Chinese Communist Party (CCP).

*The Black Book of Communism*, originally published in French at the close of the twentieth century, is the closest thing to a bible for contemporary anti-communists.¹⁰ This is the source of the unreliable figure of one hundred million dead found in the US congressional resolution. The book's central idea is that communism in all its forms shares an evil criminal essence that makes it the most murderous force in human history. There is supposedly a straight line from the Russian Revolution to mass murder under Joseph Stalin when he headed the Communist Party of the Soviet Union (CPSU). Contexts and social forces are irrelevant; what matters is communism's lethal ideas. Communism is deemed "criminal as both ideology and reality, and always identical in all times and in all places," as historian Enzo Traverso puts it in his critique of anti-communism after the collapse of the USSR and the other "actually existing socialist" societies of Eastern Europe. The interpretation found in *The Black Book of Communism* and similar sources is not in the least original: it recycles "the old McCarthyist theory of the communist conspiracy"¹¹ from the US in the 1950s. This is a way of understanding history with an unambiguous message for the present. Historian Douglas Greene sums this up nicely: communism is a "messianic and totalitarian democratic pseudo-religion" that wrongly "promises an earthly happiness." But trying to "create a paradise on earth" can only lead to extraordinary horrors. This "damns in advance any attempt to change the world."¹²

Anti-communism often lumps communism and fascism together as "totalitarianism." This kind of demonization of communism is reflected in the marking of August 23 as Black Ribbon Day and the idea that Communism and Nazism inflicted a "double genocide" on the nations of Eastern Europe. It has gone furthest in the several countries in Eastern Europe where it has been embedded in laws that prohibit the public display of communist symbols or the promotion of communist ideas. In the region, right-wing nationalists have succeeded in making communism

> the symbol of the evil of history and the ultimate perpetrator, commemorated and condemned alongside Nazism. The nation, characterised as the heroic protagonist in the narrative of historical struggles of the mythic forces of West and East, is now constructed as an East European community of victims, repressed by both totalitarian regimes, but mainly by communism.[13]

This kind of anti-communism devotes far more attention to people in Eastern Europe killed by Communists than to the many more people murdered by the Nazis. For example, in Budapest the House of Terror Museum has one room on the Holocaust and around twenty on Communism. Yet the 1941–45 war between the USSR and Nazi Germany began as the USSR's self-defence against a German invasion that was "a colonial war with no distinction between combatants and civilians, in which whole peoples were to be made into slaves, while others were exterminated," as Traverso notes.[14] The USSR did end up occupying Eastern Europe, its armies did commit atrocities, and the Communist states it established in Eastern Europe were repressive. But all this was fundamentally different from what the Nazis did.[15] Eastern European anti-communists also generally downplay how many people in their countries collaborated with Nazism.[16] Seeing communism as "history's worst evil," this kind of anti-communism opens the door to treating Nazism as preferable.[17] Even when anti-communists do not go so far as to apologize for fascism, institutionalizing anti-communism creates a hostile ideological environment for anyone who wants to encourage collective action to improve the lives of working-class and oppressed people. Their efforts can be smeared as alien agitation, hostile to the national community. This is not just a problem in countries with well-known anti-communist legislation, such as Poland and Indonesia; there are anti-communist laws still on the books today in parts of the US. Such laws are tools that right-wing politicians can use against anyone they label "communist."[18] Today, for people on the far right like Donald Trump who believe in the threat of a mythical "cultural Marxism," even liberal supporters of equal rights for queer and trans people can be so labelled.[19] Little wonder, then, that more people are pushing back against anti-communism.

## QUESTIONING ANTI-COMMUNISM

Anti-communism is an asset for capitalism's defenders. But it has not stopped the experience of living under capitalism from making growing numbers of people around the world, especially young people, increasingly critical of capitalism as a way of organizing society. Sometimes, and more often than was the case in the 1990s and at least the first decade of this century, anti-capitalist sentiment is also "anti-anti-communist." This involves both rejecting anti-communism and adopting an attitude that is at least somewhat sympathetic to the USSR and similar societies. It should not be difficult to understand why many people critical of capitalism think this way. After all, the capitalist status quo with which we are all too familiar is horrible. Its defenders demonize communism. Thus, sympathy for whatever capitalism's champions denounce can come easily, especially for people unfamiliar with the societies that anti-communists portray as evil.

Here I must pause to address the question of what to call societies organized along the lines first developed in the USSR (these societies are distinct from countries governed by parties that claim to be socialist in which private firms continue to control most economic activity, such as Venezuela, Bolivia, and Nicaragua[20]). There is no term for them that is universally accepted. Anti-communists often call them "Communist" (as have a few anti-capitalist radicals critical of them). However, this term has generally been rejected by their governments and supporters, who have maintained that these societies were not yet communist but only moving in the direction of communism as they understood it. They described this social order as "socialist," often using the term "actually existing socialism" for it. Many communists who are critical of these societies call them "Stalinist." Some anti-communists have used the same term. For now, this book will refer to them as so-called "actually existing socialism," abbreviated as AES. Here this is simply a generic neutral term for these societies, *used without accepting the claim that these societies were evolving towards communism or any other claim about them*. What they were and whether they were in transition to communism are crucial questions that this book addresses. How communism and transition to it should be understood will be explained in the third section of this chapter.

Importantly, anti-anti-communism is distinctly different from a perspective that opposes *both* capitalism and AES as ways of organizing society rooted in domination. It is the latter response that is expressed by a phrase from the radical left in the 1960s: "The 'Communist' world is not communist and the 'Free' world' is not free."[21] But where Trump and his liberal opponents put a minus sign, today's anti-anti-communists tend to put a plus. When the subject is Communism, anti-anti-communists generally combine sympathy with at least some criticism of the perceived shortcomings of Communist societies and movements. But sometimes contemporary anti-anti-communism flows into outright endorsement of some version of Communism, whether that of Stalin or Mao in the past or China and Cuba today.

Anti-anti-communism is not a new phenomenon. It was a feature of the culture of part of the New Left of the 1960s and 1970s. "We refuse to be anti-communist," declared Tom Hayden and Staughton Lynd, central organizers in the mid-1960s of the emerging movement against the US war in Vietnam.[22] Many people in North America and Western Europe who took part in the movements of that time started by adopting an anti-anti-communist stance and went on to become involved with what was often called the New Communist Movement (NCM), a sizeable current of the radical left that looked above all to China for inspiration.[23]

Today, long after the disintegration of the NCM and the end of the Cold War between the US-led "Free World" and the "Communist" states, anti-anti-communism has a somewhat different flavour, one that more often acknowledges problems in AES societies. Ethnographer Kristin Ghodsee and philosopher Scott Sehon present the situation this way:

> On the Left stand those with some sympathy for socialist ideals and the popular opinion of hundreds of millions of Russian and east European citizens nostalgic for their state socialist pasts. On the Right stand the committed anti-totalitarians, both east and west, insisting that all experiments with Marxism will always and inevitably end with the gulag. Where one side sees shades of grey, the other views the world in black and white.[24]

In other words, Ghodsee and Sehon see anti-anti-communism (their source for which is anthropologist Clifford Geertz, who rejected anti-communism in the Cold War US) as the alternative to a right-wing position. They do not acknowledge a third possibility: refusing both anti-communism and nostalgia for AES and being deeply critical of both capitalism and AES from a left-wing perspective that yearns for a better world. They are explicit about their criticisms of Communism: "this does not mean that we are apologising for, or excusing the atrocities or the lost lives of millions of men and women who suffered for their political beliefs."[25] After dissecting today's anti-communism, they conclude:

> Responsible and rational citizens need to be critical of simplistic historical narratives that rely on the pitchfork effect to demonise anyone on the Left. We should all embrace Geertz's idea of an anti-anti-communism in hopes that critical engagement with the lessons of the 20th century might help us to find a new path that navigates between, or rises above, the many crimes of both communism and capitalism.

In her 2018 book *Why Women Have Better Sex under Socialism*, which has been translated into over a dozen languages, Ghodsee argues that although "state socialism" ultimately failed, for much of the twentieth century it "presented an existential challenge to the worst excesses of the free market."[26] Its collapse led to the end of efforts to regulate markets and redistribute incomes. Moreover, these socialist experiments had many positive aspects. The state guaranteed citizens employment and housing. It provided public child care and implemented other measures to promote women's education and participation in paid work, including in jobs that had traditionally not been done by women. "There was a baby in all that bathwater. It's time we got around to saving it," Ghodsee concludes.[27] While those public services and rights undoubtedly existed, this way of evaluating them — "cherry pick[ing] from the Soviet policy pantheon," as theorist Sophie Lewis puts it[28] — treats them as if they can be considered apart from the oppressive features of AES with which they were entangled. This approach is similar to the one taken by people who argue that we should not be anti-capitalist because Western capitalist societies have positive aspects like civil liberties, multi-party elections, and unions through which workers can defend themselves against employers and fight to improve their pay and working conditions. As Lewis observes, Ghodsee never asks "the question of what an anti-capitalist, non-capitalist, post-capitalist society worthy of those names might actually look like."[29] A somewhat similar approach can be seen in *Free*, political theorist Lea Ypi's acclaimed memoir of life before and after the collapse of AES in Albania, which has been translated into over twenty languages. Ypi is unsparing about the failings of the society in which she grew up — and about how capitalism limits human freedom. At the same time, she sees Albania as having been a socialist society, emphatically rejecting the opinions of socialists who question that assumption.[30]

In recent years anti-anti-communism has become more common on the left than it was for several decades after the collapse of AES. Often this is a diffuse mood that surfaces in social industry posts.[31] But it also crops up in articles in widely read left-wing publications. For example, in 2022 journalist Liza Featherstone looked to the history of the East Bloc to criticize the US's failure to guarantee workers any paid vacation time. In an article on the *Jacobin* website, possibly the most-read English-language radical publication, Featherstone argued that Communism:

> took summer vacation seriously. Long before any other industrialized nations, the Soviet Union's Labour Code obligated employers to provide two weeks of paid vacation. The 1936 Soviet constitution specifically included a "right to rest." To that end, the Eastern Bloc communist countries not only provided the time off but invested in affordable vacation spots for workers. In the late 1930s, the government increased spending on resorts, health camps, campgrounds, and other vacation spots, including spas. Some of these offered activities, such as volleyball or mushroom hunting.[32]

Another article on the same site, about Bulgarian architecture, concludes that "socialist architecture's presence across the post-communist world reminds people that another world — however flawed — was once possible."[33] This kind of nostalgic response captures the spirit in which today's anti-anti-communism engages with AES. Similarly, in British socialist magazine *Tribune*'s interview with Sheila Fitzpatrick, "What Was the Soviet Union?," the historian describes "what happened to the promise of the revolution" as upward mobility for workers, "'affirmative action' on behalf of workers, but also on behalf of minorities, small nationalities, women, and so on," "not ... straightforward betrayal ... of the working class."[34] Writing in the socialist journal *Catalyst*, Ghodsee and Julia Mead argue that "state-socialist governments supported women's rights in ways that dramatically improved the material conditions of hundreds of millions of women's lives" in spite of "very real downsides" like "authoritarian regimes."[35] The anti-anti-communist stance is quite different from one that is ruthlessly critical of social domination and assesses both capitalism and AES from that perspective — the approach once expressed in the previously mentioned slogan "The 'Communist' world is not communist and the 'Free' world' is not free."

The soil of anti-anti-communism today is fertile ground for perspectives that are not just sympathetic to AES but enthusiastic about it. Writer Barnaby Raine observes that

> there is a new if modest proliferation of radicals now who would have baffled 1990s commentators; young people in Europe and North America who want to sound like the old Communists. On podcasts and on social media, in political parties and in unions, they salute authoritarian state power past and present. They speak, they say, in the name of socialism. They amass thousands of followers online. They are not the dwindling band of pensioners who remember subsidised cruises on the Volga. They don an aesthetic of kitsch cheek or unsentimental realism or, somehow, both.[36]

Critics on the left have dubbed them "tankies" (a term some anti-communists now also use indiscriminately to smear anyone who opposes Western imperialism) and "campists." Such a positive evaluation of AES is not restricted to some young radicals, though. We can see it, for instance, in an editorial against anti-communism by Salvatore Engel-De Mauro, at the time chief editor of the ecosocialist academic journal *Capitalism Nature Socialism*. This statement deplores the "blanket rejection of state socialism by many leftists" and praises the "historical achievements" of those societies as a basis "on which better socialist futures can be built, using critical understanding and historical insight to help pre-empt institutional degeneration, political repression, and general social harm."[37] Instead of demonstrating that AES societies were, in spite of their problems, qualitatively better than capitalism and not equally deserving of rejection, such an approach simply assumes that this is true. Political theorist Jodi Dean, one of the highest-profile writers in English associated with communist ideas today, writes in a similar vein.[38] In their *Half-Earth Socialism*, ecosocialists Troy Vettese and Drew Pendergrass insist that the lack of democracy in the USSR was a problem, since democracy was needed to make economic planning really work, but they do not question the country's socialist credentials. They also suggest that Cuba since the early 1990s is similar to the ecosocialism they advocate.[39]

Why does any of this matter today? There is a great deal at stake in how we respond to anti-communism and what we make of AES. If anti-communists are right, attempts to replace capitalism are misguided. If AES was, and in its remaining holdouts still is, a better way of organizing society, then anti-capitalists should look to such societies and the Communist political tradition associated with AES for instruction and inspiration. If AES is not such an alternative, anti-capitalists will need to look elsewhere.

## THE APPROACH OF THIS BOOK

What the AES societies were and are is a *very* different kind of question than, say, the question of what kind of society Spain was in 1492 when Christopher Columbus sailed across the Atlantic and claimed the lands he "discovered" for the Spanish Crown. Virtually no one in the twenty-first century wants to recreate late feudalism. But there are people who believe it would be good to replace capitalism with something that resembles AES at least in some ways. Some of today's communists heap AES with praise, even celebrating Stalin; others are more critical.[40] There are also communists who maintain that AES was not moving towards communism. How should we make sense of all this?

This book analyzes AES societies and Communist politics from the perspective I call reconstructed historical materialism, an unorthodox anti-racist feminist marxism[41] (I do not capitalize marxism to make the point that this is a living approach to understanding society in order to change it, one that was pioneered by Karl Marx and Friedrich Engels, brilliant imperfect thinkers in the nineteenth century, and has been developed by other people; it is not a system of thought given to us by revered Founding Fathers). This approach tries to develop what Marx and Engels called the "materialist conception of history" by bringing together their best ideas, the best ideas of later marxists, and insights arising out of contemporary struggles against oppression.

In brief, this book's perspective views human societies as produced by an animal species distinguished by how its members cooperate to transform the rest of nature in ways we consciously choose. In so doing, humans change ourselves and our culture. We have a metabolic relationship with the rest of nature, taking materials and energy from it as we remake our environments and change ourselves at the same time. This social metabolism changes depending on how the interconnected core features of human societies are organized. These are how people have babies, care for people of all ages, and produce goods and services. The social arrangements for carrying out these core activities vary and change across history and geography.

Since the appearance of gender oppression and class exploitation in history, societies have been made up of interwoven social relations such as class, gender, sexuality, and, much more recently, race. At the centre of every society is the labour done to carry out its core activities of having babies, providing care, and producing goods and services. A distinctive way of organizing people to produce is called a mode of production. A mode of production in which class division exists — feudalism and capitalism are two examples — is distinguished by the shape it gives to two overlapping phenomena. The first is productive forces: the technology, knowledge, and ways of cooperating that people use to produce goods and services. The other is relations of production. We can think of these as having two dimensions. There are "vertical" social relations between the people who actually produce goods and services, the direct producers (such as wage-workers), and the people (such as capitalist employers) who exploit their labour. There are also "horizontal" relations among members of both the exploiting and exploited classes. Exploitation involves the extraction of surplus labour from the direct producers. Surplus labour takes the form of work effort or products of labour beyond what goes into reproducing the direct producers. For example, exploiters can appropriate some of the goods that toilers produce, such as a share of what peasants grow. They can also extract sums of money, as when landlords make peasants pay rent for the land they farm. A third example, familiar to people who work for wages, is workers producing goods and services worth more than the compensation received for their labour.

To illustrate some of these ideas briefly, consider how the relationship between humans and the rest of nature was radically different in Indigenous societies in North America before European colonialism was imposed on them than it was in the societies built across the continent by the European settlers and their descendants who dispossessed Indigenous peoples. This is because most Indigenous societies were organized along the lines of modes of production we can call egalitarian-communal; there was no ruling class that enriched itself by systematically exploiting direct producers. In contrast, European colonialism at first bore the stamp of the feudal mode of production that still existed in Spain, England, and France. It then became structured by capitalism as that new mode of production became dominant in England. Feudal colonialism was mostly about plunder to enrich monarchs and nobles, exemplified by Spanish colonial authorities who used enslaved and otherwise coerced labour to extract silver and gold. British colonialism was different because Britain became capitalist. Capitalist competition is a distinguishing feature of this mode of production. Economic competition between capitalists is familiar. But there is also geopolitical competition between capitalist states. The competitive logic of capitalism drove British and US settler colonialism to relentlessly expand across the continent to acquire ever more land and resources, dispossessing Indigenous people all along the way. At first there were many settler farmers, fishers, and artisans who produced mostly for their own subsistence, along with traders. For a small number of colonists, the labour of a massive force of enslaved Africans generated great wealth. Over time, as capitalism transformed the US and the British colonies that became Canada, competing business owners producing goods to sell for profit, such as lumber, cotton, wheat, and tools, became increasingly important. Here we see another key feature of capitalism: most goods and services are commodities, produced for sale, not for the immediate use of the people who actually produce them. As part of the same process, a growing class of people came into existence who had no option but to sell their ability to work to employers in exchange for wages. This reflected another of capitalism's unique characteristics: human labour power becomes a commodity on a large scale. Capitalist competition forces employers to reorganize labour, raising productivity by making work more intense and introducing new technologies. This leads to the rapid growth of productive forces while harming direct producers and the rest of nature.[42]

Today capitalism structures our world more widely and deeply than ever. It has overwhelmed all pre-capitalist modes of production. Nevertheless, the reconstructed historical materialism I use in this book considers it *possible* — which, to be clear, does not mean likely, much less inevitable — and desirable for people to break with capitalism and at least start a transition to a kind of society that has not yet existed in history: a classless and stateless society of freedom in which people organize production to meet their needs and flourish — communism. This would be a society founded on the highly democratic cooperative control of society's wealth by the entire community. Productive forces themselves would be remade along with the new relations of production. The way society is organized would transcend both markets and state power, which both "express modes of social alienation in which human beings are unable to regulate and govern their economic and political affairs democratically, and in which institutions and mechanisms outside their control dominate and direct their life activities."[43] Philosopher Søren Mau puts it well:

> Communism doesn't imply a particular idea of the good life. Communism isn't a lifestyle or a fantasy about making every facet of an individual's life the object of political decision-making; it isn't a romantic community cult or a dream of communes and potlucks and DIY culture. Communism is the effort to establish institutions that can ensure the highest possible degree of individual freedom and democratic control over those aspects of human life that are, necessarily, shared by the members of a society. Communism is just as much for introverts and hermits as it is for enthusiastic collectivists ... The fundamental condition of communism is that the basic conditions of the life of society are brought under democratic control ... What is at stake here is thus a wide-ranging and comprehensive expansion of democracy.[44]

That such social arrangements were possible and worth fighting for was the basic idea of a new current of revolutionary and democratic politics that first emerged on the left wing of the working-class movement in the mid-nineteenth century. Marx has been this current's greatest theorist.[45] The final chapter of this book takes up the possibility of a future transition towards such a society.

No longer bound by capital's ceaseless drive to accumulate on an ever-larger scale and at an ever-faster speed, without any limits, such a society could prioritize action to address the ecological crisis and begin to repair the devastation wrought by capitalism on the rest of nature (making this a priority would not be automatic — the decision would have to be made democratically). It would transform how people live and care for one another. How this would look cannot be predicted, though past experiences in moments of revolutionary upheaval and breakthrough may provide some glimpses. The goal would be all-round human emancipation, the end of class exploitation, alienation, and all forms of oppression including those based on gender, sexuality, race, and disability.[46] Transition towards this kind of society would not automatically lead to liberation from all kinds of oppression. However, it would mightily destabilize them and facilitate efforts by oppressed groups to uproot the different forms of domination to which they are subjected.[47]

What we call such a society is *much* less important than clarity about what kind of society it would be. For Marx, as political economist Paresh Chattopadhyay argues, "socialism and communism are simply equivalent and alternative terms for the same society that he envisages for the post-capitalist epoch which he calls, in different texts, equivalently: communism, socialism, Republic of Labour, society of free and associated producers or simply Association, Cooperative Society, (re)union of free individuals."[48] It later became common among many of Marx's would-be followers to think of "socialism" as a stage of development before the ultimate goal of "communism" is achieved. The idea was that under socialism the state and "certain inequalities in property still exist," to quote Stalin, top leader of the CPSU in the 1930s when its leadership declared that the USSR had attained socialism.[49] This was how the terms *socialism* and *communism* were used in the AES societies. In the USSR, for example, under Stalin's successor, Nikita Khruschev, the CPSU program predicted that communism would be achieved by the early 1980s, a claim that was dropped early in the 1970s.[50] Nevertheless, philosopher Peter Hudis is correct to write that "the later notion that 'socialism' and 'communism' represent distinct stages of social development — a staple of Stalinist dogma — was alien to Marx's thought and only entered the lexicon of 'Marxism' after his death."[51] In this book, I will use *communism* to refer to the kind of society described in the previous two paragraphs, assuming that a society that had transcended class divisions and state power would be evolving, not static. I will call a society in transition to communism simply that, avoiding any use of "socialism." I recognize that there would have to be a process of transition between class society and communism but will not delve here into what Marx and other thinkers had to say about this and the merits of their views, which is less important than the analysis of what has happened in history.[52]

When looking at AES societies from this book's perspective that maintains that at the very least transition towards communism is possible and desirable, the most important question is whether they were in transition to communism or not. To put it differently: were social relations changing in ways that meant that the arrangements bred by capitalism and other forms of class society were starting to be replaced with new ones that had the potential to eventually flower in the withering away of class division, markets, and state power? Was there "direct control by the people of the whole administration of the community"?[53] Was there what in the early twentieth century was called "industrial democracy"?[54] In other words, were freely associating producers at least starting to implement democratic economic planning to replace the regulation of production by markets and other forces? This is the essential criterion for assessing whether transition to communism is taking place. Both political and economic democracy would be necessary features of evolution in the direction of communism because of precisely what communism would be. There would have to be democratic decision making about what goods and services would be produced and how work was organized as well as about all other concerns of the community. This far-reaching practice of participatory democracy would necessarily take place through new, profoundly democratic institutions created by the direct producers themselves — "not rule *for* the masses but *by* them."[55] These and other new public institutions under democratic control, including armed forces to defend the new society against external attacks and any counter-revolutionary attempt to overthrow it from within, would replace the states through which capitalists rule. The nature of the process would determine what would actually be accomplished. No one has expressed this more clearly than Rosa Luxemburg, who, using "socialism" here as equivalent to "communism" in the sense in which I am using it, wrote shortly before her murder that

> the establishment of the socialist order of society ... requires a complete transformation of the state and a complete overthrow of the economic and social foundations of society. This transformation and this overthrow cannot be decreed by any bureau, committee, or parliament. It can be begun and carried out only by the masses of people themselves. In all previous revolutions a small minority of the people led the revolutionary struggle, gave it aim and direction, and used the mass only as an instrument to carry its interests, the interests of the minority, through to victory. The socialist revolution is the first which is in the interests of the great majority and can be brought to victory only by the great majority of the working people themselves. The mass of the proletariat must do more than stake out clearly the aims and direction of the revolution. It must also personally, by its own activity, bring socialism step by step into life. The essence of socialist society consists in the fact that the great labouring mass ceases to be a dominated mass, but rather, makes the entire political and economic life its own life and gives that life a conscious, free, and autonomous direction.[56]

All this needs to be at the front of our minds when we analyze social relations in AES societies, centred on the mode of production and the form of state power. We cannot rely on what top leaders in these societies said or wrote about what was happening; that would not be a historical materialist approach. It is worth remembering that when it came to the study of history, Marx poured scorn on relying on what people said about what they were doing:

> Just as in private life one distinguishes between what a man [sic] thinks and says, and what he really is and does, so one must all the more in historical conflicts make the distinction between the fine words and aspirations of the parties from their real organisation and their real interests, their image from their reality.[57]

It is social reality, not what has been said about it, that we need to analyze.

Thus the perspective of this book is a communist one. It is also one with "a scientific conscientiousness, which for its sympathies and antipathies — open and undisguised — seeks support in an honest study of the facts, a determination of their real connections, an exposure of the causal laws of their movement."[58] This perspective does not mean that it is uncritical of AES — far from it. Here it is necessary to anticipate an objection from some on the left: that this way of evaluating AES is anti-communist. Writer Michael Parenti labels all criticism of AES by people who consider themselves on the left (except mild criticism by supporters of AES like himself) as "left anticommunism." This is a classic amalgam. It lumps together quite different ways of criticizing AES, including the criticism of social democrats who truly are anti-communist along with the arguments of anti-capitalists who criticize AES for not being in transition to communism, and daubs them all with the brush of anti-communism, associating them with McCarthyism. Parenti assumes precisely what he needs to demonstrate, namely that AES societies were moving towards communism. He writes dismissively that "whether we call ... [them] 'socialist' is a matter of definition. Suffice it to say, they constituted something different from what existed in the profit-driven capitalist world."[59] How they were different and how this was significant from the perspective of transition towards communism goes unexplained. Parenti responds to the argument that AES was not in transition to communism by labelling it a "'pure socialism' view [that] is ahistorical and nonfalsifiable; it cannot be tested against the actualities of history."[60] Again, this is intellectual sleight of hand: it just assumes that AES societies must have been developing towards communism. Missing is any attempt to develop a case based on the evidence of "the actualities of history" that demonstrates that they were. Parenti's kind of objection is shallow and evasive. It is a weak attempt to deflect historical materialist evaluation of AES by repeating assumptions instead of offering serious arguments.

A question raised by this book's project of understanding and evaluating AES is how do we know what we know about these societies? What sources can we trust? There are good reasons for skepticism, but also bad ones. The most common ways these societies are depicted today — the ones usually encountered in schooling, in the mainstream media, and so on — are influenced by anti-communism of the kind that runs through *The Black Book of Communism*. Portraying Communist societies as ruled by evil totalitarian forces solely "responsible for 100 million deaths, making it [communism] the most lethal force in all of human history"[61] is profoundly wrong. In academia, it amounts to a case for the anti-communist prosecution masquerading as scholarship. As Greene argues, it distorts the historical record to attribute every possible death to communism to reach the magic figure of 100 million. This gives *The Black Book* [and similar depictions] the impression of atrocity porn with inflated body counts and massacres without any regard to context. Whether the Soviet Union was at war or peace are [sic] not taken into account ... Courtois [the book's chief editor] makes no distinction between intentional killings and those who died from neglect or other causes.[62]

Less outrageous anti-communist presentations of AES societies past and present often contain plenty of inaccuracies and rely on dubious ways of explaining how AES functions. The main explanation is usually totalitarianism. This boils down to the idea of an all-powerful state run by a single party controlling all aspects of society and using terror to rule the population. As Greene notes, this "cannot explain the internal dynamics of the Soviet Union since it posits a completely static society ruled by unchallenged terror."[63] Changes within AES societies and the collapse of AES in most of the countries in which it had been established demonstrate the flimsiness of theories of totalitarianism.

That said, the inaccuracies and faulty interpretations found in so many depictions of AES do not justify the more or less uncritical attitude to these societies taken by some of their supporters (some of whom self-identify as Marxist-Leninists [MLs]). The flimsiness of anti-communist accounts does not justify naïve or dishonest portrayals of AES that ignore or dismiss well-established evidence. For example, the archives of the People's Commissariat of Internal Affairs (generally known by its Russian initials, NKVD) reveal that in 1937–38 its forces executed 681,692 people. Using these and other records that became available after the collapse of the USSR, historians J. Arch Getty and Oleg V. Naumov estimate that in the 1930s close to 1.5 million people were executed or died in the prisons, forced labour camps (Gulag camps), labour colonies, and special settlements that made up the vast carceral system of the country at the time. This does not include the deaths of peasants forced into internal exile in the early 1930s and those who died in the famine of 1932–33.[64] Such reliable research allows us to understand Parenti's regretful admission that Stalin executed "hundreds of Old Bolshevik leaders"[65] (true, but the NKVD executed *hundreds of thousands* of people in 1937–38 alone) as the minimization of repression that it is.[66] We would do well to remember historian E.H. Carr's argument that a historian "must seek to bring into the picture all known or knowable facts relevant, in one sense or another, to the theme on which he [sic] is engaged and to the interpretation proposed."[67]

There are many problems with both anti-communist and apologetic accounts of AES. But it is still possible to come to reliable understandings of what these societies were like and what the remaining few are like today. This task requires, first, careful attention to the sources used by historians and other researchers and how they use them. We also need to pay close attention to how they understand what it is that they are studying. Anyone thinking about a society, past or present, has ideas about what kind of society it is, how it works, and how change happens. These ideas are usually unconscious and contradictory. Sometimes they are consciously thought through in a systematic way (as I have sketched out this book's approach in the previous pages). We all have some kind of social theory in our heads whether we realize it or not.[68] These ideas inevitably affect how we make sense of society, how we explain events and the ways in which societies stay the same or change over time. To use the example of NKVD executions in 1937–38, approximately how many people were killed is no longer disputed. What remains a matter of debate are the causes and significance of these mass executions. Do they reveal the essence of communism (as many anti-communists say)? Were they a terrible error made by Stalin while he led the USSR along the road towards communism (as Stalin's successors said)? Were they an orgy of violence by reactionary rulers who blocked further progress towards that goal or who were a new exploiting class (as anti-Stalinist communists argue)?

Unfortunately, different ways of understanding facts like the mass executions of the Great Purge are not all that can make it challenging to make sense of AES. We are now living in societies in which facts and truth are often in doubt. There is now, as writer Richard Seymour argues, "a *radical scepticism about reality*." This is connected to "the fact that so much of social reality is now composed of mass-produced digital images, to the point where the edges separating real from unreal begin to dissolve."[69] Yet the "corrosion of trust" is not just about this dimension of everyday life. For years corporations have "been engaged in the mass industrial production of scientific doubt, whether it is about the effects of tobacco or the effects of carbon emissions." Media corporations are driven to circulate inaccurate reports. At root, the acid eating away at trust in facts and truth is being produced by what capitalism is doing to ties between people, the ties that allow us to trust each other. Since "knowledge *depends* on trust, not scepticism,"[70] the decline of trust has dire consequences for understanding society. As writer Naomi Klein puts it, "suspicion directed at the wrong target is a very dangerous thing."[71] More people become open to believing conspiracy theories and accepting far right lies. This social environment also makes more people open to the view that all or almost all of what we hear about the negative features of AES is false, nothing more than anti-communist lies and distortions. Anyone encountering debates about AES should bear this in mind.

The USSR was the first society in which the government declared that socialism had been built as a step toward communism. It was there that the distinctive model of organizing society that came to be known as AES came into existence at the end of the 1920s with what was called the "Great Break." For that reason the next chapter looks at the Russian Revolution of 1917 and what happened to it over the years that followed. The third chapter looks at the USSR from 1928 until its collapse in 1991. The next chapters examine two other AES societies, the People's Republic of China (PRC) and Cuba. We need to consider China because in the 1960s and 1970s it was seen by many people around the world as a progressive socialist alternative to the USSR, while in recent years more people who oppose US imperialism have become sympathetic to China. Cuba will be discussed because it is the only AES society in the Americas and one whose government has enjoyed wide support on the global left, including among some anti-Stalinist marxists who have viewed Cuban society as not burdened by the kind of conservative bureaucracy that ruled the USSR and the PRC. This is followed by a look at objections to my analysis of AES and a deeper examination of what kind of society AES is. The next chapter discusses why AES and the ML political tradition linked to it matter today, in a world of worsening ecological and social crises caused by capitalism. Then follows an introduction to the tradition of communist politics that is deeply critical of AES. The book concludes by asking "What can we hope for?" and whether transition towards communism is possible.

Before proceeding to look at the origins of AES I will repeat what should already be obvious to good-faith readers: none of the criticism of AES or its supporters in what follows should in any way be construed as justification of capitalism or as lending support to anti-communism. The perspective of reconstructed historical materialist critique yearning for human emancipation that I bring to bear on AES is, as the final chapter will make plain, one that needs to be applied universally in the world today.

# CHAPTER 2

# THE RUSSIAN REVOLUTION: FROM 1917 TO THE "GREAT BREAK"

## FROM THE FALL OF THE EMPIRE TO WORKING-CLASS RULE

**BEFORE ITS DOWNFALL IN 1917,** the Russian Empire encompassed a vast territory across Eurasia.[1] Its dominant class of landlords and capitalists was headed by the monarchy of the Tsar. It ruled over a society in which capitalist zones coexisted with vast rural areas of pre-capitalist agriculture. In 1914, over 82 percent of the population lived in rural areas. Most of the Tsar's subjects were peasants. The working class, made up of urban and rural wage-workers and their dependents, was a minority, 15 to 20 percent of the population.[2] Economic development in the society run by the Tsarist state lagged far behind what existed in the advanced capitalist societies of Western Europe. However, the state had enabled "partial advances in specific areas." It was "driven by military competition to introduce limited industrialization and partial agrarian reform."[3] The state was able to foster pockets of advanced capitalist industry and an urban working class. Capitalist development generated fierce antagonism between capital and labour. This conflict was intensified by the weakness of democratic rights under the repressive monarchy. It also fed into and was in turn fed by the antagonism between peasants and landlords, and by the resistance to Russian domination of other nations in the multinational Tsarist empire. This situation was potentially explosive, and World War I acted as a detonator. The war led to food shortages, the requisitioning of farm animals for the army, inflation that bit deeply into the buying power of peasant incomes and workers' wages, and widespread disaffection among soldiers and sailors.[4]

The result was a social revolution unlike any other in world history. It began in February 1917 when workers and soldiers demanding peace and an end to hunger and exploitation rose up and toppled the monarchy. The unstable Provisional Government was formed, made up of liberals along with members of the Socialist Revolutionaries (SRs, a party that drew most of its support from peasants and was divided between a radical left wing and a moderate right wing) and members of the moderate socialist party known as the Mensheviks. Workers and, to a lesser extent, peasants organized themselves in extraordinary ways. Hundreds of highly democratic soviets (councils) of workers, soldiers, sailors, and peasants were created. These were made up of delegates elected by workers from their workplaces, members of the military from their units, and peasants from their villages. Delegates were accountable to their electors and recallable at any time.[5] Having toppled the Tsar, workers then "determined to overthrow 'autocracy' on the shop floor."[6] They started to form factory committees, unions, militias, and other organizations. This created a situation of dual power: institutions of highly democratic working-class power inside and outside the workplace existed uneasily alongside the unelected Provisional Government and the power of capitalists. In rural areas, peasants also took matters into their own hands. Starting with challenges to landlord authority, peasants then started to seize and redistribute land. The oppression of women and subjugated nations was also rattled by the oppressed organizing themselves against injustice.[7]

As the year went on, society went deeper into crisis and the Provisional Government, which had no intention of attacking the class power of landlords and capitalists, failed to deliver the major changes demanded by workers and peasants: an end to Russia's involvement in the war, access to adequate food, land rights for peasants, and democracy. This led to intense political debate and accelerating radicalization; more and more people came to the conclusion that overthrowing the monarchy had not been nearly enough and the revolution needed to go further, as the writer China Mieville chronicles brilliantly in his history of the Russian Revolution, *October*.[8] Many soldiers refused to keep fighting and engaged in mass "desertion as a social movement."[9] Historian Steve Smith explains the role that the revolutionary socialist party known as the Bolsheviks — whose goal was the replacement of the Provisional Government with the rule of the working class through its new democratic institutions in alliance with the peasantry and whose foremost leaders in 1917 were Vladimir Lenin and Leon Trotsky — played in the process:

the Bolsheviks themselves did not create popular discontent or revolutionary feeling. This grew out of the masses' own experience of complex economic and social upheavals and political events. The contribution of the Bolsheviks was rather to shape workers' understanding of the social dynamics of the revolution and to foster an awareness of how the urgent problems of daily life related to the broader social and political order. The Bolsheviks won support because their analysis and proposed solutions seemed to make sense.[10]

Smith quotes a worker from a factory in Petrograd where workers had previously been extremely hostile to the Bolsheviks: "'the Bolsheviks have always said: "It is not we who will persuade you, but life itself." And now the Bolsheviks have triumphed because life has proved their tactics right.'"[11] Workers and peasants turned away from the Provisional Government. They increasingly placed their faith in the soviets and other democratic organizations they themselves had created. For their part, landlords and capitalists also gave up on the Provisional Government and sought a military dictatorship that would crush the revolution. Having lost most of its support, the Provisional Government "had expired even before the Bolsheviks finished it off"[12] with an insurrection in October 1917 that put the soviets in power.

The power of the old ruling class was shattered in much of the former empire. In its place, the highly self-organized working class became the dominant class; its democratic institutions were in control of most important social decisions. Workers and peasants, including those serving as soldiers and sailors, were transformed by the experience of overthrowing the monarchy, challenging the domination of their lives by bosses, officers, and landlords, and then taking charge of society through democratic institutions of their own creation. The revolution did not just topple the Provisional Government. The combination of soviet government and dual power in workplaces, which in a minority of cases saw workers' self-management replacing employers' control altogether, challenged the power of capital itself.[13] This made the unfolding revolution a socialist revolution. It had replaced the rule of the exploiting class with working-class rule, opening the door to a transition towards communism. This outcome was the product of a "drawing together and mutual penetration of two factors ... a peasant war ... and a proletarian insurrection."[14]

## FROM WORKING-CLASS RULE
## TO BOLSHEVIK LEADERSHIP RULE

In the months following that insurrection, soviet power spread across more of the territory once ruled by the Tsar.[15] "No political body more sensitive and responsive to the popular will was ever invented," wrote US socialist eyewitness John Reed.[16] Workers and, to a lesser extent, peasants were engaged in a historically unprecedented experience of multiparty democratic self-government through a new structure of central, regional, and local soviets. The establishment of working-class rule allowed the working class to begin to reorganize society in the direction of communism. But this was not the same as actually reconstructing society in this way. The material conditions in society — above all a low level of development of productive forces and the predominance of the peasantry — meant that there was very little potential for beginning a transition to communism, as the Bolshevik leadership took for granted at the time. One of the prerequisites for progress in such a transition is enough common wealth that people can meet their needs, including the need for free time in which to flourish, which requires shorter hours of work.[17] Another is the objective social interconnectedness of producers' labour within and between workplaces that makes possible cooperative production to meet human needs. But this was a society of very limited industrialization and deep poverty. Most people were peasants, who as a class were hostile to exploitation but had "little or no interest in socialism, and little or no interest in the collective organization of production and distribution beyond the confines of the village."[18] The Bolsheviks staked their hopes on victorious revolutions in more advanced European societies coming to their rescue with resources that would help the working class in power in Russia slowly take steps towards communism.

The Soviet Congress held in Petrograd immediately after the overthrow of the Provisional Government created a Council of People's Commissars (CPC) as a central government. Initially all-Bolshevik, it was soon joined by members of the Left Socialist Revolutionary Party (Left SRs — the left and right wings of the SRs had split into separate parties). The CPC was to be accountable to the congress's Central Executive Committee (CEC), in which the Bolsheviks had a majority.[19] The Soviet Congress met four times in 1918, as intended, with the last meeting of that year in November. Its CEC met every four or five days until mid-1918.[20] But then "it did not hold a single meeting between July 14th, 1918, and February 1st, 1920 — though decrees continued to be issued in its name."[21]

As historian Marcel Liebman notes, "by the second half of 1918 the soviets had lost their drive and their animation ... their life was due much more to the activity of their executive organs than to that of their deliberative bodies, which had become lethargic."[22] The main reason was that food shortages, job losses, and the outbreak of civil war between "Red" revolutionary and "White" counter-revolutionary forces, along with troops from Britain, France, Japan, the US, Canada, and other countries, had begun to disrupt urban society severely. Moscow's population fell from two million in May 1917 to 1.7 million in April 1918. Petrograd's dropped from at least 2.3 million at the start of 1917 to below 1.5 million in June 1918. In the latter city, nearly half of the manufacturing workforce was laid off in the first three months of 1918.[23] Smith describes the desperate conditions that soon prevailed in Red urban areas: "life was reduced to a constant search for food, fuel, shelter, and warm clothes, and to trying to avoid disease and crime ... In spring and summer 1918 and again in summer 1919 many cities came close to starvation ... every ounce of energy was drained by the exigencies of survival ... Against a background of perishing cold, poor diet, unsanitary conditions, and health facilities at breaking point, epidemic disease erupted on a devastating scale."[24] During the Civil War, the Bolshevik leadership essentially ended multi-party soviet democracy. In June 1918 the Bolshevik majority on the CEC voted to bar members of the Right SR Party, much of which backed the Whites, and the Menshevik Party, which was divided in its stance to soviet power. The CEC directed other soviet bodies to follow its example. In July 1918 the German ambassador was assassinated on the orders of the Left SR Central Committee. Bolshevik leaders then barred Left SRs from serving as soviet delegates unless they rejected their leadership's actions.[25] The Bolshevik removal of almost all members of other parties from soviet office was a feature of the wartime "*militarization* of the whole of public life" that "suppressed the soviets as really functioning bodies."[26] However, there was still vibrant democratic debate within the ranks of the Bolshevik Party.

In 1917 many urban workers had created "an astonishing combination of direct and representational democracy"[27] in their workplaces. Workers' power exercised through factory committees usually coexisted with the old management in a situation of workplace dual power. Not surprisingly, this did not sit well with employers already horrified by soviet power. This led to a sharpening of class struggle and a wave of workplace takeovers by workers intent on pushing their government to expropriate private employers who wanted to close enterprises. Their actions led the revolutionary government to carry out sweeping nationalizations. Most nationalized enterprises were run by collegial management boards, with one-third of the members appointed by workers, one-third by union officials, and the remaining third by regional bodies of the state's Council of National Economy. A small minority were under "one-man management," which became more common in 1919–20.[28]

Between the end of October 1917 and late 1918 what existed in the urban territory of the revolutionary regime was the rule of the working class, although this was incomplete because, as just mentioned, in most workplaces workers had influence but were not running their workplaces under democratic self-management. The armed forces loyal to soviet power were initially structured democratically, with troops electing their officers until March 1918.[29] Important social reforms of a kind never seen anywhere in the world were implemented. A new Code on Marriage, the Family and Guardianship included full legal gender equality and easy access to divorce; its drafters saw these moves "as but a first step toward the eventual withering away of the family and the law."[30] Same-gender sexual activity was decriminalized, as was abortion. The right to self-determination of all the peoples within Russian territory, including the right to secede, was proclaimed.[31] The control of society by the working class itself was an extraordinary achievement in spite of its incompleteness. To use the phrase Marx applied to the Paris Commune, "the great social measure" of working-class rule in Russia "was its own working existence."[32] However, the material conditions in which workers ruled meant that further steps towards communism could not be taken.

As soviet democracy was suspended, working-class rule metamorphosed into something qualitatively different. The leadership of what from 1918 was officially named the All-Russian Communist Party (Bolsheviks) — a party that was very much part of the working class — began to rise above the class in whose name it claimed to rule. Civil war and social breakdown forced the leadership to build a state under its control to defend the revolution. It began to use this fragile improvised state to control the "social body" of workers and peasants as an "authority usurping pre-eminence over society itself," to use words written by Marx in a very different context.[33] Its aim was to defend the "Beleaguered Fortress"[34] of soviet power against the domestic and foreign military forces pitted against it while doing whatever it could to promote revolutions abroad that could come to the relief of the isolated revolution in Russia.

The state that began to take shape under the pressures of civil war was a "command-administrative system" that "functioned more like a loose set of rival and overlapping jurisdictions than a centralised bureaucratic hierarchy,"[35] although power was increasingly wielded by higher-level party officials. It became "a sprawling and ramshackle edifice, the product of no architect's design." In spite of extensive economic nationalization, "there was virtually no meaningful planning of production."[36] The working class did not rule through this state: "The power that the workers had seized in October 1917 fell completely from their hands in the course of the ensuing civil war … The state retained, to be sure, certain important links with the working class but it stood above it and beyond its control."[37] Yet neither was there a new exploiting class ruling through this state.

The new state controlled the output of the workers who toiled in state-owned workplaces. By the time soviet democracy ceased to function, the great majority of wage earners in Soviet Russia were producing for enterprises owned by a state that they did not control. But state authorities had only weak control of workers' labour on the job.[38] In order to feed the urban population and the military, the state was forced to seize grain from peasants with little or no compensation, backed up with the threat of jail sentences for people who did not comply with the order to hand over all their grain above the amount they were allowed to retain for their own subsistence.[39] In short, during the Civil War, the state relied mainly on force to appropriate the products of peasant labour. It relied on workers' dependence on wages, along with political exhortation and coercion, for the appropriation of their surplus labour. But there was no cohesive social layer in command of state power, and control over society by central state institutions existed more on paper than in reality. There was still a degree of democracy as well as freedom of discussion within the Communist Party (CP), whose leadership headed the state.[40] Thus, what replaced working-class rule can be called a surplus-extracting state of proletarian origin. This was a historically unique phenomenon. It was the product of an unstable situation in which social supremacy had passed from the working class to the leadership of one segment of that class, a social layer whose power over society was not highly developed.

The most important reason for the end of working-class rule was the catastrophic disruption of urban life caused by the outbreak of civil war described earlier. Another contributing factor for soviet democracy ceasing to function was the departure of so many of the most politically active workers to military or state service, away from urban life.[41]

The impact of these catastrophic social conditions was overwhelming. However, the actions of Bolshevik leaders also contributed to the loss of working-class rule. Contrary to widespread belief, there was never a Bolshevik plan for one-party rule. Historian Alexander Rabinowitch's detailed study of Petrograd in the year after October 1917 reveals "the lack of any special concern on the part of most veteran Bolsheviks with the institutionalisation of an authoritative and exclusive directing role for party organs in government." Rabinowitch emphasizes something too often missed by studies of 1917 and its aftermath: the Bolsheviks "had to transform themselves from rebels into rulers without benefit of an advance plan or even a concept." The most powerful influences shaping the early years of soviet power and Bolshevik government "were the realities the Bolsheviks faced in their often seemingly hopeless struggle for survival."[42]

How Bolshevik leaders handled the situation was, however, shaped by their theory. A crucially important fact almost never considered seriously in interpretations of what happened after 1917 is that the Bolsheviks had long believed that the coming revolution would be one in which their task would be "the overthrow of the Tsarist autocracy and its replacement by a democratic republic."[43] It would be a bourgeois revolution made by the working class and peasantry. Such a revolution would destroy feudalism, establish a capitalist democratic republic, and open the road to the unimpeded development of capitalism in Russia and a future socialist revolution.[44] This outlook changed only at the Bolshevik party conference of April 1917.[45] The Bolsheviks had never thought that they would find themselves leading a socialist revolution and then governing a regime that was attempting to move towards communism in a society that had not already experienced a bourgeois revolution and a period of capitalist development. Consequently, as Rabinowitch notes, they had not "even a concept" of what to do next.

What they did have was a version of marxism in which the idea of a "workers' state," which is how the Bolsheviks perceived their state, was not understood as by definition workers themselves controlling society through their own new democratic institutions of class rule, which was how Marx, Engels, and Luxemburg had understood it.[46] For Lenin, "the party was the final repository of working-class sovereignty."[47] Most Bolsheviks believed sincerely that the working class was in power because their party was running the state.[48] Their theory also failed to recognize the importance of workplace self-management for working-class rule.[49] That said, "an elementary sense of proportion and perspective demands that we distinguish between Lenin's flawed conception of democracy, which he by and large upheld at least until the Spring of 1918, and the clearly anti-democratic perspective that, with his associates, he began to adopt shortly before and especially during the course of the Civil War."[50] The latter outlook is best understood this way: "under the intolerable pressures of isolation in the Beleaguered Fortress, principles" — for example, majority rule, political rights for all parties that accepted soviet power, and press freedom — "were first distorted by the strain of emergency exceptions, and *then the distortions themselves became the principles*."[51] But we must not lose sight of the fact that the main reason working-class rule came to an end in 1918 was the catastrophic social conditions. That is why in places where Left SRs and anarchists rather than Bolsheviks "consolidated their political hegemony in the period of the first Soviet government, they were no less inclined towards party dictatorship than the Bolsheviks were on a Russian-wide scale."[52] It was also dire social conditions that mainly determined the unexpected course of events between the end of the Civil War and the late 1920s, when AES was born.

## FROM COMMUNIST LEADERSHIP RULE TO A NEW RULING CLASS

To the surprise of the Communist leadership, the Reds won the Civil War only to find themselves still in command of the Beleaguered Fortress; although parts of Europe had been rocked by revolution, nowhere else had workers taken and held power more than briefly. In these unforeseen circumstances, the priorities of most members of the ruling layer shifted. Isolated in a devastated country in which forces of production were much less developed than in most of Europe, they soon came to stake their survival on industrialization, not rescue by revolution abroad, the prospects for which seemed remote. The leadership began to think in terms of using "the financial and commodity assets of the country to industrialize and modernize its economy within a [world] market framework."[53] This would be done slowly, within the framework of the New Economic Policy (NEP) adopted after the end of the Civil War. The dominant group in the party leadership around Stalin ideologically justified this with the previously heretical notion of "socialism in one country" — the idea that a society well on the way to communism could be constructed in the isolated and backward USSR. As E.H. Carr put it, "industrialization was the economic corollary of socialism in one country."[54]

Under the NEP, individual workers enjoyed strong job security rights, protection against discipline, and the ability to file grievances over wages and working conditions. They also had some control over how they worked.[55] But this did not give workers any control over the surplus extracted from them. Throughout the NEP years, the labour of the working class was alienated to a substantial degree. Since workers were unable to democratically shape the goals, pace, and methods of industrialization, the social layer at the helm of the state was bound to use the surplus labour it extracted from them for economic purposes that were hostile to the interests of the working class.

The decision to move forward with industrialization was adopted at the party's fourteenth congress in 1925.[56] In 1927 fear of war and a grain procurement crisis spurred the directing elements of the party-state elite to move more quickly: "Industrialization and fast economic growth came to be seen as the only means to persuade the British and the French that a decision for war with the Soviet Union would be a costly one."[57] The shortfall in peasants' sales of grain to the state was, in the context of the threat of war, "viewed as a threat to national security, posing risks to industrialization and defence capacity as well as to internal social stability."[58]

This led to the "Great Break." In 1928 the state began to implement its first five-year plan, setting in motion "the first example in history of a government seeking to transform an entire economy and society through planned action by the state." This was "accompanied by a political rhetoric replete with military metaphors … and with calls to workers to show heroism and revolutionary optimism."[59] The start of an all-out drive to industrialize was soon followed by "extraordinary measures" of coercion to get grain from the peasantry. Authorities started to use criminal law against peasants, with punishments including fines, forced labour, imprisonment, and the confiscation of property. "With these practices, repression ... replaced the market in the economic relations of town and countryside."[60] The party-state soon went further and began to force peasants off their land and into state-supervised collective farms. This amounted to nothing less than the dispossession of the peasantry. Together, the unforeseen combination of crash industrialization and so-called collectivization "became parts of a concerted attack"[61] on the direct producers. The assault on peasants became intense because the state needed not only to feed the non-agricultural population but also to export grain to fund the industrialization drive — even as global grain prices fell.[62] It was this "collectivization" and industrialization that produced the distinctive new way of organizing society that came to be known as AES.

The process leading to this outcome should be understood as the Communist ruling layer becoming a new exploiting class. To understand this process, we should start by clarifying that a social class is "a group of persons in a community identified by their position in the whole system of social production, defined above all according to their relationship (primarily in terms of the degree of ownership or control) to the conditions of production (that is to say, the means and labour of production) and to other classes,"[63] to use the words of historian G.E.M. de Ste. Croix. Ever since a surplus-extracting state of proletarian origin had come into existence, the Communist ruling layer had three characteristics that made it in some ways like a social class. First, it had enough control of surplus labour to make it the dominant group in society. Second, it was not subject to democratic control from below by the working class or peasantry. Third, it commanded the state's armed forces. The second of these was confirmed by its hostile response to democratic impulses that emerged outside the ranks of the party after the end of the Civil War and by the hardening of its anti-democratic stance when it adopted the NEP in 1921. Party committees increasingly made decisions, further draining soviets of meaningful political engagement.[64]

In the years after the Civil War, two changes came to make the ruling layer more like a distinct class. One was that the party-state leadership became ever-more insulated from the party membership. Party democracy was weakened by a 1921 ban on factions (groups of members formed to advocate for a platform of ideas within the party), which broke with the Bolshevik tradition of open political debate. Crucially, the Central Committee (CC)'s secretariat soon became a powerful body dominating other party structures. During the years 1921 to 1924, as historian Simon Pirani summarizes,

> the party apparatus reinforced its control over the party, and thence over the state apparatus ... it used channels of appointment and command to determine the election of delegates to party congresses; it established tight control over the distribution not only of information about the political and economic situation, but also of full information about its own instructions and policies; it systematized the upward flow of information to the secretariat; and it achieved a degree of immunity from legal proceedings for party members, and for officials in particular.[65]

The rapid and overwhelming defeat of the Left Opposition (LO) that came together in late 1923 around a platform that included criticisms of the bureaucratic regime within the party reflected, in part, just how entrenched the dominant group within the party leadership had become.[66] It did not hesitate to use the GPU (as the security police were named at the time) against the LO; later, the renamed OGPU acted inside the party "as the secret police of the emergent Stalinist leadership,"[67] which was now entirely free of any democratic control. From 1923, the group that now controlled the party benefited from an influx of new party members, many of whom joined with the aim of acquiring technical skills or simply to better their personal situation. A party that had emerged from the Civil War as an egalitarian and self-sacrificing but militarized and elitist political force committed to the defence of the new regime and to world revolution was becoming an administrative instrument for the leadership, which was now committed to "socialism in one country." Control of an obedient and much-enlarged membership would be part of how the ruling layer governed.[68] By 1927 only eight thousand of the approximately 786,000 members had been Bolsheviks at the beginning of 1917.[69]

The dismantling of democracy within the party made another momentous change possible. From 1923, the CC — in practice, its secretariat — gained the right to fill important posts by appointment. This was called the *nomenklatura* system. Provincial and district committees did the same for lower-level positions.[70] Even though this system did not function very efficiently in the 1920s,[71] it was a mechanism for a key part of the ruling layer to exercise power over the hierarchy of state managers beneath them. Efforts were also made to increase the number of state officials who belonged to the party.[72]

Democracy within the CP meant that the interests of the working class and peasantry could be reflected indirectly within the party. This could only be a hindrance to leaders intent on implementing their policies regardless of the desires of the people in whose name they claimed to rule. Party democracy was also an obstacle to the CC secretariat's control over the party organization. Thus the party leadership weakened party democracy in 1921–22. This paved the way for the apparatus led by Stalin to eliminate it altogether. Similarly, the *nomenklatura* system and the enrolment of more state officials into the party gave the secretariat more control over the party-state officialdom. The dominant elements of the ruling layer did not seek power as an end in itself. Rather, sensing the antagonism that existed between themselves and the workers and peasants whose surplus the state appropriated, what they sought was the greatest leeway to run the state as they saw fit while they groped their way towards industrialization. This meant reducing the influence of the working class and peasantry as much as possible.

In this way, the party-state elite became more cohesive during the NEP years, becoming even more like a ruling class. Another feature that the party-state elite acquired in these years was its ability to use the surplus product extracted by the state "for purposes … alien and hostile to" those of the working class "in order to strengthen and expand its rule over production and society."[73] During the Civil War, the governing layer had two overriding priorities: military victory over the counter-revolutionary forces that sought to reimpose the power of landlords and capitalists, and support for revolution abroad. These priorities mainly determined how it used workers' surplus labour and peasants' surplus product. For this reason, in spite of the ruling layer's undemocratic and often coercive methods, its wartime priorities had converged with the interests of the working class and, to a lesser extent, the peasantry. Workers and peasants would have been dealt a huge blow if the revolutionary state had been overthrown and the old exploiting class restored. But after the Civil War the priorities of the party-state elite changed, no longer coinciding with the interests of workers and peasants. This became decisively true when the state launched its hyper-industrialization drive in 1928 and then started to dispossess the peasantry.

The Great Break stamped out the remaining embers of the revolutionary blaze lit by workers and peasants in 1917. It marked the triumph of counter-revolution in a form never seen before: instead of the overthrow of the Communist party-state by open opponents of the socialist revolution of 1917, a new ruling class was consolidated that used the language and symbols of that revolution. As a group, the ruling members of the party-state officialdom controlled the state-owned means of production, exploited the urban and rural direct producers, and decided what would be done with the surplus extracted. Dispossessing the peasantry and ramping up the exploitation of the working class in order to transform society through the Great Break marked the crystallization of this layer into a distinct social class. In political economist Gareth Dale's useful formulation, this was a "modernizing counter-revolution," since crash industrialization carried out, as we shall see in the next chapter, by greatly intensifying the exploitation of workers "required an embrace of science and technology, of mechanization, rationalization and urbanization, of social and occupational mobility, and a veneration of industry and labour (including the incorporation of women into the industrial workforce, and the socialized child care on which that depended)."[74]

What caused this outcome? The Great Break was ultimately a response to the social pressures acting on the Communist leadership as it sought to maintain its state against foreign and domestic foes. Across its borders, it faced states with much more advanced productive forces and hence superior military might. Within its borders, it contended with the classes from which it was compelled to extract surpluses in order to maintain its rule: a working class with rights that allowed workers to stymie efforts to intensify exploitation, and a peasantry whose control on the land allowed its members to decide how much of their produce to consume and how much, if any, to sell to the state to feed the urban population.[75] Under the NEP, the ruling layer had sought to develop industry slowly while balancing between, on the one hand, the working class out of which and over which it had arisen and, on the other, the much-larger peasantry. All the while it had to keep an eye on the capitalist states that had tried to overthrow it during the Civil War. The Communist leadership launched the Great Break to protect its rule from a future foreign military attack and because it believed that the development of state industry was the essence of "socialist construction."[76] It was the pressure of social conditions, not ideology, that led to counter-revolution. However, the very weak commitment to democracy of what Bolshevism had become by the end of the Civil War and the belief that the development of state industry was the measure of development towards communism facilitated the rise of a new ruling class.[77]

Before we proceed to look at the society born of the Great Break, the first AES society, we need to briefly discuss a question that often comes up when discussing Russia between 1917 and 1928: was this outcome inevitable? Greene is perceptive to observe that both anti-communists and supporters of AES who think the USSR was moving towards communism under Stalin's leadership believe that the way of organizing society that took shape was bound to develop: "Whether Stalinism appears as a saviour or the Antichrist, both agree that there is no alternative to it."[78] But Greene himself disagrees strongly. He maintains that Trotsky was right that the course of events in the USSR was mainly caused by the fact that the Russian Revolution was not followed by a revolutionary victory in a more developed society that could come to its rescue; this alternative scenario was possible. This is persuasive: a wave of revolutionary or pre-revolutionary upsurges of working-class struggle featuring workers' councils similar to the soviets in Russia shook Germany, Italy, and a number of other European countries between 1918 and 1923.[79] However, what Greene's defence of Trotsky does not confront is whether the isolated social order that existed in the NEP years could have lasted much longer than it did and whether an isolated USSR could have at least partially industrialized without an enormous amount of coercion. The current in the CPSU led by Trotsky and the current around Nikolai Bukharin both thought that this was possible, though they strongly disagreed about what economic policies the state should adopt. Here it is essential to emphasize the domestic and international pressures that drove the ruling layer led by Stalin to make the Great Break. Peasants' control of the land and workers' rights drastically limited how much surplus the party-state elite could extract from the population and use for industrialization. The low level of development of productive forces made it impossible for the USSR to industrialize without intensifying the exploitation of workers and peasants; industrializing without ramping up exploitation of the direct producers was like trying to square a circle. If the rulers had not aggressively turned on the people in whose name they claimed to rule, the state would not have been able to industrialize and modernize society. As a result, it would have probably been defeated in war and the Communist state would have been overthrown or fallen. This does not mean that *exactly* what happened from 1928 on was bound to happen. However, there was no fundamentally different path to industrialization available to the rulers of an isolated USSR.[80]

# CHAPTER 3

# THE USSR 1928-91

## HOW THE GREAT BREAK WAS MADE

**WHAT THE CPSU LEADERSHIP LAUNCHED** in 1928 was a drive to industrialize unlike anything ever seen before in history. The initial plan was to increase output to a level three times what it had been before World War I. "Not having much capital to throw at the problem, the Soviet state threw cheap labour,"[1] observes Sheila Fitzpatrick, a historian sympathetic to the USSR. It is not that the government did not try to bring in more funds for buying advanced technology from the West by selling goods abroad. However, its efforts collided with what was happening in the world economy shortly before and during the Great Depression that began in 1929. The value of the USSR's currency fell, the prices for its exports dropped, and it became more difficult to borrow money to buy imported goods.[2] This led the party-state leadership to squeeze the direct producers more intensely.

In urban areas, there was a "sharp, unplanned drop in the standard of living."[3] Nominal wages rose but prices rose faster. In Moscow, by 1932 real wages had plunged to 52 percent of the 1928 level, recovering by 1937 to 63.5 percent. This pattern was seen across the country. Access to health care and education improved but housing conditions got worse as massive numbers of people migrated into cities and towns to take up new jobs. Food was rationed between 1929 and 1935. Meat consumption by workers in Moscow declined by 69 percent, and dairy products by half.[4] Working conditions also got much worse.[5] Managers exhorted workers to voluntarily work harder for the cause of "socialist construction." Their relative lack of success meant that the state relied mainly on trying to extract more labour from workers by raising output quotas, cutting wage rates, fostering "socialist competition" between groups of workers and later between individuals, and offering money or scarce goods to workers who exceeded their quotas and/or "volunteered" for more work. The party-state instituted harsh penalties for absenteeism. Workers who missed a day of work without just cause faced automatic firing, loss of ration cards, and loss of housing provided through the enterprise. In 1938 penalties were made even stiffer, including dismissal and loss of housing for being more than twenty minutes late, as well as eviction for workers who quit their jobs without permission. The length of maternity leave was also cut. The state turned unions into institutions for administering benefits such as sick leave, vacations, and children's camps, not organizations through which workers could defend themselves on the job. Previously unemployed male wage earners and large numbers of women who had not been working for wages were mobilized in the colossal push. Yet even more important as a source of labour power were people who had been farming.

Driving peasants off the land had not been part of the plans of Stalin's leadership, contrary to what anti-communists sometimes allege. But before long the peasantry had been largely dispossessed. This was done with great brutality and led to many deaths.[6] As we have seen, in 1928, in response to a decline in the amount of grain sold by peasants to the state, Stalin pioneered "extraordinary measures": requisitioning grain but paying for it (the Russian word used for agricultural procurement was *zagotovki*). By late 1929 these measures had become standard procedure. The authorities made it compulsory for peasants to sell grain to the state. But the state often did not keep its side of the bargain when it came to paying for grain with money and goods. Better-off peasants were forced to hand over reserves of grain saved from previous harvests. Between five and six million of them, roughly 4 percent of all peasant households, were labelled *kulaks* (rich peasants) and forced to join so-called collective farms (*kolkhozy*).[7] Many members of these targeted households were deported and resettled in remote regions. Others fled to urban areas instead. The party-state undertook an accelerating campaign to push all peasants to sign up to join collective farms even though there were far too few tractors, trucks, other materials, and agricultural specialists for such farms to operate successfully. "Dekulakization" acted as intimidation to comply with collectivization. Historian Moshe Lewin describes what became

> an established pattern: a *zagotovki* campaign in the autumn, with governmental reprisals growing as peasants offered stubborn resistance; then a new wave of mass arrests and deportations, as a shock treatment to prepare the next stage; finally, in the last stage, inducing new millions of peasants to join *kolkhozy*.[8]

What was dubbed collectivization was, in reality, a chaotic and violent process of dispossession. Such resistance as peasants were able to mount, in which women played a leading role,[9] was overwhelmed by state repression. By the end of the 1930s the property of the peasantry, minus many animals slaughtered in the process, had been taken into state hands. As we shall see, the cost in lives had been terrible, and agriculture had been hit hard. But the new ruling class had found a way to make sure the rapidly expanding urban working class would be fed and achieved "the regimentation and control of the countryside, and the smashing of potential peasant resistance."[10]

The CPSU leadership hailed the Great Break as an all-out effort to build socialism. In reality, it was an effort by rulers to use their state power to rapidly industrialize a less-developed country by ramping up the exploitation of workers and exploiting and dispossessing the peasantry in a way never before seen in history.

## WHAT WAS BUILT

This furnace of exploitation and dispossession succeeded in forging greatly expanded forces of production. The party-state leadership used state power to marshal as much labour power and natural resources as it could for its industrialization and modernization project. By the end of the 1930s, 99 percent of non-agricultural output came from state-owned enterprises.[11] The priority was "heavy industry ... the expansion of coal, iron and steel production, engineering, chemicals and electrical power." This went from about two-fifths of total output in 1928 to some three-fifths in 1940, rising by the 1980s to three-quarters.[12] Existing industries grew dramatically while others that had existed barely or not at all were expanded or created. The manufacture of modern military equipment was the top priority, and its needs shaped the development of other industries, such as the production of metals and machine tools. For example, by 1940 the USSR produced four times more steel than it had in 1928, much of it of the kinds needed for the armaments industry.[13] Electricity generation shot up from some five gigawatt hours in 1928 to forty-three in 1939, rising by 1959 to 265 and by 1979 to 1,238 (for comparison, output in the UK for those years was, in rounded figures, 16, 36, 115, and 279).[14] Freight and passenger rail traffic ballooned, as did the construction of modern highways.[15]

The enormous effort devoted to building up the armed forces to defend the state against its geopolitical rivals — initially the major powers of Western Europe and Japan, later the US and then also China — was successful. The tanks, aircraft, artillery, and other equipment that were designed and mass produced in the 1930s and during World War II made it possible for the military to eventually stop the Nazi invasion of the USSR that began in 1941, drive the German armies from the USSR, and fight westward to Berlin. In the decades after the war, the USSR was able to use its productive forces, including advanced science, to develop the jet aircraft, nuclear weapons, guided missiles, and other armaments needed for credible preparation to fight a war with the NATO countries.[16]

The achievements of AES also included a much more urban and educated population. In the 1930s the number of people living in cities and towns grew at a faster rate than had been seen up to that point in the history of the world. By 1961 half the population was living in urban areas, and by 1989, two-thirds.[17] Khruschev launched a major effort to build more housing. In the decade after 1956, over one hundred million people were able to move into new apartments of their own instead of living in apartments shared with other families or in student or workplace dormitories.[18] In the decades after World War II, spending on other aspects of what can be called the broad welfare state — education, health care, pensions, paid maternity leave, child care, stipends for post-secondary students, and other kinds of social provision — also grew.[19] Lewin notes that society also acquired such features as considerable "personal physical security, libraries, a broad reading public, interest in the arts in general and poetry in particular, the importance of science."[20] On a more mundane level, by the end of the 1980s almost all households had both a refrigerator and a television.[21] Social development was reflected in people's bodies, with average height for both urban and rural residents rising, beginning with children born in the second half of the 1930s. Mortality rates fell and life expectancy rose by the 1960s to a plateau that lasted until the collapse of the USSR.[22]

This development of productive forces, military might, and accompanying social achievements, to which admirers of the USSR point, are undeniable. However, they were only accomplished with terrible human and ecological costs.

## THE COSTS OF CLASS SOCIETY

In spite of what the CPSU proclaimed, the achievements of AES were those of a society structured by class exploitation. It was fundamentally surplus labour extracted from the urban working class that built AES. (The dispossession of the peasantry did boost the supply of labour power available to work outside of agriculture. However, the net contribution of agriculture to industrial development was little or nothing because of how many resources had to be diverted to the countryside to compensate for the loss of animal fertilizer and horsepower resulting from peasants killing so many farm animals during "collectivization."[23]) This was class exploitation. The working class sold its ability to work to the "central political bureaucracy" that had "at its exclusive command the basic means of production," as dissident marxists Jacek Kuron and Karol Modzelewski phrased it in their analysis of AES from within.[24] The working class had no way to make decisions about how much of their labour would go towards producing for their own consumption, how much would produce for other purposes, and what those purposes would be. There was no democratic allocation by workers of their surplus to industrialization or anything else. All such decisions were the exclusive preserve of top party-state officials. These officials were not subject to the slightest democratic control, not even the minimal degree that exists in countries with political systems that allow citizens to vote for candidates from more than one party to represent them. Elections to state bodies under AES almost always involved voting for a single CPSU candidate chosen by party officials.[25] Class exploitation to build AES was organized through the party-state's dictatorship.

This exploitation was interwoven with gender and other forms of oppression. With respect to women's liberation, in the words of historian Wendy Goldman, "the tragedy was that the Party continued to present itself as the true heir to the original socialist vision," as it did around many other issues. "Cloaking its single-minded focus on production in the empty rhetoric of women's emancipation, it abandoned its promise to socialize household labour and to foster freer, more equal relations between men and women."[26] Women were pushed to participate in paid work outside the home while also doing the unpaid labour of the household. State authorities also exhorted them to have more children to help build socialism. The mid-1930s saw a "pro-family" social conservative policy turn as the ruling class sought to encourage population growth and social discipline: homosexuality was criminalized, abortion was banned, and divorce was made more difficult to obtain. Beginning in 1944 women were awarded medals for having large numbers of children. Although abortion was made legal in some circumstances in 1955 and fully legalized in 1968, divorce law was reformed, and eventually some birth control devices became available, gender inequality remained deeply entrenched.[27]

Officially, the state was opposed to racism and committed to the equality of the various nations and ethnicities within its borders. Yet the stability of the USSR trumped their nominal rights. Starting in the mid-1930s, the state also stressed the "cultural and political superiority of Russia."[28] Between then and the early 1950s, over three million people were deported within the USSR on the basis of belonging to ethnonational groups whose loyalty to the state was deemed suspect by the authorities. These groups including Germans, Chechens, Koreans, Poles, Finns, and Crimean Tatars. The state treated "each and every member" of them "as a carrier of the same suspect traits that he or she transmitted, necessarily, to the next generation. That is a racial logic at work."[29] Anti-Semitism was also an ongoing feature of society, flaring at the end of the 1920s, between 1947 and 1953, in the early 1960s, and in the final years of the USSR.[30] African and Asian visitors to the country also experienced racism.[31]

The achievements of AES were also inextricably bound up with a huge level of other forms of violence, repression, and destruction. Most obvious was the execution of close to 700,000 people in the Great Purge of 1937–38, mentioned in Chapter 1. The total number of people executed between the start of the Great Break and 1941 may have been as high as one million,[32] the killing a consequence of counter-revolution. Stalin's leadership inflicted terror on the direct producers to prevent resistance to its remaking of society. It also wiped out most of the remaining "Old Bolshevik" veterans of 1917, people who might remember what the revolution had originally been about. Having unleashed such violence, the top leadership was then "caught up inside the process" and "could not always turn terror in the way it wanted."[33]

Unfortunately, these executions were just one way in which death was inflicted on the population as a consequence of the Great Break. The dispossession of the peasantry and the state's extraction of so much grain from the countryside led to a terrible famine in 1932–33.

Party-state leaders viewed peasants' attempts to retain grain for their own subsistence as sabotage. In response, they doubled down on enforcing grain procurement quotas. This led to famine in Ukraine and other grain-producing areas. The state did not set out to cause starvation but did little in response to the famine. Stalin and other top leaders interpreted Ukrainian peasant resistance as Ukrainian nationalist opposition to their central government. They responded with state terror, which made the famine worse in Ukrainian-speaking areas. The death toll from starvation and hunger-related disease amounted to several million people.[34] The total death toll of the modernizing counter-revolution can be estimated by demographic analysis. The number of excess deaths between 1928 and 1938 (the number above what would have been expected given population trends before the Great Break) has been estimated at around ten million, half or more of which were adults.[35] This covers death from execution and starvation as well as illness, disease, accidents, and other causes linked to the deportations, imprisonment, and other dimensions of social upheaval during those years.

Mass incarceration was another repressive repercussion of the Great Break. Between the late 1920s and the early 1950s, millions of people served time in a prison, labour camp, labour colony, or special settlement (where residents were not officially detained but also not permitted to leave). Their labour, mostly in atrocious conditions, contributed to building AES. In 1953, the year Stalin died, numbers peaked at about 5.5 million persons, 2.9 percent of the population.[36] That year revolts in the camps influenced the decision of the CPSU's top leaders to relax repression. In the years that followed, many prisoners were released. However, until its end the USSR remained a highly repressive society. The only unions allowed were the official state-run ones; self-organization of other groups independent of the party-state was not permitted; censorship was extensive; and people were jailed, put in psychiatric hospitals, or exiled internally for social or political criticism.[37]

One final cost of building AES must be noted: ecological destruction. For the ruling class, whose paramount goal was industrialization, there was no "place for the environment as something to be preserved or defended, but only as an object to realize production and modernization targets, that is, almost exclusively as a resource for industry."[38] The state's reorganization of agriculture and its harnessing for the drive to industrialize and urbanize also subjected the land to damaging farming practices. This led to the widespread pollution of land, water, and air; biodiversity loss; the depletion of lakes and rivers; soil erosion; the clear-cutting of forests; and other kinds of damage to ecosystems.[39]

Examining the costs to people and the rest of nature of building AES in the USSR is very revealing about how this way of organizing society was not liberatory. Since the social relations within a society powerfully influence its relationships with other societies, examining the USSR's relationship with class and national liberation struggles outside its borders further illuminates the USSR itself as well as demonstrating its impact on emancipatory struggles globally.

## THE USSR AND GLOBAL STRUGGLES

In spite of the marxist language they used, the CPSU leadership's overriding concern was the continuation of their rule, which entailed promoting the security of their state. Encouraging revolutions that resembled what had taken place in 1917 was anathema to them. Nor were they generally keen about any other kind of revolution, even by forces committed to creating societies modelled on the USSR; revolution meant instability and potentially problems for the security of the USSR.

In 1919 the Bolsheviks and like-minded revolutionary socialists from other countries created the Communist International (Comintern). This was an international organization of parties committed to social revolution based on workers' councils, along the lines of what had happened in Russia. As the CPSU leadership evolved as a ruling layer, its politics shifted away from promoting world revolution and towards calculations based on its own distinct interests, now expressed in terms of "socialism in one country" — the building by the party-state officialdom of a modern industrialized society in the USSR. These interests came to dominate the increasingly CPSU-controlled Comintern. The Comintern leadership adopted policies favoured by Stalin and his cothinkers, imposed compliant leaders on its component parties, and expelled dissenters.[40]

In 1928, the Comintern adopted a highly ultra-left line for what it dubbed the "Third Period." CPs were directed to create "red unions," which meant splitting their members and supporters away from existing unions to form new unions led by CP members that would implement CP policies. They were also to denounce social democrats as "social fascists" instead of allying with them in struggles around immediate concerns, including fighting fascism, and trying to show in practice that revolutionary politics were the best way for working-class people to change society. This sectarian refusal to cooperate with other working-class forces contributed directly to the failure of the powerful Social Democratic and Communist parties in Germany to unite and stop the Nazis from taking power.

In 1935 Comintern policy swung wildly in the opposite direction as the USSR's rulers sought to ally with Britain and France against Germany. Now CPs were to form "popular fronts" against fascism that even embraced liberal capitalist forces; no demands that might scare away such forces were to be raised.

Then, to the dismay of many Communists globally, in 1939 the USSR and Nazi Germany signed a pact. Publicly, it was a non-aggression pact; its secret section paved the way for Germany and the USSR to divide Poland between them and for the USSR to conquer and annex Estonia, Latvia, and Lithuania. The USSR deported exiled Communists who had fled the Nazis back into their hands, including some even before the pact was signed. From the outbreak of World War II until Germany attacked the USSR in 1941, the Comintern advocated a negotiated peace with the Nazi state and downplayed anti-fascism.

After the Nazi state turned on the USSR, all-out support for the war against the Axis powers then became the order of the day. All other commitments, including the defence of workers' rights and opposition to colonialism, were to be subordinated to popular fronts for the war effort. In 1943 the CPSU leadership initiated the dissolution of the Comintern, whose lingering association with world revolution they now saw as a hindrance to the USSR strengthening its relations with Western powers in order to influence the shape of the postwar world in its favour.

In the years following the end of World War II, the USSR's control of Eastern Europe and the coming to power of the CP in China led the top leaders of the CPSU to come to see CPs in countries outside the "socialist bloc" as less important for the security of their state than they had been deemed before the war. As a consequence, the USSR's rulers came to tolerate more political independence from these parties while still expecting them to champion the USSR and support its foreign policy objectives. These objectives generally favoured social stability, not revolution of any type.

Some examples will illustrate the USSR's relationship to global social struggles. First, three revolutions in Europe:

- In Spain in 1936, a right-wing military coup against the Popular Front government touched off a social revolution, with workers and peasants in some areas taking democratic control of their workplaces and the land, alongside civil war between the fascist Nationalists and anti-fascist Republican forces. The USSR came to the aid of the Republicans by sending weapons and a small number of troops, while the Comintern mobilized support internationally. At the same time, the CPSU leadership worked to build up the Spanish CP, which pursued a popular front strategy with the limited goal of defending capitalist democracy. That strategy led the Spanish CP to strive to suppress those workers and peasants who wanted to both fight fascism *and* advance social revolution. The top foreign policy priority of the rulers of the USSR at the time was to form an alliance with Britain and France against Nazi Germany, since they feared Hitler intended to eventually attack the USSR. Because the capitalist governments that Stalin wanted to ally with were, unsurprisingly, hostile to social revolution in Spain, the CPSU's leaders set out to smother the revolution. This involved destroying or marginalizing the anti-Stalinist marxist and anarchist forces that challenged Communist influence. NKVD agents in Spain went so far as to kidnap and murder anti-Stalinist marxists and anarchists.[41]
- In Hungary in 1956, then an AES society and part of the USSR-led Warsaw Pact, protests for democracy and national independence grew into a revolution in which workers organized councils reminiscent of the soviets of Russia in 1917. Afraid that a victorious revolution could inspire workers in other AES societies to follow the Hungarian example, the CPSU leadership decided to crush the uprising with force. Its army did so, killing over two thousand people. Revulsion at this counter-revolutionary violence led to many CP members resigning from their parties internationally.[42]
- In 1974–75, Portugal, a member of NATO, was shaken by a revolution sparked through a coup by modernizing military officers against the authoritarian government that was trying to hang on to the country's colonies. The USSR did what it could to aid the Portuguese CP, whose actions during those years aimed to increase its presence in government. This led the CP to oscillate between mobilizing people in order to boost its political influence and demobilizing them to show that the party was a trustworthy player in government. It was

hostile to the independent self-activity of workers, peasants, women, and students, as well as to the revolutionary left. What the USSR's leaders wanted was not social revolution but a weaker NATO.[43]

The USSR's response to two revolutions outside Europe reveals a similar approach:[44]

- The CPSU's leaders did not encourage the Chinese CP (CCP), led by Mao Zedong, to take power. Far from it: after the end of World War II, Stalin tried to sign a treaty with the Nationalist government that the CCP was fighting. This was in keeping with the conservative preference for geopolitical stability of the top leaders of the CPSU. As the Chinese Communists grew stronger and it looked like the US would not rescue the Nationalists, the USSR stepped up its support for the CCP. However, even as the CCP's armed forces drew closer to a complete victory, Stalin tried to persuade Mao to include non-Communists in a new government and not to remake society along AES lines.[45]
- In Ethiopia in 1974, an anti-feudal revolution by a military committee, the Derg, took place. The government of the USSR kept a cautious distance even as the Derg endorsed Marxism-Leninism as its ideology, set its goal as establishing an AES society, and repeatedly asked the USSR for weapons. This was because CPSU leaders were concerned to maintain good relations with neighbouring Somalia, where the USSR had military bases. The USSR's policy changed in 1977 after Mengistu Haile Mariam secured his place as the Derg's definitive leader, killing a number of other leaders with whom he clashed. The USSR then started to supply Ethiopia with weapons, followed by sending its own and Cuban troops to help Ethiopia win the war that broke out between Somalia and Ethiopia. That the Derg was killing many of its ML opponents and many other people was no obstacle.[46]

Although the USSR supported many national liberation struggles in the Third World to at least some extent, its support was certainly not consistent. For example, after Germany invaded the USSR, the CPSU's leaders, acting through the Comintern and the CP of Great Britain, directed the CP of India to unconditionally support the British war effort, drop agitation against British imperial rule, and oppose the Quit India campaign launched by the independence movement led by Gandhi.⁴⁷ In 1948, the USSR's government supported the creation of the settler-colonial state of Israel. Later, it was an "intermittent and inconsistent patron" of the Palestine Liberation Organization.⁴⁸ One final example: even though the USSR had funded one of the two ML groups fighting for Eritrea's independence from Ethiopia, it later backed the Derg regime against them.⁴⁹ As with its stance towards revolutions, when it came to Third World challenges to colonialism and imperialism, the top concern of the ruling class in the USSR was never advancing global freedom struggles.

## WHAT KIND OF SOCIETY?

Having analyzed how AES came into existence, surveyed what was accomplished in the USSR and at what cost, and examined the USSR's relationship to social struggles globally, we must now assess this society. This was a society whose ruling class was able to use state power to carry out its project of industrialization and modernization, made possible by its exploitation of urban and rural direct producers. The rulers succeeded by organizing what economist Jacques Sapir calls a mobilization economy: a general mobilization by the state of all available resources, on a non-commercial basis. In this respect it echoed previous experiences of war economies in other countries where states orchestrated production for their non-commercial goals, while going further than any of these had (this is why economist Oskar Lange dubbed the USSR a *"sui generis* [one of a kind] war economy"⁵⁰). In the USSR, the state guaranteed that all products ordered from and delivered by its many enterprises would be accepted; markets did not determine what would be sold or not sold.⁵¹

This has usually been seen as a "planned economy." The essential idea of planning is that resources are allocated in advance to meet consciously chosen objectives rather than allocated in response to market or other demands. In reality, it was not "planning in any meaningful sense," as economist Mike Haynes argues. Haynes suggests that the idea that AES was based on a planned economy involves two myths. The first myth is that there was planning to meet people's needs even though there was no democracy. However, planning without democracy is "the very opposite of human liberation — it is an expression of extreme alienation."⁵² Theorist Raya Dunayevskaya elaborates on this point: in the USSR, "planners express in the Plan the total domination of workers by the machine. In reality, therefore, the State Plan is nothing but the organization of the proletariat to produce under the domination of the machine." What Marx called "dead labour" — the products of human labour not subject to the control of the direct producers themselves — "dominates over living labour," as it does where workers produce commodities for privately owned companies.[53]

The second myth is that what took place was actually planning. "At best what we see is clumsy centralized direction ... Looking back, Moshe Lewin wrote that 'there is no doubt that the whole process was an immense improvisation, guided by the rule of thumb, hunch, and all too often despotic whim.'" Nevertheless,

> a logical set of priorities did emerge ... These were determined by the needs of defence and competitive industrialization. They were embodied in the differing power and status of the various commissariats that grew up to direct development ... Relations between them were characterized by imbalance, waste and contradictions. To resolve these and other difficulties a second economy grew, informal but tolerated, and run by *tolkachi*, or fixers, and the use of influence, or *blat* ... But here too there was a rationale to the use of informal power and influence. Military competition and the needs of competitive industrialization were again the ultimate arbiters of what happened within the economy. They constituted the barely veiled logic that lay behind the targets of the leaders. They were also the factors that established who had power and influence, and who did not. They thus guided the deployment of formal power and informal *blat*.[54]

The more closely one examines how the economy worked, the clearer it becomes that "planning" was a fiction. Gosplan, the central planning agency, issued multi-year "plans," but its annual plans, containing binding targets for all economic units, were much more important. What units actually produced over years was often far from what the multi-year plan specified.[55] Both plans and how they were implemented reflected central state priorities: "If steel, say, was in shorter supply than originally planned, it was the production of bicycles that would lose out, not that of tanks or machine tools," observes economist Philip Hanson.[56] More important than Gosplan was Gossnab, the central agency responsible for supplying units with everything they needed for production — in other words, Lewin comments, "for doing what market mechanisms did" in other countries.[57] Gossnab was both "the cause and manager of constant shortages" and became the hub of the "murky world" of fixers acting on behalf of the enterprises that employed them.[58] This was a world of competition. It was not competition to sell goods and services in markets but, as Sapir points out, there most definitely was competition between economic units for the materials and labour power that their managers needed to produce whatever it was that Gosplan directed them to produce.[59] Thus the mode of production in AES featured economic mobilization by the central political bureaucracy of enterprises that were to some extent pressured to compete with each other for inputs.

All this rested on a hierarchical and authoritarian way of organizing how people worked, their labour processes; there was no hint of workers' self-management of workplaces or even encouragement of some control by workers over how they carried out their tasks. There was a high degree of alienation — objective powerlessness — in workplaces.[60] Workers were completely deprived of any officially recognized way of organizing collectively to defend or improve their pay and working conditions. For the party-state's rulers, the result was "a fatal combination: a depoliticized, but alienated and bitter work force which, because labour power was desperately scarce, could neither be induced nor compelled to work efficiently."[61] Strikes and other kinds of collective action were severely repressed. But managers and upper-level state officials could not stop workers from missing work, putting in little effort, or changing jobs. Workers were able to exert a degree of control at work because of the endemic scarcity of labour power in this mobilization economy.[62]

These workplace realities were a huge barrier to the ruling class raising the productivity of labour in the cities and countryside. This was less of a problem during the Great Break and the all-out effort to win the war against Germany than it became after Stalin's death, when the ruling class shifted to ruling in a much less repressive way. Growth in the production of goods and services slowed in the 1960s and declined further in the 1970s, roughly parallel to trends in the world economy. The ruling class was unable to benefit from changes in the global economy that saw multinational corporations, aided by Western states, find new ways of raising their profits by taking advantage of cheap Third World labour and materials and prying their way into new markets (although the USSR was not cut off from the postwar world economy, as is sometimes thought[63]). This was due to the size of the USSR's military-industrial complex — "the linchpin of the economy"[64] — the pressures of military competition with the NATO bloc, and the structure of the bureaucratically directed mobilization economy.[65] The way in which the mobilization economy worked meant that enterprises that produced lower-quality or less output than others, or goods and services for which there was less demand, were not pressured by competition with other enterprises to reorganize production. Instead it was the central state that was saddled with the consequences.[66]

The economic stagnation that eventually resulted from how production was organized played a major role in creating the conditions that led to Mikhail Gorbachev's effort to restructure AES society starting in the mid-1980s. This touched off the train of events that spiralled into political crisis and the dissolution of the USSR in 1991. Also feeding into the breakdown of the social order created by the Great Break was its imperialist character. The oppression of nations originally incorporated by Russian conquest into the Tsarist Empire had been sustained in a different form within the borders of the USSR. These borders expanded during and after World War II, and the USSR came to dominate Eastern Europe. In 1979 the USSR's armed forces invaded Afghanistan. The war of occupation that followed, alongside nationalist protests in Eastern Europe and within the Russian-dominated USSR, all contributed to the USSR's final crisis.[67]

Precisely what kind of society this was will be examined in Chapter 6. What is clear from this analysis is what it was not. The USSR was portrayed to its citizens and to the world as "a new world power, founded on laudatory ideals, and backed up by tangible programs and institutions: full employment, subsidized prices, paid vacations for workers, child care, health care, retirement pensions, education, and the promise of advancement for oneself and one's children."[68] The industrialization and dispossession carried out after the Great Break accomplished in a decade what had taken centuries or decades in Western Europe. Yet neither under Stalin nor under his successors did social relations change in ways that meant transition to communism was happening. Throughout its existence the USSR was a society structured at its core by class exploitation and alienation. State power was pervasive, and through it the exploiting class, the central party-state bureaucracy, ruled. Its leaders "exercise[d] the totality of political and economic power, depriving the working class not only of the means of power and control, but even of self-defence."[69] No wonder, then, that they did not promote social revolution for workers' power outside the USSR. Neither class relations nor state power ever weakened from 1928 on. As we have seen, the direct producers did not in any way control and plan production to meet their needs. To return to Luxemburg's eloquent phrasing, they were not "ceas[ing] to be a dominated mass." They were not "mak[ing] the entire political and economic life [their] own life and giv[ing] that life a conscious, free, and autonomous direction."[70] Thus, as Lewin puts it, "To persist in speaking of 'Soviet socialism' is to engage in a comedy of errors … If, confronted with a hippopotamus, someone insisted that it was a giraffe, would he or she be given a chair in zoology? Are the social sciences really that much less exact than zoology?"[71]

**CHAPTER 1**

# CHINA 1949-PRESENT

**IN THE 1960s AND 1970s**, the leadership of the CCP proclaimed their country a socialist society en route to communism and criticized the government of the USSR as turncoat "revisionists." Many people on the left globally saw China as a progressive alternative to the USSR. Most of this support gave way to disillusionment as China's rulers befriended their US counterparts and welcomed foreign investors. More recently, the rivalry between a rising China and the US has led more people on the global left to again sympathize with the CCP's leaders.

The path that led to the establishment of a society along AES lines in China was completely different from the one that led to AES first coming into existence. As we have seen, AES in the USSR was birthed by a modernizing counter-revolution carried out by the rulers of a state whose origins lay in a social revolution made by workers and peasants. AES in China was created by new rulers who saw socialism in terms of the USSR and who came to power in 1949 by leading a revolution qualitatively different from what had happened in Russia in 1917. Today China is a very different society than it was in the late 1970s, when the CCP government began to expand the role of market forces and open the country up to global capitalism. However, because the CCP still maintains that China is a socialist society, one with a "socialist market economy," this chapter will deal with China from 1949 to the present.

## THE PATH TO AES AND HOW AES WENT TO MARKET

In the 1800s, China's Imperial state ruled over an overwhelming rural feudal society. China suffered defeats at the hands of the British military and was forced to accept demands that gave European, Japanese, and US governments and firms a great deal of economic and political power in the country. The Qing dynasty was overthrown in 1911 and replaced by a republic. This feeble new regime was utterly unable to challenge imperialist domination or implement serious modernizing reforms. Rival regional warlords soon emerged. Capitalism remained marginal, concentrated in commerce and finance more than production. Many firms were foreign owned. The landlord class that dominated rural areas was "capable of little more than pursuing the most ruthless traditional forms of socioeconomic exploitation, unchecked by traditional political or moral sanctions."[1] Whether peasants were tenants or independent smallholders, they were mostly very poor. Both tenants and independent farmers had to combine growing cash crops and food for their own subsistence. They, along with landless agricultural workers, suffered from the decay of the state's irrigation, flood control, and famine prevention measures caused by imperialist disruption and war.[2] Urban wage-workers — estimated as under 2 percent of the working population in the early 1930s[3] — and the rest of the urban poor were exploited by both Chinese and foreign capitalists. This was a "historical situation ... marked by the weakness of *all* social classes."[4]

In 1919, a student-driven movement of anti-imperialist modernizing nationalist protest swept through cities and towns. This revived the anti-imperialist but pro-capitalist Nationalist Party, which had been formed in 1912 by activists involved in the overthrow of the Qing dynasty. Some participants in the movement who were inspired by the Russian Revolution concluded that imperialism and capitalism were inextricable and formed the CCP in 1921. The Comintern leadership soon directed the CCP to join the much larger Nationalists, a directive opposed but ultimately obeyed by CCP leaders. The Comintern's move was influenced by how some CPSU leaders were prioritizing their state's survival over promoting socialist revolution internationally. They wanted to establish an alliance with the Nationalists as the leading anti-imperialist force in China. Confusion about communist strategy in countries where capitalism was not yet dominant was also a factor in the Comintern decision. In 1923, the Nationalists allied themselves with the USSR. The following year, a rising wave of struggles by workers and peasants strengthened both parties. These class struggles threatened foreign and domestic capitalists and the landlord class. The growing threat from below drove Chinese capitalists towards the Nationalists, whose army was in large part led by officers drawn from the landlord class. As the power of the Nationalists grew, they also "emerged more and more as the party of property and order."[5] In 1927, having built up the military power and capitalist support he needed, Nationalist leader Jiang Jieshi (Chiang Kai-Shek) turned on the CCP and the workers' and peasants' movements, killing hundreds of thousands of people in a few years. The Stalin-led USSR had enabled this disaster by providing training to the Nationalist army, while the Comintern leadership had directed the CCP to subordinate itself politically to the Nationalists.[6]

Remnant members of the CCP survived by fleeing to remote rural areas. There they began to root themselves in the peasantry and develop a strategy of guerilla warfare, with Mao Zedong becoming a central leader. The CCP gained experience governing the areas in the province of Jiangxi, which they came to control, and built a Red Army. Forced in 1934 to flee the more powerful Nationalist army, a small minority of its forces survived a gruelling year-long "Long March" to the province of Shaanxi. In 1931 Japanese forces occupied the province of Manchuria, making further incursions into China in the years that followed. Popular pressure on Jiang to unite the Nationalists with the CCP against the Japanese eventually succeeded. However, the brutal and conservative Nationalists were hardly an effective force for rallying peasants and workers against the invaders. With Mao now its key leader, the CCP was able to respond to the full-scale Japanese 1937 invasion of China by positioning itself as the leading defender of the nation.[7] Among peasants in different regions, they organized "a nationwide resistance movement and imbued it with a sense of national mission that otherwise would have been absent."[8] War made peasants' lives even worse, which increased the appeal of the CCP's land reform policies, though these were not radical: rent control, a cap on interest rates, and progressive tax reform.[9]

Japan's surrender in 1945 ended World War II. Negotiations between the Nationalists and the CCP about a postwar coalition government, a goal sought by the US government but which neither Chinese party wanted, went nowhere, and civil war between the rival parties resumed in 1946. Despite having more soldiers and superior equipment, the Nationalists' initial gains were illusory. Their overextended units were vulnerable to the guerilla tactics of what was now named the People's Liberation Army (PLA), their troops were unmotivated, and their commanders were incompetent. Ably combining both guerilla and more conventional military tactics, the CCP's PLA won victory after victory in 1948. PLA morale was high due to the support of its peasants-turned-soldiers for CCP patriotic social justice policies and vision of liberation.[10] As it became increasingly clear what the outcome of the war would be, and with inflation extremely high, Jiang's government lost all credibility, including among many capitalists. In 1949, Jiang and forces loyal to him fled to Taiwan. In October 1949 Mao declared the creation of the People's Republic of China (PRC).

The CCP had carried out a revolution that had broken the state through which the Nationalists had governed on behalf of landlords and capitalists. In its place, and basing itself on the PLA, it started to build a new state. This revolution had been accomplished mostly through war fought by armed forces under the CCP's command, not mass struggle from below democratically organized by the exploited masses themselves. Peasants were active participants but there were no equivalents to the councils and other democratic organizations through which workers and peasants had made the Russian Revolution.[11] This was not a problem for CCP leaders, who had adapted the politics of Stalin's CPSU to Chinese conditions.[12] The CCP enjoyed widespread support but was not subject to democratic control by peasants and workers. The party itself was a militarized organization and was not internally democratic as the Bolsheviks had been until the early 1920s.[13] This was also a "rural revolution in which workers had played little part."[14] In the cities, "neither major strikes nor urban uprisings paved the way for the Red Army," which was "composed essentially of peasants and officered by other peasants and intellectuals."[15] In fact, in 1949, as the PLA moved to take control of the country's major cities, the CCP leadership told urban workers to keep working.[16]

The CCP did not immediately reorganize society on AES lines. The party leadership first expropriated the landlord class and redistributed land to the peasantry.[17] A large minority of enterprises were state-owned or joint state-private firms while the rest remained in the hands of private business owners.[18] Whatever form ownership took, though, workers were not in control on the job and the CCP endeavoured to orchestrate labour-management cooperation and tamp down workers' militancy. In some cases, "What was all the talk about 'Liberation,' workers asked, if wages and the organization of work remained as they had been before?"[19]

In 1953, CCP leaders initiated a five-year plan and announced the start of a transition to socialism. The reorganization of production that this involved was modelled on the USSR after the Great Break, and the USSR provided aid for the effort. At its centre was the rapid expansion of state-owned industry, with even more emphasis on heavy industry than in the USSR. Many new enterprises were created, and over the next three years most urban private firms were nationalized.[20] The party-state leadership had originally believed that it would need to industrialize China before it could move agriculture from private ownership, with some cooperative farming, to collectivization. It understood peasants' attachment to their land and was aware of the disastrous experience of forced collectivization in the USSR, which it did not want to repeat. However, agricultural production failed to grow at the pace required by the plan. This was a problem because "extracting from the countryside a sizeable economic surplus for investment in the cities"[21] was crucial for the industrialization project. Slow growth in agriculture was an obstacle to industrialization, which was key to building armed forces that could defend the state against Western imperialism. Imposing quotas on the peasantry did not result in the amount of farm output delivered to the state reaching the desired level. In response, in 1955, Mao turned to collectivization as the way to raise agricultural productivity. Collectivization met with little resistance and was carried out successfully. This success stemmed in part from how the party-state's rulers were able to use the party's large and well-organized rural membership and its history of struggle in the countryside to persuade peasants to go along with giving up their family landholdings. The CCP's leaders were also fortunate that so many peasants were poor and receptive to dramatic change.[22] In 1956, the party-state leadership proclaimed the victory of socialism in China (it did not use the term AES, a term later used in the USSR and Eastern Europe, to describe Chinese society).[23]

The tumultuous events of the following two decades — the era known as the Cultural Revolution, which will be touched on below — will not be discussed here, since the purpose of this section is simply to outline how AES came to China and how AES later became today's "socialist market economy."[24] After Mao's death in 1976, the faction led by Deng Xiaoping that won the fight to lead the CCP was confronted with economic stagnation, widespread popular dissatisfaction with poor living standards, and urban movements for democracy. Starting in 1978, the central political bureaucracy responded with "reforms" to AES. Its aim was to use market forces to develop forces of production while preserving the party-state's control of society. The state encouraged the creation of private businesses and "collective" enterprises that operated much like them. The result was a rapid spread of commercial activity in both urban and rural areas. It also began to expand exports and imports.

It welcomed foreign investors, who stood to profit by exploiting low-paid workers kept in line by the party-state's unions and who, from 1982, were denied any right to strike. Rural China was transformed by a shift from collective to private farming over only a few years. While the land was not formally privatized, leases that came to be as long as fifty years "effectively established a de facto [in effect] free market in land, with 'contracted' lands rented, bought, sold and mortgaged as if they were fully alienable private property."[25]

Over time, in an experimental trial-and-error process — sometimes referred to with the saying "crossing the river by feeling the stones" — the party-state leadership gradually restructured society. It privatized many state-owned enterprises, laying off large numbers of workers, though state agencies often had influential links with now-private firms.[26] It commercialized other enterprises so that they operated as market-oriented state-owned firms listed on stock exchanges.[27] The party-state has overseen the creation of multinational corporations and fostered their growth,[28] so much so that "large Chinese firms are now among the leading global investors."[29] Today a "*strong state* is deeply entwined with a fundamentally *marketized economy*" in which "the most strategic industries (e.g. metals, energy, pharmaceuticals) are tightly controlled by the state and dominated by central state-owned enterprises."[30] Firms seen by the state as less important "are governed through regulations rather than direct oversight by the government."[31] Most production is for-profit, with state agencies stabilizing and steering markets in line with the priorities of the central leadership of the party-state. People have to buy almost all of the goods and services they need.[32] The central political bureaucracy is now at the centre of a ruling class that includes many company owners, among them billionaire corporate executives who belong to the CCP. China has changed enormously from what it was under Mao but its social arrangements still retain significant features of AES, above all the repressive one-party state that tightly administers society. We might call this "market Stalinism."[33]

## ACHIEVEMENTS OF AES IN CHINA

There can be no doubt that the CCP accomplished a great deal. Its first major achievement was freeing China from semi-colonial domination by European powers and Japan: "the removal of imperialist control from China's territory and institutions marked the first time in over a century that Chinese were in charge of China's territory, polity, and economy."[34] The CCP ended what was often called the "century of humiliation." At the same time, the CCP established the rule of the central state in place of regional fragmentation, a goal that both the Nationalists and CCP had sought since the fall of the Qing Empire.

Extinguishing imperialist domination made possible the CCP's other major accomplishment: the industrialization of China under AES. Between 1949 and 1957, "CCP officials succeeded in accumulating more industrial capital than Chinese bureaucrats and private business had managed in their pursuit of 'modernization' during the whole of the previous century."[35] Historian Maurice Meisner highlights key aspects of China's industrialization under Mao:

> Between 1952 and 1976, the output of steel grew from 1.3 to 23 million tons; coal from 66 to 448 million tons; electric power from 7 to 133 billion kilowatt-hours; crude oil from virtually nothing to 28 million tons; chemical fertilizer from 0.2 to 28 million tons; and cement from 3 to 48 million tons. By the mid-1970s China was manufacturing jet airplanes, heavy tractors, and modern ocean-going vessels in substantial quantities. The People's Republic was also producing nuclear weapons and long-range ballistic missiles; it first launched a satellite in 1970, six years after its first successful atomic bomb test.[36]

All this was achieved despite a US trade embargo that lasted until 1972. Aid from the USSR was important at first but was suddenly withdrawn in 1960 after disagreements between the rulers of these two AES societies boiled over into mutual denunciation (the main reason for the rift was Mao's desire for "full autonomy for China's own policies"[37]).[38] Researcher Kim Yong-uk helps puts China's industrialization in sharper perspective: "the CCP rulers were pursuing the mind-boggling aim of constructing a heavy industrial and military industrial base comparable with those of the United States and the Soviet Union in a country with a level of development comparable to Afghanistan in the 2000s."[39] As alluded to by Meisner, the party-state's extraordinary industrialization allowed it to produce armaments to upgrade the PLA into a military more modern than the forces that had won the civil war against the Nationalists.

AES in China also led to some significant improvements in the lives of peasants and workers. The party-state brought public health and basic medical care to most of the population for the first time. Although peasants were not eating better in the mid-1970s than they had in the early 1950s, death rates, including infant mortality, plummeted and average life expectancy in China rose from forty to sixty-four over those years. Most of the population became literate for the first time. In 1950 the state adopted a law on marriage that affirmed gender equality (while setting the minimum age to marry as eighteen for women and twenty for men), permitted divorce in most circumstances, and prohibited forced marriages.[40]

There have been extremely important changes in Chinese society since the shift to market Stalinism that began in the late 1970s. The chief accomplishment of the decades in which the CCP leadership has overseen a shift to a political economy mostly made up of private firms and integrated China into the capitalist world economy has been an extraordinary development of productive forces. After first becoming a massive hub for the labour-intensive, relatively low-technology manufacture of goods for export to markets around the world, China is increasingly becoming a country capable of the most technologically sophisticated production. While there are many limits to using gross domestic product (GDP) as a measure of economic activity, in 2022 China's GDP was USD$30 trillion, the largest in the world (US GDP was estimated at $25.5 trillion).[41] Electricity generation ballooned to 8,839 billion kilowatt hours, up from 411 in 1985 (for comparison, in 2022 the US generated 4,297 billion kilowatt hours).[42] While capitalists have done extremely well for themselves from economic development since the end of the 1970s, median daily income per person leaped from $1.02 in 1981 to $10.72 in 2019, an increase of 951 percent (in the US the figure in 2019 was $65.04).[43] Life expectancy has risen to seventy-five and a half.[44]

China's rulers are understandably proud of the country's enormous economic accomplishments since the late 1970s, which, building on the achievements of the Maoist era, have raised the PRC to a leading place in the world. The contrast between China in 1949 and China today is truly extraordinary. However, under both Mao and his successors, workers and peasants have paid a terrible cost for these accomplishments.

## THE COSTS OF CLASS SOCIETY

The achievements of AES in China were inseparable from class exploitation and the forms of oppression interwoven with it. The Chinese

Revolution did away with the old ruling class and put in place a new ruling class made up of top party-state officials, including enterprise bosses and military leaders.[45] The central political bureaucracy of the party-state extracted surplus labour from workers and peasants to create and develop AES. Collectivization represented the near-total dispossession of the peasantry. Almost all land, animals, and tools came under the control of farm administrators (families were left small plots for personal use). Peasants were paid what amounted to wages in the form of "work points" awarded for tasks completed, with tasks done by women generally rated as worth fewer points than those performed by men. Points were later redeemed for a share of the surplus produce remaining after the state had taken its share of the harvest, as well as for small amounts of money. In a change from the situation before collectivization and before 1949, almost all peasant women were drawn into labour in the fields.[46]

Outside agriculture, workers were hailed as "masters of the country" in Maoist rhetoric. Yet they had no say over how much of their labour would go towards their compensation and how much would go towards producing goods and services for the party-state. Nor could the working class decide what would be produced. All such decisions were made by state officials over whom workers had no control. In truth, "the CCP's dictatorial authority was always exercised *in the name* of the proletariat, never by the proletariat themselves. Workers had no democratic control over production."[47] Nor could they negotiate the terms of exploitation through unions: by the mid-1950s unions had lost the minimal degree of independence they had enjoyed after 1949 and been completely converted into institutions for raising workers' productivity.[48] The exploited classes were also deeply divided by the *hukou* system of household registration. To limit migration to urban areas, where social programs were much better than in the countryside, in 1958 state authorities assigned all citizens "agricultural" or "non-agricultural" registration, though this was enforced only from 1961. People with agricultural status who nevertheless worked outside rural areas toiled in very low-paid and insecure jobs.[49]

After the Marriage Law was adopted, the party-state did little to combat women's oppression (and from 1954, enforcing the law was treated as unimportant[50]). Women in urban areas were sometimes urged to take on waged work, just as their rural counterparts worked in the fields. This paid work was to be done on top of their unpaid domestic labour. During the Great Leap Forward (GLF) at the end of the 1950s — a frenetic push to speed up the pace of the development of productive forces — the state made efforts to "socialize housework" as a way to get women to do more work outside the home. But the public dining halls, child care centres, kindergartens, and other facilities set up for this purpose were short-lived; state authorities shut down most of them after the CCP leadership ordered an end to the disastrous GLF. Under AES more women got jobs in male-dominated occupations but the reality of gender relations was far from the equality of official pronouncements.[51] Throughout these years heterosexism was also strong. Same-gender sexual activity was seen as "bourgeois decadence" and punished by the state as "hooliganism" against the social order.[52]

Six percent of the PRC's population was not ethnically Han. Dozens of recognized minority groups were granted local autonomy by the constitution but no right of self-determination. Equality was declared but "in practice a hierarchical binary existed, with minorities on one side and the Han on the other."[53] The sharpest manifestation of ethnonational oppression by the central state under Mao was probably the treatment of Tibet after a 1959 rebellion there was crushed (Tibet had been in effect an independent state before the Chinese state took control in 1950–51, imposing CCP rule while leaving Tibet's feudal theocracy intact).[54]

The attempt to speed up economic development in the chaotic GLF had a ghastly unintended consequence: devastating famine on a huge scale. Though the party-state leadership did everything it could to keep the urban population fed, starvation in rural areas between 1959 and 1962 was caused by rural officials' efforts to meet unrealistic central state targets for farm output, the impact of the large-scale shift of workers from agriculture into industry, and the continued export of grain, along with food waste and drought. Although there is much debate about the number of excess deaths caused by the famine, one scholarly estimate of fifteen to twenty-five million would make this famine "the deadliest in modern history in absolute terms" (there are also higher estimates).[55]

To this hideous toll stemming from the CCP's forced pace to develop AES must be added deaths from state repression. This was not centrally directed in the way the Great Purge was in the USSR, but it was nonetheless deadly. Official statistics put the number of people killed in the campaign against "counter-revolutionaries" of 1950–53, during which

Mao set quotas for executions, at 712,000. In 1968–69, state authorities went about restoring order at the end of the "Cultural Revolution" (CR), which had touched off in 1966 when Mao called on supporters to mobilize against his opponents in the CCP leadership and to reenergize AES. The conflicts that followed ended up spiralling out of control, sometimes escalating into armed clashes. Repression by the PLA and other forces of order was responsible for most of the 1.5 to 1.8 million deaths associated with the CR.[56] Chinese AES was also very much a carceral society. Its construction included the building of a system of labour camps during the 1950s. By 1960, the number of people incarcerated in the camps has been estimated at between twelve and twenty million, which was between 1.8 and 3.0 percent of the population. The camp system collapsed during the upheaval of the CR but was then rebuilt.[57] Throughout the Maoist years AES society was highly repressive, with citizens not allowed to organize independently of the party-state, although state authorities' control broke down temporarily during the CR.

As in the USSR, building AES in China was ecologically destructive. The state had to feed a growing population, including a larger non-agricultural workforce, without much use of chemical fertilizers or farm machinery. Higher agricultural output was also needed to help fund industrialization. These demands led to more forests and grasslands being turned into farmland. Yet over these years the total amount of arable land actually decreased because of the impact of ecologically destructive practices. Deforestation was also driven by the demand for more wood for fuel and timber. The growth of manufacturing and construction likewise caused considerable pollution.[58]

The shift in the late 1970s to market Stalinism profoundly changed China, but the exploitation of the working class has continued. What has changed is who exploits workers. It is no longer just the central political bureaucracy that extracts surplus labour: today private business owners, both Chinese and foreign, employ over 80 percent of urban workers. No matter who employs them, the party-state prevents workers from organizing independent unions through which they could try to alter the terms of exploitation. NGOs that advocate for workers' legal rights have also been shut down.[59] In agriculture, which now accounts for only a minority of the labour force, the shift from collective to private farming has modified the character of exploitation. Some people lease no farmland and are simply exploited as agricultural wage-labourers. For peasant farmers, exploitation takes the form of rent or, for those who lease land but must also work for wages, both rent and wage-labour.⁶⁰

The shape of gender oppression has also mutated. The shift to a "socialist market economy" has "opened spaces and possibilities previously blocked but also reconfigured forms of sexist discrimination and violence … Seen as inferior to men*, women* suffer from oppression, discrimination, harassment, and domestic violence — especially in the countryside."⁶¹ The One-Child Policy, in place from 1979 to 2015, was a harsh imposition on women's bodily autonomy. Now the state — like a number of other states today that want their populations to grow and are unable or unwilling to do this by attracting immigrants — is adopting "pro-family" policies designed to push women to have more babies, including providing small payments for children, reducing access to abortion, and making divorce less easy to obtain.⁶² Women's participation in paid work has declined, with those who work for pay still expected to also do most of the unpaid work in the home too.⁶³ Since the late 1970s the weight of heterosexism has lightened. Hooliganism was removed from the criminal law in 1997, and homosexuality is no longer classified as a mental disorder.⁶⁴ But more recently, concerns among top state officials about a "masculinity crisis" in China have led to "anti-sissy" measures with oppressive effects on trans and queer people.⁶⁵ This move is part of a "state-promoted conservative turn — in both rhetoric and policy — that emphasizes heteronormative family values and women's domestic responsibilities."⁶⁶

Ruling-class fear of social disorder can also be seen in the oppressive regime of control that has been imposed on Muslim residents in the region of Xinjiang. Because they are Muslims, Uyghurs and other Turkic people have been targeted by the party-state's version of the global anti-Muslim "War on Terror." This has included "DNA mapping, obligatory spy apps on private smartphones, widespread video surveillance, regular body searches, mass detentions in reeducation camps, and forced labour." These measures attest to "the increasing racist and Han supremacist tendencies in the CCP leadership."⁶⁷

The central political bureaucracy, now headed by Xi Jinping, has become much less tolerant of dissent than it was earlier this century. Some of the techniques used in Xinjiang, "the CCP leadership's laboratory for repressive tools,"⁶⁸ have also been deployed elsewhere. Repression has again come to the fore in how the Chinese ruling class governs. But now it uses the most sophisticated information technology available to try to prevent people from organizing to engage in collective action, to silence criticism of the status quo that it deems unacceptable, and to punish people when they disobey.[69] With repression and its paternalistic "Common Prosperity" policy, the party-state leadership "says to citizens, 'I will give you good things, but you won't be able to demand them *through action*.'"[70]

Finally, the dramatic development of productive forces since the late 1970s has done enormous ecological damage, far greater than that done in the preceding decades:

> If China's smog is appalling, the contamination of its rivers, lakes, reservoirs, underground aquifers, and farm soils can only be described as apocalyptic … No other nation has wrecked its environment so quickly and on such a scale … As fast as China became the workshop of the world, it also became the toxic waste dump of the world.[71]

China's vast amount of manufacturing and construction activity has been powered mainly by fossil fuels, above all coal. What has taken place in China since the start of this century has been "the greatest expansion of coal burning in world history,"[72] carried out in full knowledge of the implications for global climate change. Researchers at Climate Action Tracker rate China's actions as "Highly Insufficient." They point out that its greenhouse gas emissions "remain sky high with no sign of substantial emission reductions before the 2030 peaking timeline … Energy and electricity demand forecasts continue to grow, prolonging China's dependence on fossil fuels, despite substantial progress in renewables and end use sectors."[73]

The other side of the coin of the CCP's world-changing achievements over the past three-quarters of a century has been the exploitation of the workers and peasants whose interests the party claims to serve, interwoven with various forms of oppression and high levels of state repression. Along with these has come ecological devastation, especially since the party-state's turn to markets. Chinese society has been transformed, but not in ways that weaken class exploitation and state domination. Examining the PRC's relationship with global struggles deepens our understanding of the nature of the society built by the CCP leadership after 1949.

## CHINA AND GLOBAL STRUGGLES

In the 1960s, after the PRC rulers' desire to be able to steer their own policy course without pressures from their counterparts in the USSR led to an open rift between the two states, Mao and his fellow leaders became notorious for their talk of world revolution and denunciation of imperialism and the USSR's "revisionism." As people who had led a revolution of national liberation, CCP leaders' outlook on class and anti-imperialist struggles internationally was not identical to that of their counterparts in the CPSU. China under Mao provided support to national liberation struggles, such as Vietnam's, but did not support them consistently. Before, during, and after the 1960s the main concern of the ruling veterans of 1949 and their successors has always been to enhance the power of their state in relation to more powerful states, above all the US and, while it existed, the USSR.[74] This has led them to adopt wildly different political stances over time. The CCP's leaders did not relate to struggles outside China through an organization like the Comintern and never tried to create one. Like the USSR, the PRC could, when it suited its rulers' purposes, offer some combination of political education, military training, weapons, money, and advisors to political forces it wanted to support. The CCP also propagated its version of ML ideology (discussed in Chapter 7) around the world.

After they took power, CCP leaders promoted their strategy of guerilla warfare to achieve national independence and then build AES to radicals in what was then often called the "Third World." For example, in the early 1950s they trained Malayan and Burmese CP members and encouraged their armed struggles. Then, when top party-state officials adopted for China a "new self-projection as a non-interfering source of international harmony"[75] to build alliances with the rulers of other countries in the South, they urged CPs in those countries to stop fighting. Following the rift with the USSR, the CCP reversed course and offered support for the resumption of armed struggle. Two decades later, Deng withdrew support for Communist insurgency in Malaysia when he sought closer economic and diplomatic relations with its government.[76]

Before its break with the USSR, the CCP's overall global orientation was in synch with that of the CPSU. This included backing the USSR's crushing of the Hungarian Revolution.[77] But after the break, the CCP leadership became increasingly hostile to the USSR. Armed clashes between soldiers of the two states in 1969 intensified the animosity. CCP leaders' tactics, motivated by considerations of national self-interest in general, and by the very real threat of the Soviet Union in particular, were elevated to the level of a doctrine proclaiming that the interests of revolutionary movements everywhere were identical with the national interests of "socialist China." It was a doctrine that bore the imprint of Stalin's doctrine of "socialism in one country" as well as one that reflected the profoundly nationalist content of Maoism.[78]

China's rulers then adopted stances that surprised many of its international supporters. They developed friendly relations with the US, which they had previously denounced vociferously. This was part of a "global diplomatic strategy based on the rather traditional principles of national sovereignty, peaceful coexistence, and the establishment of friendly relations 'between states with different social systems.'"[79] The party-state leadership backed the government of Pakistan against the revolt that created Bangladesh. They rallied to the government of Sri Lanka (then Ceylon) against the 1971 uprising by the People's Liberation Front, a ML organization. In the civil war in Angola, they even supplied arms to the same forces that were actively supported by South Africa and the US and fighting against the side supported by the USSR.[80] Under Deng and his successors, the PRC moved away from socialist rhetoric in international affairs and shed entanglements with political forces seeking to overthrow their governments as it moved to deepen its integration into global capitalism.[81] Today the Chinese government celebrates its good relations with all manner of governments willing to align with it against the US, including the far-right government of Victor Orbán in Hungary.[82]

In the twenty-first century the CCP's support for movements fighting Western imperialism is a distant memory, as is its pirouette in the 1970s to backing governments and movements aligned against the USSR and with the US. But at no time did the rulers of the Chinese party-state act consistently to advance national liberation and class struggles globally. Their most important international concern has always been their state's position in relation to the states seen as most threatening to their interests. This priority corresponds to the party-state leadership's domestic project, which brings us to the crucial question about the kind of society built since 1949.

## WHAT KIND OF SOCIETY?

The AES society built by the CCP leadership after the Chinese Revolution was one in which the central political bureaucracy of the party-state functioned as a new exploiting class. After breaking the grip of semi-colonial domination and the power of landlords and business owners, it adopted the USSR's model of AES and carried out the industrialization and modernization of the country. It did so by extracting surplus labour from peasants and workers. For all the talk of socialism and communism, "the really operative goal was rapid industrial development, and the actual governing values were those most conducive to industrialization — the values of economic rationality and administrative efficiency."[83] From the 1950s until the end of the 1970s, the PRC was a mobilization economy — not identical to the one in the USSR, to be sure, but fundamentally similar. The top officialdom of the party-state then moved away from this non-commercial model. It gradually expanded the extent to which markets organized the production of goods and services and social reproduction (all the activities involved in having and raising the next generation of workers and in ensuring that people who are currently employed are able to keep working for their employers) until market forces became decisive. At the same time, it continued to rule over society and retained a major role for state-owned industries and state steering of the private sector. Much has changed in the lives of direct producers since the late 1970s. However, they have been no less exploited than they were before.

As in the USSR, under AES in China the party-state attempted to direct economic life, but there was no planning in the meaningful sense of the concept. Genuine planning involves setting an integrated set of achievable goals on the basis of adequate knowledge about what it would take to achieve those goals and what labour power and resources are available; this is impossible without mass democratic participation. In China, central state authorities channelled labour power and resources towards their priorities while enterprise managers attempted to meet the production targets issued to them. Democracy was just as absent in the PRC as in the USSR. However, economic direction by central state authorities was looser. When the first five-year plan was launched in 1953 the central institutions of economic management were only "half formed."[84] During the GLF the system was decentralized. The production targets that were still issued "lost touch with reality," ending any pretense of "planning."[85] This was followed by a recentralization, with enterprises ordered to stop selling or bartering their products with each other. This began a recurring cycle between centralization, which increased order at the cost of rigidity, and decentralization, which increased production but led to imbalances and instability. During the chaotic years of the CR and after, Mao promoted provincial and local "self-reliance" — not relying on resources from other regions — to reduce the need for central coordination. Sometimes this boosted production. It also led to more duplication and waste, more shortages, more competition between industries and enterprises for raw materials, and a lack of overall coordination that made a mockery of the very idea of a planned economy — what one analyst calls "plan anarchy."[86] Yet through the fluctuations of a mobilization economy even more poorly coordinated than the one in the USSR, there was a pattern of priorities. This was visible in the growth of heavy industry's share of total production in spite of Mao's calls for balance between heavy and light industry and agriculture. As in the USSR, the cause was, in the words of one economist, "the needs of defence"[87] — more precisely, the pressure to build the kind of extractive and manufacturing industries needed for a powerful military. From the 1980s onwards, the gradual spread of market competition and the integration of China into global markets changed the scope and character of the state's ongoing efforts to direct economic activity.[88]

Throughout the rule of the CCP, the labour of most direct producers has been alienated. The labour of rural producers — whose toil in "collective" agriculture was recognized with work points — was not under their own control, although party-state authorities had less control over what people did in the fields than they did over work in factories and offices, on construction sites, and elsewhere. The work of people who openly worked for wages has always been organized in hierarchical and authoritarian ways. While exhorted to participate in management's drives for higher production under Mao, workers themselves never democratically ran their workplaces. However, management control sometimes broke down during the upheavals of the CR. The restoration of order by the PLA then put military officers in charge in many workplaces. After they were withdrawn, managers' ability to compel their subordinates to work was often weak; managers were afraid of being punished by their superiors for some political failing, could offer few incentives to motivate workers, and in most cases had limited ability to discipline their subordinates.[89] Starting in the 1980s the party-state rulers was able to solve this bosses' problem by empowering managers and gutting workers' job security rights. Some workers protested but resistance was limited by the repressive power of the party-state to prevent workers from forming and sustaining independent organizations.[90]

Exactly what kind of society China was between 1949 and 1978 and what it became in the years since the end of the 1970s will be discussed in Chapter 6. Without question, though, in spite of what CCP leaders have maintained, China has never been in transition to communism. The Chinese Revolution ended semi-colonial domination and unified almost all of the territory of the former Qing Empire under CCP rule. It established a one-party state that implemented social reforms and industrialized and modernized the country. This laid the basis for the extraordinary development of productive forces that has happened since the late 1970s, which has given China's rulers great global influence. These are major changes in social arrangements. However, none of them have involved direct producers themselves taking charge of society and beginning to democratically plan production to meet their needs. None have eroded class exploitation and state power. As historian Yiching Wu observes,

> From the start, Chinese Communist rule took a harsh and authoritarian form that involved strengthening the one-party system, increasing political repression, and tightening control of information. A highly repressive garrison state was created in which institutions of the party, the military, and the state were closely intertwined. Because of the CCP's successful seizure of power by military means, the party was really a rebel army that transformed itself into a state, and military-style bureaucracies and militaristic concepts and practices played prominent roles in the country's everyday social and political life.[91]

One communist activist in China put it this way: "the form of China's existent political power is essentially that of a bureaucratic structure; the privileged stratum that controls this structure is a mountain weighing on the Chinese people ... their high salaries are the blood and sweat of the workers, peasants, and rusticated youth."[92] Whether under Mao or his successors, this bureaucratic structure was never one through which workers and peasants could start to reorganize society in their own interests. As Meisner recognizes, as China became more "socialist," the state became all the more dominant. For with the expropriation of the propertied classes, the nationalization of industry, and the collectivization of agriculture, not only was the state the political master of society, but it became its sole economic master as well … the Maoist state machine became increasingly separated from the society it ruled, its bureaucracy grew ever larger and more alien, and the division between rulers and the ruled became ever more pronounced.[93]

The picture has changed since 1978: there are now billionaire Chinese capitalists as well as many less wealthy business owners, so the state is no longer the "sole economic master" even though its influence within the private sector is strong. Yet today Chinese society is no more changing in ways that point towards a classless and stateless society of freedom than it was under Mao.

# CHAPTER 5

# CUBA 1959–PRESENT

**THE ONLY SOCIETY IN THE AMERICAS** where AES has been established is Cuba. As in China, AES came to Cuba as the result of a different kind of revolution than the one that happened in Russia. However, this revolution was not led by Cuba's CP but by left-wing nationalists who later adopted ML ideology. Cuba has changed since the fall of AES in the USSR and Eastern Europe but its path has differed from China's. Ever since the Cuban Revolution of 1959, much of the global left has been supportive of the Cuban government, which to this day continues to defy the US and proclaim its commitment to socialism. All this makes the case of AES in Cuba important to examine.

## THE CUBAN ROAD TO AES

Cuba was a colony of Spain from 1511 until 1898. Only in 1880 was slavery abolished, with formerly enslaved Afro-Cubans providing service as "apprentices" to their former owners until 1886. The year 1898 marked the end of the third war by Cubans to free themselves from colonial rule. When the Liberation Army was close to victory, the US government, which had offered to buy Cuba from Spain, decided to intervene against the Spanish. As a result, the war was ended by a treaty between the US and Spain, with Cubans frozen out of the process altogether.

This was no intervention to support Cubans determining their own future as a nation; instead, the objective was ensuring that the US would control a nominally independent Cuba. US capitalists owned plantations in Cuba that yielded sizeable profits from the production of sugar, the agricultural industry that increasingly dominated the island's economy. Companies in the US refined sugar and produced cigars and rum using raw materials from Cuba. Cubans also imported a wide range of goods from the US. After the war's end, US soldiers occupied Cuba until 1902.[1] They departed only after Cuba's constitutional convention reluctantly adopted an appendix to the constitution of the new republic, the Platt Amendment (named after its author, a US senator), that gave the US a "prerogative to exercise permanent, indirect rule in Cuba."[2] US troops returned from 1906 to 1909 and again from 1917 to 1922. In parallel to neocolonial political rule, the Cuban government signed treaties with the US that "cemented Cuba's role as a sugar export economy to the US market and as an importer of US manufactured goods."[3] By 1907, only a quarter of the land in rural Cuba was owned by Cubans; most of the rest was in the hands of US firms and individuals. By the 1920s, most of the sugar harvested in the country came from US property, and most of the profits from sugar went into the bank accounts of US companies.[4] Thus, capitalism in Cuba was decisively shaped by US capitalists. A growing proportion of the rural population became landless, and not all of the dispossessed were able to survive by working for wages in the sugar industry.[5] Boosted by immigration, the urban population swelled as part of the development of "what was by Latin American standards a relatively advanced, secular, and socially liberal society."[6]

The Great Depression in the 1930s led to the worst economic crisis in Cuban history. The president, Gerardo Machado, had been elected in 1924 as a reformer opposed to the Platt Amendment but then used "intimidation and bribery ... to run for his second term unopposed and as the only candidate representing every major political party." He was soon ruling as a dictator who had critics arrested and in a number of cases killed, and he faced rising opposition.[7] Then in 1933, revolution in Cuba: a bus drivers' strike in Havana escalated into a widely supported island-wide general strike calling for Machado's resignation. The US assistant secretary of state for Latin America, in Cuba to negotiate a deal between Machado and his opponents, threatened the president — now seen as incapable of maintaining order for US capitalists — with US military intervention. After Machado went on radio to denounce US interference, army officers told the president that they would overthrow him if he did not resign. Machado left the country. Workers and peasants rightly saw his exit as their victory and were inspired to fight for more. Many workers who had gone on strike against Machado now struck against their employers. In this climate of social upheaval, a group of non-commissioned officers led by Fulgencio Batista who were concerned about poor pay and career prospects as well as about Machado loyalists in the army then mutinied and took control of the military. This led to the creation of a provisional government under Ramon Grau, an anti-Machado academic. By this point, sugar workers were occupying dozens of sugar mills and running them under workers' control. In some places workers also took over small towns, railways, and rural areas around the mills.[8] "It was this continued mobilization from below that pressured the new government to act on the progressive agenda that had emerged over the last few years."[9] The government began to implement social reforms, including a minimum wage, lower utility rates, and voting rights for women. These met with resistance from capitalists and the US government. The US refused to recognize Grau's government, which was divided between left-wing nationalist populists and more timid reformers. Batista led the military to restore order with lethal violence on the sugar plantations. Early in 1934 he pressured Grau into resigning, to be replaced with a president acceptable to the US. After the military had quelled the revolution, the US and Cuban governments did away with the widely hated Platt Amendment as a sop to the defeated Cuban people.[10]

For the following twenty-five years, Batista dominated political affairs, whether wielding influence as the head of the military, as elected president (1940–44), or as president after leading a military coup (1952–58). The 1940 constitution that enshrined a host of liberal and social rights, testament to the impact of the 1933 revolution, was popular but toothless because it was not enforceable. US imperial domination siphoned out profits from capitalist economic activity in Cuba. Corruption flourished, mostly homegrown but made worse by criminal organizations from the US that found Cuba a good place to do business. The sugar industry, in which Cuban ownership grew, remained central. It provided workers with seasonal employment followed by months of unemployment and was subject to fluctuations in the price of sugar on international markets and from US demand. Cuban capitalists tended to send their profits abroad or direct them into speculation or real estate, which limited capitalist development in Cuba. So too did state regulation in response to economic instability and workers' militancy.[11]

Conditions of economic stagnation and dictatorship clashed with aspirations for better lives in the working class, which was some seven-tenths of the population in a society whose population in the early 1950s was 57 percent urban. These conditions also corroded backing for Batista among the middle class and capitalists.[12] But moving from dissatisfaction to action for change was not easy. Unionized workers who were against Batista were blocked by the union officialdom from organizing for political change through their unions; most union officials maintained tight control of the unions using bureaucratic and corrupt means and supported the president in exchange for being allowed to engage in collective bargaining with employers. The reputation of the Popular Socialist Party (PSP, the name taken by the Cuban CP in 1944) was tainted by its support for Batista in the 1940s and its entanglement in corrupt politics. This and its loyalty to the USSR limited the PSP's appeal among the growing number of workers, peasants, and middle-class people who wanted to see Batista leave office.[13] Batista's 1952 coup was a last straw for some of them, and small groups of soldiers and civilians took up arms against the dictator. One after another their efforts to topple Batista failed.

Then, in 1957, the July 26th Movement led by Fidel Castro, a left-wing nationalist populist, began to gain strength. The movement succeeded in building and sustaining a small guerilla force in the Sierra Maestra mountains. This base allowed the movement to survive the blow of the failure of its general strike attempt in the spring of 1958 and go on to create other fronts of guerilla activity. Its defeat of an army offensive that summer forced the army to retreat. This won the movement overwhelming political support among the many opponents of a dictator who was generally despised. Even the Catholic Church hierarchy and associations of sugar capitalists were now against Batista.[14] The army, "a fundamentally mercenary and corrupt institution with no solid social base or ideological and political motivation,"[15] was now collapsing. As 1959 began, Batista fled the country and the rebels took power.

The July 26th Movement's revolution had been made against a fragile capitalist state. Like the Chinese Revolution of 1949, this was a revolution mainly carried out by armed fighters acting on behalf of the masses, although in Cuba the level of popular participation was lower than in China. It was not a revolution made by mass struggle from below, democratically organized by workers and peasants themselves. Castro's rebels enjoyed widespread working-class support but the level of workers' self-activity was much lower than it had been in 1933.[16] In this environment, the leaders of the July 26th Movement, a "declassed" leadership with "no strong organizational or institutional ties … to any of the country's … major social classes,"[17] did away with what remained of the existing state and began to build a new one.[18]

Castro's new government of left-wing nationalist populists (a few of whom had ML politics) and liberals adopted a host of reforms, including wage increases, decreases for urban rents, and lower utility rates. It reacted to direct action to redistribute land with a law against such self-activity and then brought in a moderate agrarian reform law.[19] However, since much of the affected land was owned by US firms or citizens, this sparked the ire of the US ruling class. The signing of a Cuba–USSR trade deal in early 1960 was followed by US-owned oil companies refusing to refine oil from the USSR. The government responded by taking control of the operation of these refineries while leaving them as the property of their US owners. In turn, the US abrogated its agreement to buy Cuban sugar. The Cuban state then seized the assets of other US firms. The US retaliated by launching an economic blockade. The government then expropriated and nationalized the property of most Cuban capitalists.[20] As these events unfolded in 1959–60, with the population radicalizing and participating in rallies and the government setting up new community organizations under its control, supporters of other political currents either resigned from the government or were pushed out by the Castro leadership. Castro and his team also took control of the unions and mass media, setting up a new state security agency with help from the USSR. In April 1961, a US-orchestrated invasion of the island by right-wing exiles was easily defeated and Castro declared the Cuban Revolution "socialist."[21]

This was not evidence of a Communist conspiracy, as some anti-communists contend. Nor did Castro have "a precise long-term strategy with a previously determined specific goal."[22] Rather the decision by Castro and other top leaders to remake Cuba on AES lines, without a timeline, was "most likely the result of a conjunctural choice made by the fall of 1959."[23] Researcher Samuel Farber observes that

> Castro's brand of populist caudillismo [a kind of politics centred on a strong and unaccountable leader], detached from any significant institutional ties to Cuba's principal social classes, had an elective affinity with Soviet-style Communism. But only the presence of certain historical circumstances (e.g., US pressures, the widely shared belief in the international rise of Soviet power, and political pressures coming from the Partido Socialista Popular and the group around Raul Castro and Che Guevara) converted that affinity into choice and commitment.[24]

That the Cuban Revolution ultimately created an AES society was the result of choices made by a revolutionary leadership with a particular ideological complexion and an alliance with the pro-Moscow PSP, acting while under pressure from the US.

The actual adoption of the USSR's economic model along with a move to develop heavy industry began in 1961. In the same year the government brought the July 26th Movement, the PSP, and the student-based Revolutionary Directorate together in one political organization. Initial attempts at "planning" with the assistance of advisors from the USSR and Eastern European AES countries flopped. These were followed with a combination of mobilization efforts influenced by China's GLF in most enterprises, alongside contemporary techniques from the USSR in others. A modified version of the former approach was then rolled out. After this failed it was replaced at the start of the 1970s with the version of the centralized direction of production in use in the USSR, overseen through the one-party state by the party with ML ideology that had been created in 1962 and renamed the CP of Cuba in 1965.[25]

## ACHIEVEMENTS OF AES IN CUBA

The Cuban Revolution led to a number of far-reaching accomplishments. The first momentous change was the end of the US domination that had done so much damage to the country. Even though Cuba had to rely on the USSR and other AES countries to buy most of its sugar and other exports and as its suppliers of oil and many other imports, its relationship with them, which lasted until the end of the 1980s, did not drain the surplus produced by workers out of the country as had the US-Cuba relationship. In fact, the USSR's rulers subsidized Cuba for the sake of their geopolitical interests.[26]

With Cuban workers' labour no longer enriching US and Cuban business owners, the party-state was able to mobilize it for other objectives. The goal of industrialization was relinquished in 1964 in favour of a return to sugar; this was intended as a temporary move to make possible a resumption of industrialization, but the resumption never happened.[27] However, the state did succeed in building comprehensive public health and education systems. These improved the lives of the citizenry, with rural residents benefiting the most. By 1995 life expectancy had reached seventy-five, up from fifty-nine in the early 1950s. But both health and education systems have deteriorated considerably in the years since the collapse of AES in the USSR and Eastern Europe, an event that had a huge impact on Cuba because of how dependent Cuba had been on trade with and aid from those states. The expansion of advanced education has also enabled the development of high-technology productive forces in biotechnology, used to produce pharmaceuticals.[28]

The mobilization of women to work outside their homes for wages in much larger numbers weakened the patriarchal gender relations of families previously dominated by male wage earners. Women now had to live with the "still patriarchal but less intimate and far more impersonal authority of the one-party state and its institutions of control."[29] In 2022 a new Family Code was adopted by referendum. This undid previous bans on same-gender marriage and adoption while strengthening the rights of women and children.[30] The revolution also weakened the burden of racism for Afro-Cubans. The new state soon did away with segregation in schools, clubs, beaches, and parks. People who experienced racism also benefited from the state's moves to redistribute income and resources even though these were not designed in specifically anti-racist ways.[31]

Today, freedom from the US control that the country endured before 1959 remains a major achievement of AES in Cuba. While its much-vaunted broad welfare state is now much more meagre than it was at its peak, its services continue to contribute to the well-being of the citizenry. As in the USSR and the PRC, though, the accomplishments of Cuba since the adoption of AES have taken place through class exploitation and various interwoven forms of oppression.

## THE COSTS OF CLASS SOCIETY

The new government led by Castro built a party-state along AES lines that extracts surplus labour from workers and peasants. The direct producers have never had any control over the uses to which their labour has been put; all such decisions are made by the central political bureaucracy. Nor have they ever democratically controlled their workplaces. Workers cannot even use unions to contest how exploited they are because union officials and management are so closely connected and unions are geared to raising productivity. Unions in Cuba, like the official mass organizations for women and other groups, are arms of the party-state. There is no legal right to strike. In the growing private sector, which now employs a sizeable minority of workers, workers' legal rights are much weaker than in the state sector.[32]

As mentioned above, gender oppression and heterosexism have in some ways been weakened in Cuba. However, for several decades after

1959 the actions of the Cuban leadership made heterosexism worse than it had been before the revolution. For many years the party-state demeaned same-gender sexuality and treated "effeminate" men as a problem, even operating forced labour camps for gay men and other "deviants" from 1965 to 1968. Women continue to carry out a disproportionate amount of the unpaid labour of social reproduction, the burden of which has swelled in the years of economic crisis since the fall of the USSR. They also continue to experience a lot of gendered violence.[33]

Racism against Afro-Cubans and other non-white people persisted after the establishment of AES. From the 1990s on, racism has worsened, since Afro-Cubans have been disproportionately affected by the effects of the economic crisis. Soon after the revolution, the new state's leaders shut down the well-established Afro-Cuban mutual aid associations. This move was followed by the state's declaration that the problem of racism had been solved. From this has flowed a strict commitment to "race blind" policies rather than measures specifically designed to do away with racial oppression. All these actions have had the effect of perpetuating racism.[34]

The party-state's near-total prohibition of people forming grassroots groups independent of state institutions, which include its official mass organizations like its unions and the Federation of Cuban Women,[35] remains a barrier to oppressed people coming together to identify and act against their oppression. This restriction is an important facet of state repression in Cuba. Today the central political bureaucracy no longer holds much of the popular support it once enjoyed as a consequence of the revolution's achievements. As a result, it must rely more on repression to maintain its rule. Writer Raymar Aguado Hernandez notes that after "widespread protests" in July 2021, the largest anti-government protests in the country since 1959, "this hermetic and repressive order was greatly fortified. There were thousands of arrests and cases of police brutality ... a new penal code that criminalized dissent was enacted, and many activists were pressured or forced into exile."[36]

To acknowledge these negative aspects of Cuban society is not, as defenders of the Cuban state often claim, to side with imperialism. Nor does it mean denying what the Cuban Revolution accomplished or that the welfare state that still exists in Cuba today has beneficial effects on people's lives. It is simply to recognize the evidence that class exploitation, oppression, and state repression are very real features of this AES society.

## CUBA AND GLOBAL STRUGGLES

Since 1959, Cuba has been widely seen by leftists as, in Farber's words,

> a consistently anti-imperialist force and a stronghold of progressive and national liberation movements ... However, a careful examination of Cuban foreign policy reveals that while it is true that Cuba has followed a consistent policy of opposition to the imperialism sponsored by the United States and its Western allies, it has not followed that policy toward other imperialist aggressors. In fact, the Cuban government has taken the side of oppressor states on various occasions.[37]

This record is particularly relevant to evaluating Cuba because some of its supporters on the global left place much weight on its government's international commitments.

After 1959, the Cuban government initially adopted a bold anti-imperialist orientation distinct from the foreign policy of the USSR. Cuba's Latin American policy "involved open and aggressive support for guerilla movements and harsh denunciation of the traditional Communist Parties on the continent that criticized and opposed such policies."[38] Not surprisingly, this sincerely held stance led to arguments with CPSU leaders, who were against this strategy. The Cuban leadership saw them as timid comrades.[39]

The Cuban party-state's orientation changed in the late 1960s. Castro supported the 1968 invasion of Czechoslovakia by armed forces from the USSR and other Eastern European AES states. For this, Cuba was rewarded with more military and economic assistance from the USSR. The new orientation involved Cuban leaders giving less support to Latin American guerilla struggles and no longer providing it openly. They soon began to work with the USSR to support Third World anti-imperialist forces in ways that were politically agreeable to the CPSU leadership.[40] The Cuban priority became support for African nationalist movements. In the 1970s and 1980s Cuban leaders devoted a great deal of effort to this cause, on occasion acting independently of the USSR. In 1975–76 they took the initiative to send some thirty thousand soldiers to Angola to support the People's Movement for the Liberation of Angola (MPLA) in its war against the MPLA's opponents, who were being aided by South African troops and backed by the US.[41] In 1988 an even larger force of Cuban troops again fought alongside MPLA soldiers against South African and US-backed Angolan forces. Between 1975 and 1991, over 430,000 Cuban troops and civilians served in Angola. This major commitment stemmed from the sincere opposition of the Cuban Communist leadership to Western imperialism and the South African apartheid state. But Cuba's role in the country was not entirely limited to support of a national liberation struggle: Cuban forces took sides in a bloody 1977 conflict within the MPLA rather than declining to intervene in that fight out of respect for Angolan national self-determination. The Cuban approach in the Horn of Africa was also quite different from its more clear-cut stance in Angola. Cuba originally supported Eritrean forces fighting for independence from Ethiopia. Then, after the Derg came to power in Ethiopia, the Cuban state switched sides. After Somalia, whose government Cuba and the USSR had been backing, invaded Ethiopia in 1977, seventeen thousand Cuban troops were sent to fight against Somalia. These realignments by Cuba were the same as those of the USSR.[42] Many anti-capitalists around the world have also been disturbed by Cuban support for the People's Party government of Guyana, which in 1980 murdered internationally known revolutionary socialist Walter Rodney, and by Cuba's friendly relations with the Franco government in Spain and the repressive rulers of the Islamic Republic of Iran.[43] The Cuban state's political alignment with Russia after its invasion of Ukraine in 2022, which it justified in terms of opposing the expansion of NATO, is a recent example of how it has on occasion sided with imperialist aggression.[44] These and other similar cases demonstrate that the Cuban CP leadership's orientation to struggles globally has been shaped by "its perception and definition of what it needs for its own survival and what is in the best interests of the Cuban state,"[45] not by consistent anti-imperialism let alone communist politics.

## WHAT KIND OF SOCIETY?

AES came to Cuba in a way that was entirely different than the circumstances in which it first emerged in the USSR. AES in Cuba was the outcome of a revolution, as it was in China. However, unlike in China, the revolutionary leadership that succeeded in toppling Batista's weak state was not already committed to establishing AES. The new order had a lot of popular support because AES was established by the leaders of a movement that had overthrown a widely loathed dictator and put in place a new state that freed Cuba from US domination and delivered real improvements in the living standards of most citizens. Capitalist development in Cuba had, despite its many harmful features, already turned most people into wage-workers and generated productive forces in Cuban society that were more advanced than those that existed in the USSR in 1928 or China in 1949. This meant that Cubans were spared the kind of mass death and misery that happened in the USSR and the PRC as a result of forced industrialization and the dispossession of peasants.

These specific aspects of Cuban reality put their stamp on AES in Cuba. Nevertheless, the social relations established there were always in essence similar to those in other AES societies. One communist critic, arguing in the 1980s against fellow anti-Stalinist marxists who saw Cuba as qualitatively better than AES elsewhere, noted that Cuba had a "mixture of mass participation bodies in which the masses have no voice; 'democratic' structures which operate in the shadow of an elite dozen top leaders; 'trade unions' which see their role as speeding up production; and … systems of 'elections' in which political discussion, manifestos, factions and parties are all outlawed."[46] The party-state built a mobilization economy in which, by the end of the 1960s, the production and distribution of goods and services was carried out under state ownership to an even greater extent than in other AES countries.[47] After its initial effort to emulate the USSR's version of central economic direction, "the central plan was discarded, and a series of special plans were put in operation, all competing for scarce resources without any central coordination."[48] This was followed by a lasting shift to central direction. At no time has there ever been democratic planning of production by the direct producers. This lack of democracy discourages "authentic feedback, accurate information, and really independent initiatives from below, which imply a loss of control by the authorities."[49] Over time, the central political bureaucracy channelled a larger share of investment into manufacturing for domestic use rather than agriculture (sugar still accounted for most of the country's exports and the scale of industrialization was limited). Military spending came to account for a smaller share of the state budget than it had in the 1960s but remained high.[50] In the last decade of the century the loss of aid from the USSR and the guaranteed purchasing of sugar by AES countries forced a change in the state's economic priorities. Tourism facilities and related services have greatly expanded. Importantly, the party-state now allows more private economic activity, and about one-third of the workforce now works in the private sector, in enterprises that employ up to one hundred workers each.[51] But there has not yet been a shift to market Stalinism of the kind that took place in China. Workplaces have been organized on hierarchical and authoritarian lines ever since AES was established in Cuba. As a result of the alienation of their labour, workers often "have no reason to care or 'give a damn.'"[52] Historian Alexander Hall Lujardo observes that "the ruling class imaginary" in his country is "incapable of understanding that despotism has disastrous results on productivity."[53] The low motivation that stems from alienated labour has been compounded since the 1990s by the erosion of the state-provided "standard of living that, while modest and austere, eliminated economic uncertainty and anxiety as well as extreme hardship."[54]

Journalist Lisbeth Moya Gonzalez, who, like Hall and Aguado, is part of the "critical left" in Cuba, observes with frustration that many "foreign leftists strive to protect the myth of Cuban socialism and … associate all types of dissent with the historical project of the political right and with imperialist designs." While acknowledging those threats, Moya contends that "to imagine Cuba as a bastion of democracy and social justice, treating it as a souvenir or an idealization of utopia, does the country no more favours than to demonize it and portray it as a barracks."[55] If we abandon such self-deception and analyze Cuba from a reconstructed historical materialist perspective, it becomes clear that the leadership of the Cuban Revolution liberated the country from US imperialism and went on to reorganize society in AES ways that improved the lives of most of its people. However, a transition to communism never began and the social relations of AES have been barriers to workers and oppressed people organizing themselves to define and defend their interests.

# CHAPTER 6

# SO, WHAT KIND OF SOCIETIES WERE THEY?

**SOCIAL RELATIONS IN THE AES** societies in the USSR, PRC, and Cuba have never changed in ways that moved away from class exploitation, alienation, and oppression. The direct producers have not in any way "ceas[ed] to be a dominated mass" or made "the entire political and economic life" their "own life and giv[en] that life a conscious, free, and autonomous direction."[1] In other words, no transition towards communism was happening.

In these societies, as in other AES societies,[2] the central political bureaucracy of the state is a ruling class that exploits the labour of direct producers. These rulers' efforts to develop productive forces after a phase of industrialization have been hamstrung by their inability to raise the productivity of labour over the long term. As we have seen, under AES, party-state managers are unable either to persuade or compel workers to work ever more efficiently in a sustained way. This is a feature of AES, not a bug. It becomes an insurmountable obstacle to the central political bureaucracy realizing its goals of economic and social development. The turn to market Stalinism proved to be a solution to this problem for the rulers of the PRC, one that dismantled defining aspects of AES.

These historical experiences show that theorist Cornelius Castoriadis was right to claim that "the realization of socialism on the proletariat's behalf by any party or bureaucracy whatsoever is an absurdity, a contradiction in terms, a square circle, an underwater bird."[3] Ante Ciliga — a leader of the CP of Yugoslavia who, while living in the USSR in the 1930s, was imprisoned for more than five years for opposition to Stalin's regime — was similarly perceptive. Commenting on people who believed that industrialization in the USSR meant progress in the direction of communism, he suggested that "by dint of admiring factory-chimneys, [they] no longer perceived living beings and the social relations existing between them."[4] Unfortunately, this has been true for too many socialists since AES first emerged. Yet ever since the party-state officialdom in the USSR became increasingly like a ruling class during the 1920s there have been people who, from a communist perspective, opposed this degeneration and the new way of organizing society that took shape under Stalin.[5] Even when a new ruling class had only just crystallized in the USSR, in the confusing tumult of the Great Break, there were marxists who recognized what had happened.[6]

Of course, supporters of AES object to the analysis that these societies were or, in a few remaining cases, are not in transition to communism. Some communist critics of AES also think that this analysis goes too far. These challenges deserve consideration. Before proceeding to look more deeply at how we should understand what exactly AES is, this chapter will present and respond to the main objections raised by supporters of AES and by those communist critics of AES and other leftists who see this kind of society as superior to capitalism.

## OBJECTIONS AND RESPONSES

In online and in-person debate among leftists about AES, ideas are often presented in unserious and sometimes hostile ways, but they can nonetheless be grouped into five key objections: the dismissal of communist critique of AES as anti-communist, the "productive forces" objection, the "distorted but still in transition" argument, the "state property" objection, and "at least it was better than capitalism."

### "That's Anti-Communist" or "Purity Fetishism"

The most common response is the kind levelled by Michael Parenti, discussed in Chapter 1: dismissing the analysis and those who argue for it as anti-communist. As we have seen, this is a shallow charge. It assumes precisely what those who make it need to prove: that AES societies were in some way in transition to communism. It is not a serious argument to say that of course these societies were moving towards communism, or at least had started to do so, because Communist governments, many citizens of AES countries, and many anti-communists have all thought they were.

A recent variation on this theme charges perspectives such as the one developed in this book with the sin of "purity fetishism," "an incessant passing of judgment grounded on a superficial assessment of whether reality measures up to pure ideas or not." Writer Carlos Garrido accuses radical critics of AES of holding these "siege socialist" societies up to standards of perfection and of being unreasonably harsh about their shortcomings. Garrido claims that neither "authoritarian" measures taken by a socialist state "to protect the revolution" nor "opening up to foreign capital to develop its productive forces" are "an annihilating negation of socialism." People afflicted with "the purity fetish" are unable to see "socialist construction as a process, one which will, undoubtedly, develop contradictions which will in time be likely overcome." But within Garrido's philosophical wording is an argument no better than what Parenti offers in a plainer style. It simply asserts that AES societies — including China today — are in transition to communism no matter what. It even suggests that they feature "socialist democracy for the common people."[7] This kind of theory underpins social industry posts such as this tweet: "The Western Left: We will accept Communism once it actually 'works.' China: Raises their entire population from poverty. The Western Left: Not like that …"[8]

What this outlook involves but never acknowledges is a fundamental redefinition of communist thought, one that rejects the core ideas of Marx, Engels, Luxemburg, and many other communist thinkers before Stalin. It invokes their names and uses some of the same words that they used, but the words are now in service of *an entirely different project*. A transition to communism is no longer seen as starting with the direct producers taking control of society and unfolding as they themselves democratically remake social arrangements in ways that cause markets, class divisions, state power, and oppression to wither away. Instead, communism becomes a goal that can supposedly be reached at the end of a process that the direct producers do not control in the slightest — one that involves the strengthening of despotic "socialist" state power through which new rulers exploit the direct producers in whose name they claim to govern. Socialism is seen as a stage in that process, one defined by comprehensive state ownership of productive forces and a sufficient level of industrialization.[9] People who think of themselves as marxists who endorse this view of AES as a society on the road to communism have unknowingly reverted to the older tradition of communist politics rejected by Marx and Engels when they developed a new "viewpoint which first wedded the new communist idea to the new democratic aspirations," merging "revolutionary socialism with revolutionary democracy" for the first time.[10] As a political group to which Marx and Engels belonged put it in a statement in 1847, "We are not among those communists who are out to destroy personal liberty, who wish to turn the world into one huge barrack or into a gigantic workhouse ... we have no desire to exchange freedom for equality ... [Let us put] our hands to work in order to establish a democratic state wherein each party would be able by word or in writing to win a majority over to its ideas."[11]

It is worth mentioning that defenders of AES of the kind discussed here often try to bolster their case by pointing to the consequences of the USSR's industrialization under Stalin: an "industrial base" that later "produced the weapons of war that eventually turned the tide" against Nazi Germany.[12] In response, two points are pertinent. First, this historical fact about one of the consequences of the Great Break does nothing to demonstrate that the USSR was a society in transition to communism. That a society industrialized does not demonstrate that such a transition was underway. Second, the Nazi victory in Germany was not inevitable. If the Comintern had not stuck to Stalin's ultra-left line of 1928–34, which maintained that social democrats were "social fascists," the mass Social Democratic and Communist Parties in Germany, along with other forces, might well have come together in a united front against fascism and prevented Hitler from coming to power. In his study of the history of the Communist movement, Fernando Claudin, a member of the Political Bureau of the Spanish CP from 1947–65, argues that "the whole political evolution of Germany from 1930 ... gives grounds for assuming that the course of events could have been entirely altered if ... the Comintern and the German Communists, correcting their previous policy, had applied a flexible tactic of anti-Fascist unity."[13]

Finally, it is regrettably necessary to note that some people who argue in the manner of Parenti and Garrido also insinuate or allege that it is "Western chauvinist" or racist to view AES societies in what was once usually called the Third World as not in transition to communism.[14] The idea here is that to analyze AES in this way denigrates the achievements of non-white people oppressed by imperialism. However, an analysis that AES societies were founded on class exploitation is not connected to racist notions about the people of these societies. As long as there is no explicit or implicit idea that these societies are the way they are because of "racial" characteristics of the people in question,[15] there is nothing racist about the analysis. As the previous chapters and much other writing on AES shows, it is entirely possible to acknowledge the achievements of these societies and the impact of imperialism on them while at the same time demonstrating that they were not in transition to communism.

## The Productive Forces Objection

Another objection is that the rapid development of productive forces under AES proves that this kind of society is in transition to communism. Earl Browder, top leader of the CPUSA from 1930 until he ran afoul of Stalin's leadership in the USSR in 1945 and was removed from office,[16] put it this way in a public debate in 1950:

> the role played by America in the 19th century in leading the development of the world's productive forces under capitalist society has passed to Russia in the 20th century in the development of the world's productive forces to a stage higher than capitalism, which is the foundation of socialism ... if the proposition is valid that the growth of productive forces is the basis for progress, then the new system in Russia called socialism is the most progressive that history has ever produced. This is progress on a hitherto unknown level. It is revolutionary progress.[17]

The history of AES in the USSR and elsewhere has not been kind to this position, although supporters of the PRC today argue in a similar vein about that country.[18] But whether we are dealing with the USSR under Stalin or China under Xi, the essential problem with this position was pointed out by Browder's opponent in the 1950 debate, Max Shachtman:

> The *Communist Manifesto* over a hundred years ago went out of its way to pay tribute to the bourgeoisie which, as it said, "has accomplished wonders far surpassing Egyptian pyramids, Roman aqueducts and Gothic cathedrals," but Marx and Engels didn't, therefore, call capitalist society a socialist community ... The statistics of production by themselves tell us nothing whatever about the social nature of production.[19]

Quite simply, the rapid development of productive forces may be part of a transition to communism but is in no way, shape, or form unique to this process. It is not evidence of transition underway. Nor is it a defining feature of transition to communism.

## Distorted but Still in Transition

In the late 1970s, sociologist Albert Szymanski published a book defending the USSR against Maoist claims that capitalism had been restored there. His case is a sophisticated defence of the idea that the USSR in what turned out to be its later years was in transition to communism — *sophisticated* both in that word's meaning of elaborate and in its sense of sophistry. Szymanski believed that the USSR was a "state socialist" society that had been making "continuing (if sometimes erratic) progress towards communism ... since the 1930s" but was marred by a "concentration of power and to a lesser degree privileges, in the hands of experts."[20] There was, he contended, no ruling exploiting class because the leadership did not "appropriate the economic surplus of the producers for their own ends."[21] To support this interpretation, he pointed out that the inequality between the higher incomes and benefits of "the managerial and government power elite" compared to those of workers in the USSR was less than the gap between the incomes and benefits of capitalists and workers in the West. The elite's compensation was also small in comparison to the size of the surplus in the USSR. Living standards were growing, economic inequality was shrinking quickly, and there was an "increasing depth and breadth of political debate and participation."[22]

Szymanski's case has factual problems. For example, it ignores the fall in male life expectancy underway from the mid-1960s, downplays the perks enjoyed by members of the central political bureaucracy, and greatly exaggerates the "depth and breadth of political debate and participation" — at the time, liberal, conservative, and left-wing dissidents were still very much being persecuted, and few citizens were enthusiastic supporters of AES and its rulers' ideology.[23] But its fatal flaw is its inability to recognize class exploitation and a ruling class. Over a decade earlier, Kuron and Modzelewski's analysis of AES had pinpointed the problems of interpretations like Szymanski's. What really mattered was not the personal wealth of party-state officials. As they noted, "direct personal consumption is not an end in itself of the ruling class under any system." The crucial reality was the central political bureaucracy's "relationship — as a group — to the means of production and to other social classes (above all, the working class)."[24] As a group, they, not the direct producers, controlled the state-owned means of production and decided how work would be organized, how much surplus labour workers should generate, and to what uses it would be put. This made them an exploiting class.

## *The State Property Objection*

There are communists who are critical of AES, sometimes highly so, but who insist that such societies had taken a significant step towards communism because their productive forces were state owned. They also believe that the ruling layer of party-state officials was not a social class. This objection is quite different from the previous three because its view of AES is much more critical. People who raise it see such societies as having begun transition towards communism only to be blocked by bureaucratic degeneration or as bureaucratized from the outset. From this perspective, the obstacle to further progress towards communism is the ruling layer of party-state officials. Its perks, bureaucratic methods, and conservative ideology make it a mighty barrier but, from this perspective, it is not a ruling class. Many of the critics who see AES this way conclude that only a revolution by the direct producers can do away with the ruling layer; others believe that it can be removed by a reforming popular movement, or even reform itself out of existence. The originator of the analysis of the USSR as a bureaucratically degenerated society in transition to communism was Trotsky. After his assassination on Stalin's orders, orthodox Trotskyists built on what had been Trotsky's evolving analysis to develop their accounts of AES. Some, like writer Isaac Deutscher, were less critical of this social order and its rulers than Trotsky had been. What unites these anti-Stalinist marxist accounts is a shared belief that near-total state ownership of the means of production means that AES societies had, in spite of their bureaucratic features, started transitions to communism.[25] Today, many leftists who are critical of AES but see it as having begun to move beyond capitalism (often calling it "state socialism") understand it in a similar way, though they are often unaware of the lineage of this outlook.

For people committed to understanding society in a historical materialist way, there are grave problems with this perspective. State ownership does not in and of itself put a society in transition to communism. Engels, writing while Marx was still alive, argued that

> the modern state, no matter what its form, is essentially a capitalist machine ... the ideal collective capitalist. The more it proceeds to the taking over of the productive forces, the more

it actually becomes the collective capitalist, the more citizens it exploits. The workers remain wage-workers, proletarians. But the capitalist relation is not done away with; it is rather brought to a head.[26]

Similarly, union leader James Connolly wrote in 1899 that "state ownership and control is not necessarily Socialism — if it were, then the Army, the Navy, the Police, the Judges, the Gaolers, the Informers, and the Hangmen, all would all be Socialist functionaries, as they are State officials." Essential instead was "the co-operative control by the workers of … land and materials."[27] Writing before AES emerged, they and many other marxists understood that state ownership of the means of production is merely a legal property form. As Marx argued,

> to define bourgeois [capitalist] property is nothing else than to give an exposition of all the social relations of bourgeois production. To try to give a definition of property as of an independent relation, a category apart, an abstract and eternal idea, can be nothing but an illusion of metaphysics or jurisprudence.[28]

Put simply, Marx understood property in terms of how a dominant class organizes society's production of goods and services, not whether legal ownership is formally private or state. The fact that the vast bulk of a society's productive forces are state-owned tells us nothing about the social relations structuring production: how is production organized, and to what ends? That is what we need to understand in order to assess if a society has taken even a step towards communism. Trotsky believed that the industrialization that followed the Great Break proved that a transition was underway in the USSR.[29] Shachtman's argument, quoted earlier, refutes this belief. Industrialization under AES was not part of a process in which class divisions and state power were beginning to dissolve as direct producers democratically planned production to meet human needs. As for the view that the central political bureaucracy was not a ruling class, my point in the previous section about what Szymanski fails to see is equally relevant here. To think that a party-state leadership capable of drastically remaking the society it dominated — including dispossessing the peasantry, as in the USSR and the PRC — is not a social class suggests that the observer is wearing theoretical blinkers.[30]

## "At Least It Was Better Than Capitalism"

The final objection worth briefly mentioning concedes that AES was not moving towards communism. From this viewpoint, communism or progress towards it may even be seen as impossible. Yet it sees AES societies as "progressive" — better than capitalism and worthy of at least some political support because of "good things" their governments have done.[31] Its supporters also often point out, correctly, that the living conditions of most people in the former USSR got much worse after the end of AES.

From the perspective adopted in this book, this is a misguided approach. Once capitalism developed to the point that it created the possibility of a working class leading a social revolution and at least beginning a transition to communism, no form of class society has deserved the endorsement of supporters of human emancipation. The possibility of communism makes class society in any form historically obsolete and indefensible. Specific social institutions with positive effects on human well-being — for example, public health and education systems and job security provisions — do not make a society as a whole worthy of support. Institutions can be defended insofar as they improve people's lives, without endorsing a social order. Even if one were to concede that communism is impossible, there would be no reason to endorse AES or any other form of class society. Ongoing subordination of imperialized societies (those dominated by imperialism) ought to be opposed, along with acts of naked aggression against them. But principled opposition to imperialism does not require giving political support to the rulers of Cuba or any other imperialized country. For supporters of liberation "the touchstone of politics" should be, as it was for Marx and Engels, "the class struggle — the struggle of the lower classes against oppression and exploitation, in the present as in the time of Spartacus or Napoleon."[32]

## WHAT MODE OF PRODUCTION?

Up to this point, this book has demonstrated that AES societies were not actually in transition to communism at all. They were class societies where the ruling class, the central political bureaucracy, exploited the direct producers. Although these societies were not identical to each other and changed over time, they were still fundamentally similar and can be analyzed together.[33]

We have seen that under AES almost all direct producers work for wages.[34] They are legally obliged to work and generally cannot meet many of their needs without doing so.[35] Direct producers, whether urban or rural, do not democratically run their workplaces. Nor do they decide how much of their time on the job goes towards their own compensation and how much goes toward surplus labour. They have no say over how much of the total work effort of all producers is allocated to each of the various sectors and subsectors for producing goods and services. Their labour is alienated and exploited by a ruling class, the central political bureaucracy of a state that the direct producers do not control. These are the vertical dimension of the social relations of production.

The ruling class runs a mobilization economy. It mobilizes labour to achieve its objectives, in an extreme version of what the state does in a Western capitalist war economy when it dictates to private companies and public-sector enterprises how they are required to participate in co-ordinated production for the war effort and imposes tight restrictions on workers and employers (as happened during World War II[36]). Under AES, the state directs enterprises to produce whatever it is that they are told to produce; the degree of central coordination varies between countries and across time. The state guarantees that what is ordered and delivered will be accepted. In this system, enterprise managers are often forced by shortages to compete for the labour power and other inputs they need. These are relations within the ruling class, the horizontal dimension of the relations of production, as well as some vertical relations.[37]

The other aspect of these relations has to do with how AES countries are influenced by the capitalist world system. Neither the USSR, the PRC, or any of the smaller AES societies were ever free of its pressures. This pressure generally did not take the form of competition to sell commodities in foreign markets. Nonetheless the pressures of geopolitical, ultimately military, competition were real and inescapable. The Great Break itself was in large part a response by CPSU leaders to the economic and military superiority of Western European capitalist states. As two economists who have studied the goals of central economic direction in the USSR conclude, "Soviet rulers in the period 1928–1988 ran the economy in pursuit of military might, with consumption as the secondary objective."[38] This was what lay behind the prioritization of building up heavy industry under AES, which had far-reaching consequences for other sectors.

Geopolitical competition, competition between states, does not just influence which goods and services are produced under AES; it also affects how party-state officials organize labour. For example, Kim's research on China under Mao reveals how party-state officials compared production in particular sectors in China with production in those sectors in the US, the USSR, Japan, and other countries. They compared

> not just the total quantity of output or the total value of output, but also the rate of increase in labour productivity ... As China attempted to adjust the productivity of the concrete labour of its workers (in terms of mass of products and automation) to the level of its competitor countries, this acted as a form of intense pressure towards equalization and synchronization.[39]

What is more, they also compared the labour of workers in the PRC with labour in its geopolitical competitors

> using monetary values expressed in international currency ... One result was that even though China's heavy industry was not incorporated into processes of international exchange, international competition was nearly always the decisive factor in how and where living and dead labour was put to use within China, regardless of the domestic needs of the country (neither the needs of the bureaucracy nor the people) ... According to the *Cambridge History of China*, throughout the entirety of Mao Zedong's rule, "three quarters of investment was dedicated to producing machines that could produce more machines." The resemblance between this sentence and expressions used by Marx in *Capital* is truly striking.[40]

This is how AES societies were inside global capitalism, not outside it. To the extent that the central political bureaucracy in the PRC and other AES societies directed surplus labour into investments driven by competition between states in a capitalist world and tried to raise the productivity of workers' labour towards the levels of labour productivity in other countries, it was imposing the logic of capitalism.

As a result of the social arrangements within AES societies and their relationship to the world system, the mode of production under AES is, in fact, capitalism. This highlights what the study of the history of capitalism has long shown: capitalism can exist in many forms. It can be thought of as a variegated system.[41] State activity is always one dimension of this system. The "armed and tribute-collecting power of states, their 'interventions' and 'policy formations'... have been universal and necessary aspects of the whole of capitalist history."[42] These activities modify how capitalism's logic of economic competition operates, and they always have. Consider how in Germany and Japan in the late nineteenth century, the state led efforts to industrialize and catch up with rival countries. Similarly, states did the same in a number of Third World societies in the twentieth century. AES took "the fusion of the state and capital" to extreme heights.[43] Today, to pick just one of many possible examples, states at times treat some corporations as "too big to fail" and take action to make sure those companies do not collapse. States often subsidize certain firms. They also operate state-owned enterprises. Under AES, capital's economic logic is distorted even more than it is in a state-orchestrated war economy in which most production is carried out by privately owned businesses. The party-state's guarantee that what enterprises produce and deliver will be accepted is a major source of distortion. Capitalism in AES societies is also distorted when the party-state is unable to use the threat of layoffs to squeeze more surplus labour out of workers, as it is in any other capitalist society where workers have strong job security rights or employers face a shortage of labour power.[44] In spite of these distortions, AES societies always were and are capitalist because the surplus labour that the ruling class extracted from direct producers was allocated in ways that were powerfully influenced by competition between states in the global capitalist state system and because the ruling class did its best to raise labour productivity to match the levels that existed in advanced capitalist societies. A useful label we can use to name how AES societies are structured is state capitalism.[45]

A note about terminology: Anti-communists sometimes refer to these societies in a general sense as Stalinist. In response, some anti-anti-communists reject the term altogether or limit it to the USSR between the end of the 1920s and Stalin's death in 1953.[46] Obviously there were major changes in the USSR after the death of Stalin, but AES societies, including the USSR, were fundamentally similar in crucial ways for as long as they existed. What they had in common was many social relations organized along lines first established in the USSR after Stalin's Great Break. For this reason, communists and other leftists with a radical critique of AES have often called these societies Stalinist as a shorthand. This is a reasonable use of the term so long as we remember that the USSR after 1953 and the other AES societies were not identical to the USSR under Stalin.[47]

## THE HISTORICAL SIGNIFICANCE OF STALINISM

It is almost impossible to overstate the impact and significance of how a way of organizing society that emerged from the stamping out of the last embers of the Russian Revolution came to be misunderstood by most of its friends and foes alike as socialism, a society on the road to communism. Socialism became widely identified with the kind of society first built under Stalin. Living in bureaucratic dictatorships that called themselves AES turned many of the citizens of these countries into anti-communists. It still does, in the few remaining AES societies. Among the people made anti-communist by AES have been many who at first hoped to reform their societies so that they would live up to the fine ideals enshrined in their constitutions, only to discover just how deep-rooted the objectionable features they wanted to remove were. Millions of people outside the AES world who committed to doing away with capitalism, colonialism, racism, and other forms of oppression looked to one or more of the AES societies as a model for the future they wanted. They devoted years of their lives to parties and movements aligned with AES. Many of them abandoned the struggle for their laudable goals after learning more about what AES was really like, or after encountering serious problems with the politics of the Communist movement. Only a small minority have rejected AES and Communism from a communist perspective, in the manner of Peter Fryer, a journalist for the CPGB's *Daily Worker* who experienced first-hand the crushing of the 1956 Hungarian Revolution by the USSR's military. Fryer concluded self-critically (while using some highly objectionable language of a kind common at the time):

> *Hungary was Stalinism incarnate.* Here in one small, tormented country was the picture, complete in every detail: the abandonment of humanism, the attachment of primary importance not to living, breathing, suffering, hoping human beings but to machines, targets, statistics, tractors, steel mills, plan fulfilment figures … and, of course, tanks. Struck dumb by Stalinism, we ourselves grotesquely distorted the fine Socialist principle

of international solidarity by making any criticism of present injustices or inhumanities in a Communist-led country taboo. Stalinism crippled us by castrating our moral passion, blinding us to the wrongs done to men [*sic*] if those wrongs were done in the name of Communism. We Communists have been indignant about the wrongs done by imperialism [i.e., Western imperialism]: those wrongs are many and vile; but our one-sided indignation has somehow not rung true.[48]

AES widely discredited the communist cause in the twentieth century. The collapse of most of these societies has been generally understood as the end of communism rather than the disintegration of what was really the very opposite of communism, a peculiarly distorted kind of capitalism. The fate of AES has made the idea of a society different and better than capitalism hard to imagine. "The failure of struggles for the future in the past affects not only the present but also the relationships between these temporalities";[49] in other words, our sense of the present and what might be possible in the future is shaped by these failures. On top of this, envisioning the alternative to capitalism as a society that resembles AES, at least in some respects, has long disfigured communist and socialist politics. This is one of the ways in which, nearly a century after the Great Break, AES and the Communist tradition linked with it are still live issues. It is this subject to which we now turn.

# CHAPTER 7

# WHY DOES IT MATTER TODAY?

**WE LIVE IN DANGEROUS TIMES.** Climate change and the other dimensions of the ecological crisis caused by capitalism are doing tremendous harm to humanity and the rest of nature, and our situation is worsening globally. Rivalry between the declining US and its allies and the rising PRC, with which Russia is aligned, has the potential to boil over into open war. Ultra-right-wing forces are gaining strength in every part of the world. What does it matter, then, that AES societies were not in transition to communism? After all, most of them are long gone.

Much as it would be easier to not have to think about AES, understanding this way of organizing society *is* significant today for everyone who wants a better world. It matters in two ways. The first involves the influence of AES itself. The second is the Communist or Marxist-Leninist (ML) political tradition associated with AES, which remains a contender for the allegiance of anti-capitalists.

## STALINISM VERSUS HUMAN EMANCIPATION

Nothing has done more damage to the idea that communism is a desirable alternative to capitalism — or to the very belief that people can liberate themselves from injustice by making revolutionary social change — than Stalinism. Anti-communism has benefited enormously from the oppressive features of all AES societies, from the huge numbers of people who died as a result of party-state actions in the USSR under Stalin and the PRC under Mao, and from large-scale killings by other ML governments, such as the Derg in Ethiopia.[1] These realities remain an albatross around the neck of the communist cause. Although anti-communists often exaggerate death tolls and depict life under AES as worse than it was, the facts are bad enough. Many people who know little about AES do at least have the good sense to appreciate that this way of organizing society is not one we should try to replicate. But so long as such people believe that AES has something to do with communism, they will reject them both. This is how AES breeds aversion to communism.

This aversion is bad enough, but AES has also adulterated anti-capitalist politics much more than is usually appreciated. In the words of historian Vladimir Tikhonov, who is concerned about how some "nostalgic citizens of the post-Soviet states" believe that AES was "authentically socialist,"

> confusion of the developmentalist regime of the Soviet type with socialism in the Marxian sense of the world is a dangerous trend. It narrows the breadth of the revolutionary imagination, leading those in conflict with the really existing capitalism of today to imagine a better society of tomorrow chiefly along the lines of the much-flawed "really existing socialism" of bygone days.[2]

Thinking of AES as being on the road to communism warps how people understand both that goal and, even more, the process of transition towards it. This is obvious for AES's Communist supporters. It is also true to a lesser degree for communist opponents of Stalinism who believe that AES societies were in transition but blocked by bureaucratic rule.

The chief way in which anti-capitalist politics are adulterated by the influence of AES has to do with state power. The idea that state ownership of the vast bulk of the means of production is what makes a society in transition to communism (whether or not the society is seen as "socialism" in the ML sense of the term pioneered by Stalin) was, as we have seen, foreign to Marx, Engels, Luxemburg, and many other socialists, including anarchist communists, before the 1920s. That said, defining socialism in terms of state ownership was not "the invention of Stalinism." It was "systematized by the Fabian-Revisionist-State-socialist current of social-democrat reformism"[3] born in late nineteenth century Europe, which believed that socialism could be achieved gradually by the state nationalizing private firms and implementing social reforms. This was the current whose leading thinkers included Sidney Webb, Beatrice Webb, Eduard Bernstein, and Ferdinand Lassalle; it came to dominate left-wing parties, including the Labour Party in Britain, the Socialist Party of America, and the Co-operative Commonwealth Federation in Canada. But from the 1930s on, the influence of AES greatly boosted the belief that state ownership is what defines socialism.

This notion increasingly replaced the idea that what is essential is political and economic democracy, "direct control by the people of the whole administration of the community."[4] Seeing the path to communism through the prism of AES makes for a profoundly distorted vision. It leads to the idea that a society can be in transition without being democratic. Instead of being indispensable, democracy becomes an optional extra. Alternatively, this vision can lead people to redefine democracy in contorted ways that have nothing to do with "*control from below* in all social institutions,"[5] the measure of democracy shared by communists such as Marx and Luxemburg. Calling AES "democratic" when workers no more rule there than they do in other capitalist societies is as uncommunist as the liberal idea that a society is fully democratic when people elect governments while that democracy "leaves untouched vast areas of our daily lives — in the workplace, in the distribution of labour and resources — which are not subject to democratic accountability but are governed by the powers of property and the 'laws' of the market, the imperatives of profit maximization," as political scientist Ellen Meiksins Wood argues.[6]

In short, viewing the goal and the path towards it through the prism of AES, as many socialists and communists still do, makes for a statist vision of an alternative to capitalism. In this vision democracy is at best desirable but unnecessary and at worst derided. This is bound to influence the actions of people who adopt this outlook. There are also more direct ways in which the ideas of the Communist tradition have consequences in the here and now.

## MARXISM-LENINISM: A RULING-CLASS IDEOLOGY

Marx did not come up with a theory called Marxism.[7] What he produced over the course of his life was an astonishingly original, evolving, and incomplete revolutionary theory of and against class society, and above all its latest form, capitalism. This was not, argues philosopher Daniel Bensaïd, "a speculative philosophy of history," "an empirical sociology of classes," or "a positive science of the economy." It was not an all-encompassing theory of nature and society. It was "not a doctrinal system, but a critical theory of social struggle and the transformation of the world."[8]

Nor did Lenin invent a theory called Leninism. He was not a theorist in the way that Marx was. What he did was take the marxism of the Second International (the organization of socialist parties formed in 1889) and put it to work in building a revolutionary socialist party in Russia. That party, much changed by the explosion of working-class struggle in 1917, was able to lead workers to power, only to find its leadership soon running a devastated country wracked by civil war. Lenin's theoretical contributions were almost always responses to practical political challenges.[9]

"Marxism-Leninism" was the name given to the school of thought first codified by the rulers of the USSR in the 1920s, after Lenin's death, and consolidated in the 1930s. It was not a merger of the theories of Marx and Lenin; in fact, many of its notions were contrary to their ideas. Rather, Marxism-Leninism was, to use Bensaïd's aforementioned phrase, a "doctrinal system" produced by Stalin and ideological functionaries of the USSR. They adapted the Bolsheviks' version of marxism in the form it had come to have in the early 1920s to fit the purposes of the ruling layer that was becoming a class. In developing theory, Marx's abiding concern was to understand society in order to guide revolutionary working-class struggle to transform it. This was also Lenin's approach to theory (although at the end of his life the pressures of governing the Beleaguered Fortress were bending his outlook in a different direction[10]). Marxism-Leninism was different: this was a worldview for the central political bureaucracy of the USSR. In the words of philosopher Georges Labica, Marxism-Leninism is "a state philosophy, a philosophy for the state, a statification of philosophy."[11] Its outlook on how societies change is contradictory: "determinism for the masses, voluntarism for the leadership," as economist Nigel Harris observes (voluntarism exaggerates what people can do by sheer force of will, regardless of their material circumstances).[12] Technology determines how societies change, but at the same time the willpower of leaders can move mountains. History is a natural process governed by the unfolding of objective laws that operate independently of individual humans.[13] Yet the actions of the Communist party, and above all its leadership, are treated as the key to revolutionary change. According to Marxism-Leninism, during the transition to communism the state becomes stronger, not weaker. Even under communism there will be a state unless the society no longer faces foreign military threats.[14] Later, Mao developed his own, more voluntarist version of ML thought that differed in some ways from the CPSU's version — "an internal critique of Stalinism that fails to break with Stalinism."[15] The same description fits the thought of other ML thinkers who disagreed with aspects of the official Communist theory propagated by the USSR, such as Guevara.[16]

Marxism-Leninism is not just the ideology of party-states in AES societies. Exported through the Comintern and the educational and publishing institutions of AES states, in other countries around the world it was the theory of CPs and some other leftists. Outside the AES world, it became the ideology of leaderships that aimed to remake their societies along the lines of AES or at least remained officially committed to this goal. Depending on the party and the time, they believed that this destination would eventually be reached either by taking the road of parliamentary politics or by armed struggle. Today the influence of Marxism-Leninism within the global left is much weaker than it once was. Nevertheless, Marxism-Leninism remains one of the theoretical outlooks available to people who are looking for ways of understanding capitalism and guiding action to do away with it. In one form or another, often in Third World versions that emphasize radical anti-imperialism more than the version taught by the CPSU from the 1950s on, it is the ideology of a range of prominent young socialist online content producers, like those behind the YouTube channels Second Thought and Hakim. It also influences organizations like the People's Forum in the US and Tricontinental: Institute for Social Research, along with Communist parties and some other political groups.[17] It also influences some of the ecosocialists who today argue for "Climate Leninism."[18]

What the assorted varieties of Marxism-Leninism have in common is an inadequate understanding of what societies are and how they change. Technological determinism is false: "the *social* consequences of technological invention can never be deduced from technological considerations alone."[19] Voluntarism is just as flawed: what people can accomplish in any given place and time is limited by the social relations and productive forces of their context.[20] Marxism-Leninism envisions the strengthening of state power and even smuggles the state into the communist horizon itself. In contrast, Marx recognizes that state power is always an alienated way of organizing social life, one whose gradual overcoming through a profound process of democratization would have to happen for transition to communism to take place.[21] Marxism-Leninism also puts the actions of a party, a minority, at the centre of efforts to reach its goal. In so doing it displaces the self-emancipating struggles of workers and peasants themselves, which were at the heart of the politics of communists such as Marx, Engels, Luxemburg, Lenin, Trotsky, and some anarchists.[22] These deep theoretical problems have negative consequences for the political activity of people whose efforts to change the world are guided by Marxism-Leninism. The rest of this chapter examines ML politics for moving beyond capitalism and for struggles to improve the lives of people in the here and now.

## STRATEGY FOR REVOLUTION?

Since the mid-1930s, when the Comintern adopted the tactic of forming popular fronts that would be so broad as to include so-called "progressive" capitalists, the most influential versions of Communist politics have sought to change society by participating in left governments (and sometimes governments that cannot be called left in any sense) that administer capitalist societies through existing state institutions. This is rationalized as a tactic supposedly appropriate for the current stage of history (dubbed "national democratic," "advanced democratic," "anti-monopoly alliance," or some such term). The struggle for socialism is seen as belonging to a future stage.[23] In the 1970s the leaderships of some European CPs as well as minorities within other CPs opted for "Eurocommunism"; later, when the USSR's collapse threw CPs into crisis, more Communists adopted similar politics. This involved distancing themselves from the CPSU, criticizing the USSR, and becoming more friendly to other left-wing forces and to the expression of different viewpoints among Communists while usually continuing to pursue popular front politics.[24] Other CPs stuck with more orthodox Stalinist popular front politics. Today, most ML parties uphold some version of popular frontism. For example, the current program of the CP of Canada advocates building a "democratic, anti-monopoly, anti-imperialist alliance" that would seek to elect a "people's government," including Communists, in Canada's House of Commons. Ever more wide-ranging reforms implemented by such a government, backed by popular mobilization, would over time increasingly tilt the balance of power in society towards the working class and its allies. Support for socialism would grow, leading to "the revolutionary transformation to socialism."[25] The possibilities and limits of such politics are what need to be considered.

What does this kind of ML politics look like in practice? The record of Communists in government in India, South Africa, and Chile gives ample evidence with which to assess it.

In India, the most important experiences of Communists in government come from the states of Kerala and West Bengal. In the southwest state of Kerala in 1957 the CPI and CPI-supported independent candidates took office, showing that Communists could do so "by peaceful means in a free and fair election in a bourgeois democracy" during the Cold War.[26] The victory was short-lived: in 1959 this government was dismissed by the Congress Party central government, which colluded with the US Central Intelligence Agency to undermine the Kerala CPI.[27] More durably, the CPI (Marxist) and its allies held office from 1967–70. The CPI(M) was formed in 1964 as a split by the left wing of the CPI; they were more critical of the Congress Party than the CPI and aligned with China rather than the USSR. The combination of its efforts and peasant movement pressure yielded land reform that over decades benefited almost half of peasant households, although deep inequalities remain regarding the control of land.[28] The CPI(M)-led Left Democratic Front has governed Kerala for most of the years since 1980. Its policies contributed to significant improvements in the lives of peasants and workers in the state. However, its acceptance of neoliberal capitalism in practice has also contributed to Kerala increasingly becoming "the virtual opposite of a relatively egalitarian society proud of its high literacy, women's education, health indices, and enlightened intellectual and literary traditions."[29] In the eastern state of West Bengal, the Left Front of the CPI(M) and its allies governed without interruption from 1977–2011. As journalist Praful Bidwai summarizes,

> The first phase, from the late 1970s to around 1990, was marked by worthy, if modest, social welfare and land reform measures delivered through administrative means, combined with limited people's participation. The second phase broadly covered the decade of the 1990s. It saw popular demobilization and a turning away from redistributive policies, leading to alienation of the poorer strata. The last phase, beginning in the twenty-first century, was marked by a further rightward shift and embrace of neo-liberalism, with predatory land acquisition and industrialization policies.[30]

While social reforms are beneficial, even at their best these governments have done nothing to cultivate the popular power that would ultimately be needed to break with capitalism.

The South African CP (SACP) has had members in African National Congress (ANC) governments and cabinets since the end of white minority rule in 1994. Soon after it took office as the national government, the ANC began to implement neoliberal policies of privatization and opening the country to foreign investment. Under the ANC, the country has become "the most financialized economy in the Global South excluding Asia. If neoliberalism was born kicking and screaming in Chile, it confidently strode into maturity in South Africa."[31]

Throughout the years since the end of apartheid, the SACP has demonstrated "unwavering commitment to the ANC."[32] The SACP, argues journalist Benjamin Fogel, "has shown again and again since 1994 that not only has it failed to serve as a check on the ANC but has also sided with the worst elements in the party for short-term political gain."[33] In 2012, when police killed thirty-four striking miners, "SACP leaders were quick to absolve the authorities of any blame."[34] In 2014 they helped drive the National Union of Metalworkers (NUM) out of the Congress of South African Trade Unions (COSATU) after the NUM called for a left alternative to the ANC-dominated "triple alliance" of ANC, SACP, and COSATU. The party officially backed Cyril Ramaphosa, "a billionaire beloved by the Davos set," for president.[35] This course continues to be justified by SACP leaders in terms of the requirements of the "national democratic" stage of the struggle for socialism.[36]

Most disastrous is the role of the Chilean CP during the Popular Unity (PU) left-coalition government headed by Salvador Allende, which was overthrown by a US-backed military coup in 1973. PU's program was one of social reforms within Chile's constitutional framework of capitalist democracy.[37] Nevertheless, the capitalist class was extremely hostile to the government and to workers' struggles. PU was divided in how to respond to capital's moves: pause reforms to cultivate middle-class support or move faster and support workers' strikes and land occupations? The CP backed the go-slow approach. When some workers began to create new, radically democratic organizations in their workplaces and neighbourhoods — organizations with the potential to develop into an alternative to the existing state, which they later did, creating a situation of dual power — the CP leadership directed members to have nothing to do with them. It even praised the military for its patriotism when a joint PU-military cabinet was formed.[38] It did so again three months before the coup that put a military dictatorship in power, all the while "backing Allende's policy of dialogue with the Christian Democrats and revolutionary restraint."[39]

How should the politics put into practice in these and other cases be characterized? They are a politics for governments that administer capitalism. Such governments may implement social reforms that improve most peoples' lives but they are equally capable of adopting harmful policies if they decide they need to do so to appease particular capitalists or cater to capitalism's priority of profit. Thus these politics are reformist. In other words, they are limited to making social reforms within the framework of capitalism, whether the reforms are major (for example, nationalizing the property of some firms without compensating their owners) or minor (raising the minimum wage, for instance).[40]

Whatever the rhetoric used by CP leaders, and no matter what Communist activists sincerely believe, these are not politics that can guide efforts to move society towards a transition from capitalism in the direction of communism. A government in office in a capitalist state, which also includes military, police, judicial, penal, and other institutions, is incapable of getting such a transition underway. It cannot break the grip of capital on social life — the prerequisite for launching a transition towards communism — and put exploited and oppressed people in charge of their own destinies. This is because the power of capital cannot be broken gradually. If the ability of capitalists to make profits is seriously threatened, "a genuine economic and social earthquake is then touched off," "a profound socio-economic crisis" that can only be resolved by reimposing capitalist order or by social revolution that puts the direct producers in control of society.[41] Such a rupture would at some point have to involve new, radically democratic institutions of popular power — akin to the soviets, factory committees, and workers' militias in Russia in 1917 — replacing the state institutions that maintain the rule of capital no matter who is in government.[42] The kind of ML politics discussed here do not provide a guidebook for a parliamentary road out of capitalism. As Luxemburg argued over a century ago, politics of this kind are a strategy not for "a more tranquil, calmer and slower road to the *same* goal" that revolutionary socialists seek "but a *different* goal. Instead of taking a stand for the establishment of a new society they take a stand for surface modification of the old society."[43] This is true regardless of what their supporters intend or what they say about socialism or revolution; actions are decisive, not words.

The non-revolutionary nature of these politics was shown dramatically by the CP in France in 1968. That year police violence against student protesters led to a general strike by over nine million workers, some of whom occupied their workplaces. France was thrown into a deep political crisis. How did the CP, a mass party with considerable influence in the working class, respond? By doing its best to "stifle one of the greatest spontaneous mass movements in history."[44] Writing not long after the events, writer Daniel Singer evocatively describes its role: "The PCF has appeared from the beginning of this story as the villain, as the main obstacle to a revolutionary conclusion, or, depending on your standpoint, as the hero, the unexpected pillar of the regime, the surprising darling of the traditional upholders of capitalist society."[45] Likewise, as mentioned in Chapter 3, the Portuguese CP played a similar role during the revolution in that country in 1974–75.

In the popular front tradition dating back to the mid-1930s, this kind of ML politics usually seeks an alliance between the working class, the middle class, and a sector of the dominant class seen as "progressive," "national," or "patriotic." Again, the current program of the CP of Canada is typical. It speaks of including "small business owners, and independent, non-monopoly capitalists" in the "democratic, anti-monopoly, anti-imperialist alliance" whose components all share "common interests in opposing the reactionary policies of finance capital and its governments."[46]

The consequences of this approach to alliances are not hypothetical; the strategy has been put into practice since the 1930s. One that has frequently occurred is the adoption by Communists of ardent nationalism, even in settler-colonial imperialist societies. This is because nationalism is seen as part of what is needed to glue together a cross-class alliance. For example, after the Comintern proclaimed the popular front tactic in 1935, the CPUSA campaigned in elections under the slogan "Communism is Americanism of the 20th Century" with an image of the Stars and Stripes beside a red flag with a hammer and sickle.[47] In the 1980s, the CP of Canada used the slogan "Put Canada First" when running candidates.[48] Another consequence is not raising demands that "progressive" capitalists would not accept. To keep them onside requires not proposing anything that would threaten their profits significantly let alone disrupt the accumulation of capital, like militant mass strikes or occupations.

Most disastrously, allying with a sector of the ruling class has led to terrible defeats. In the Spanish Civil War, the CP's popular front approach "gave hegemony in the Republic to the bourgeois and reformist forces that sought to compromise with the enemy," as former Spanish CP leader Claudin notes.[49] It pitted Communists against the revolution that had broken out and unintentionally contributed to the fascist victory. In Indonesia, the CP formed a close alliance with the country's nationalist leader, Sukarno. It grew enormously, becoming the largest CP outside the AES countries. It also went along with banning strikes and opposed direct action by peasants to redistribute land. In 1965, the CP was unprepared when the military high command turned on it, killing hundreds of thousands of people.[50] In Sudan, the CP participated in the coalition government formed in 1964 after an uprising ended military rule. This government was toppled by a military coup in 1969. The new nationalist president, Gaafar Nimeiri, banned all parties except the CP, a few of whose members were given ministerial positions. But after Nimeiri had dealt with the conservative religious right, he turned on the CP and arrested its leaders.[51]

None of this is to dismiss the importance of forging unity across the many lines of division that fragment the working class. This class is broader than many people realize, being made up of everyone who depends on working for wages and has little or no management authority, along with unwaged people who depend on wage earners' income. It is fragmented by divisions rooted in racial, gender, and other forms of oppression as well as differences of pay, occupation, culture, and so on.[52] Nor is this criticism meant to ignore the issue of alliances between workers and peasants or other social layers outside the dominant class. What is in question is the popular front approach that believes in allying with a mythical sector of "progressive" capitalists.[53]

## FIGHTING FOR REFORMS

Outside the AES countries, many thousands of Communists have worked hard and sometimes heroically to defend the interests of exploited and oppressed people. Some have given their lives in the struggle. However, the kind of politics being discussed here do not provide guidance for fighting in the most consistent and effective way possible in the here and now against capital's assaults and for social reforms. Efforts to ally with "progressive" capitalists exert a moderating influence that diverts people away from fostering militant strikes and other forms of mass direct action, which are crucial for extracting gains from employers and governments. Usually the popular front approach is also accompanied by trying to permeate or influence the layer of full-time officials at the top of unions and other organizations of workers and oppressed people. This fails to recognize that such officials are a distinct social layer with different interests than their members. The officialdom needs to preserve its organizations if it is to keep functioning as a group of full-time officials. For this reason, even officials with radical politics are subject to pressures that tend to make them averse to militancy. They usually shy away from actions, such as strikes and protests that defy the law, that could threaten the institutions on which they depend.[54] This is also true of the officials who lead mass reformist parties. Supporters of the dominant strain of ML politics have sometimes supported rank and file workers organizing outside official union structures. However, this is seen as a tactic "in the mobilization of the official machinery, not an alternative to it, a stimulus to the leadership, not its antagonist,"[55] as one historian has written of the union politics of the CPGB in the decades after World War II.

There are myriad examples of the bitter fruits of Communist reformism. When in 1974 a historic railworkers' strike, "a *response* to growing dissent throughout the railway workforce and its expression through new militant organizations which the workers themselves created,"[56] affected all of India, the leaders of the country's two main Communist parties were not enthusiastic. The CPI was in a bind because it supported the Congress central government and repression of the strike was led by the Congress figures to whom it was closest. The CPI(M) did more to support the strike but its leaders were preoccupied with rebuilding the party in West Bengal and wanted to avoid a major clash with the central government from which their party would not benefit much.[57] On a much smaller scale, another example is the last mass movement in which the CP of Canada had real influence. In 1983, attacks by a right-wing provincial government in British Columbia touched off large protests and some strikes. During this movement, the CP "would nudge" the union officialdom "from time to time (although it would always clear this nudging with the top beforehand), but it would also play a role in keeping unruly leftists in line," including by "defusing enthusiasm for a general strike."[58] The case of Australia is interesting. In the 1970s, after the members most loyal to the USSR split to form another party, the CP of Australia (CPA) was for some time more left-wing and open to unorthodox ideas than most other CPs, thanks to the influence of the high level of workplace militancy and political radicalism in Australia at the time. CPA members were important in the remarkable New South Wales Building Labourers Federation (NSW BLF), "easily the most radical union — in terms of industrial militancy, democratic rank and file control and determined action around a broad sweep of political causes — in the post-war period in Australia."[59] But from 1976, as class struggle began to subside, the CPA reversed course. Its orientation in struggles both inside and outside workplaces became "increasingly conservative."[60] When the BLF's top brass, backed by employers, moved against the NSW BLF, the CPA did not "fully mobilize" in its defence, leading to "numerous resignations."[61] Many similar cases of reformist Communists failing to fight as effectively as possible for gains under capitalism could be cited.[62]

## TO THE LEFT OF THE MARXIST-LENINIST MAINSTREAM

While the most influential variant of ML politics has been the kind discussed so far, it is not the only one. Supporters of other variants have pursued different approaches. These include strategies that involve armed struggle, a more militant orientation to workplace and community struggles, and/or rejection of the idea that there is a "progressive" sector of capitalists that Communists should seek to include in alliances. Supporters of these left challengers to mainstream ML politics often draw inspiration from the ultra-left "Third Period" policy of the Comintern from 1928 to 1934 in spite of its divisive and self-defeating impact, which included contributing to the failure of the workers' movement in Germany to prevent the Nazis from taking power. In some cases the different approach is seen as a response to specific conditions that make the mainstream ML approach unviable in a particular country, at least for now. In other cases it is seen as relevant more broadly or even universally.

In Europe the leading example of ML politics that hearken back to the Third Period line is the CP of Greece (Greek initials: KKE). While getting over 7 percent of the vote in the 2023 general election, the party is, as political theorist Stathis Kouvelakis observes,

> stuck in a sectarian attitude that has kept it away not only from any form of unity of action with other left-wing forces (tirelessly

denounced as "crutches of the system") but also from all the major popular mobilizations of the recent period ... This sectarian line is at one with the systematically cultivated nostalgia for the USSR, and even for Joseph Stalin, whose complete works (in sixteen leather-bound volumes) have been republished by the party's publishing house and offered for sale at the promotional price of €208 ... It also refuses any sort of "transitional demand" considering that "workers' power" is the preliminary condition to resolve any problem. For instance, after the recent Tempi train disaster, it refused to call for the nationalization of the railways — arguing that whether privately or publicly owned, they would still serve the capitalist system. In reality, despite often effective union work (particularly in the private sector, deserted by bureaucratized unions), its radical rhetoric serves to disguise a practice of political passivity. Its actions are entirely focused on "building and strengthening" the party and its various fronts (trade union, youth, cultural, etc.), which are simply used as transmission belts for it.[63]

In India, the CPI (Maoist) presents itself as a revolutionary alternative to the country's other CPs. Using a strategy of "people's war" based on the experience of the CCP in China before 1949 (a very different society from India today), the CPI (Maoist) tries to carve out "liberated zones" in rural areas by engaging in guerilla warfare, with the ultimate aim of surrounding the cities from the countryside. Historian Jairus Banaji points out that this treats

> revolutionary movements [as] developing in a class vacuum, in complete isolation from industrial workers and the more organized groups of wage earners and employees in the economy at large. The bulk of the Indian labour force remains unorganised into unions, and it is stupefying to imagine that a revolution against capitalism can succeed while the mass of the workers are in a state of near-complete atomization.

Banaji notes that the CPI (Maoist)'s view of democracy "as a fraud" along with its

> failure to encourage and develop a culture of working class organisation and debate, to encourage forms of intervention

that contest capitalism in concrete ways, and build a movement that can address the widest possible range of issues starting from the desperate struggle for survival of the millions of landless in India, are all part of the legacy of a left that was moribund intellectually and deeply conservative in its culture.[64]

There are similarities between the CPI (Maoist)'s politics and those of the CP of the Philippines (CPP), although the CPP actively participates in elections through the National Democrats movement and leads a range of both underground and above-ground organizations as well as maintaining its New People's Army.[65] The Popular Front for the Liberation of Palestine and the Democratic Front for the Liberation of Palestine are organizations whose founders were ML supporters of guerilla warfare.[66] In the US and elsewhere, there are small groups that consider themselves revolutionary alternatives to the CPs once loyal to the USSR.[67]

There are significant differences between these versions of ML politics and the ML mainstream. However, at the centre of their politics, these left variants still substitute a party for the struggles of direct producers themselves. The politics of the ML mainstream and its ML critics also share other important features.

## CAMPISM AND CREDULITY

Another dimension of ML politics that we need to examine is its strong proclivity to give political support to states and movements in conflict with Western imperialism even though they are reactionary. This is the spirit of "The enemy of my enemy is my friend." It is an instinct deeply embedded in ML political culture, one of whose founding assumptions was that its supporters owed a duty of unswerving loyalty to the leaders of the USSR. At the end of the 1930s this led most Communists, even those with reservations, to endorse the USSR's 1939–41 alliance with Nazi Germany because of their faith in Stalin and the leadership of the Comintern.[68] After the end of their 1941–45 alliance with the other states that had fought against Germany during World War II, the USSR's rulers declared that the world was divided into two camps, one imperialist and the other anti-imperialist.[69] Although the USSR is long gone, old habits die hard. Many Marxist-Leninists see the fundamental political division in the world as one between the US and its NATO allies on one side and, on the other, a camp of states that allegedly challenge imperialism, of which "socialist" China is the mightiest. This has led some Communist organizations to support the Russian invasion of Ukraine. Others do not go that far but oppose NATO in a manner that ends up aligning with the Russian government and repeat arguments similar to those made by Putin.[70] The overall stance can be called anti-NATO "neo-campism." In this outlook, "systematic alignment behind Moscow" has been "replaced by … positioning against Washington, a stance entailing a strong propensity to act upon the logic of 'the enemy of my enemy is my friend' and hence to be barely critical of governments and forces opposed to the United States — militarily or by any other means."[71] These include, but are not limited to, the rulers of China, Russia, Cuba, Venezuela, Iran, and Syria.

The anti-NATO neo-campist view of the world involves serious misunderstandings of global capitalism today. One feature of capitalism is that it is organized hierarchically in an imperialist chain, as Lenin argued over a century ago. This chain can be thought of as made up of a number of tiers, descending from the US, "the imperialist superpower, to secondary imperialist states, to sub-imperial powers, to subordinate/peripheral states." What states other than the US do is not "explicable merely through reference to diktats emanating from Washington."[72] This means that the declining US is not the only imperialist power. China is not just capitalist; it is also a rising imperialist power, although still weaker than the US.[73] People who fail to understand these dynamics can easily end up politically backing states in conflict with the US that are just as much part of capitalism as the state at the top of the imperialist chain. One result of this stance is a refusal of international solidarity with people fighting for democracy, social reforms, and radical change within China, Russia, and other societies whose rulers clash with the US.[74]

Another consequence of the culture of anti-NATO neo-campism is a readiness to believe dubious claims made by forces in conflict with the US or another NATO power, such as Russian government exaggerations about the strength of fascism in Ukraine.[75] Along with this goes an unwillingness to accept strong evidence about objectionable actions by "the enemy of the enemy," such as the Chinese party-state's oppression of the Uyghurs.[76] These difficulties in evaluating evidence flow from the worldview of anti-NATO neo-campism. They are also fed by the excessive skepticism and suspicion about reality that is a dangerous feature of our times, discussed in Chapter 1. As ecological and economic conditions get worse in the years ahead, we can expect geopolitical friction between the US-led bloc and its rivals to become more intense. This will make it even more important for anti-capitalists to navigate a course independent of all ruling classes. In the face of this challenge, the "enemy of my enemy is my friend" impulse in ML politics is extremely misorienting.

## DEMOCRACY IN MOVEMENTS

The final dimension of ML politics we need to examine is the practice of democracy. When it comes to how Communists participate in unions and movement activity outside the workplace, it is not difficult to find examples of people working hard for democratic ways of making decisions and carrying out activity, understanding democracy here in the sense defined in the opening section of this chapter, in terms of people's ability to control the organizations to which they belong. These methods foster a high level of active participation in making decisions about what to do and how to do it, rather than just in carrying out decisions made by leaders. They aim to develop people's capacity to think and act for themselves. Many members of a group assembling in a meeting, considering different proposals, debating their merits, and voting on what to do is one example of what this kind of grassroots democracy in action can look like. The efforts of CPA members in the NSW BLF stand out as a sterling example of democratic organizing by Communists. For me, the late Stan Dalton comes to mind. Dalton was fired for his efforts to defend shelter workers and unhoused people at Toronto's Seaton House. His commitment to militancy, democracy, and solidarity made him a thorn in the side of the timid officers of his union.[77]

Yet the admirable efforts of such Communist organizers cannot be credited to any distinctive element in the ML tradition. On the contrary: insightful guidance for democratic organizing is not to be found in the writings and speeches of Stalin or Comintern leaders of his era, nor Mao, Che, or other ML figures.[78] This is no accident, since they were rulers or champions of profoundly undemocratic societies. When the goal is a society of the AES kind, democracy is at best an optional extra. Communists who have practised highly democratic ways of organizing have been drawing on other resources. These have included, for example, an older tradition of working-class self-organization; Marx and marxists who took democracy very seriously; and other traditions of liberation, including the Black freedom movement in the US.

More commonly, Communists have paid little attention to democracy in their activity in community groups and unions, especially in those they have come to lead. Sometimes they have operated in highly anti-democratic ways.[79] At worst, there are cases of Marxist-Leninists using violence against people in movements who politically disagree with them. Larger scale examples include the murder of Trotskyists and other non-Communist anti-colonial fighters in Vietnam in 1945,[80] the killings in the 1980s and 1990s by the Shining Path, the Peruvian ultra-sectarian Maoist party, of organizers who disagreed with them,[81] and the CPP's killings of other leftists in the Philippines beginning in the 1990s.[82] Communist parties and other political organizations themselves have often been only minimally democratic, with members having little ability to hold leaders accountable or determine what policies the party will adopt and act on.[83] Marxism-Leninism's conception of how to achieve socialism pivots around the actions of a ML party, not the creation by direct producers of new, radically democratic institutions to replace the state power and management structures through which exploiters rule. The party partially or completely substitutes itself for the self-emancipating struggles of exploited and oppressed people; from here it is not a leap for the party leadership to substitute itself for the membership. In short, the ML vision of the path to socialism is not one in which democracy is central and essential. To the extent that ML organizations have been modelled on the ruling party of one or another AES society, they have been highly undemocratic. This is a major weakness if one answers the question "How does a people or a class become fit to rule in their own name?" in the way that Marx and like-minded communists have. In the words of writer Hal Draper, "*Only by fighting to do so. Only by waging their struggle against oppression — oppression by those who tell them they are unfit to govern. Only by fighting for democratic power do they educate themselves and raise themselves up to the level of being able to wield that power.*"[84] Democratic ways of organizing are indispensable in this process, through which ordinary people change themselves on a mass scale.

This approach to democracy, like the other aspects of the influence of AES and Marxism-Leninism with which this chapter has dealt, makes the legacy of Communism for the contemporary left a largely negative one. Communists have undoubtedly given much to movements and struggles under capitalism.[85] However, they have done so *in spite of* the malign influence of AES on thinking about an alternative to capitalism and the path to it, and *in spite of* the many weaknesses of ML social theory and politics. For those who thirst for liberation, the ML tradition is a poisoned well. Such appeal as it has to anti-capitalists today has much to do with the period of history we are living in, one in which few people believe it is possible to create a better society in the future unlike any that has ever existed. This difficulty gives strength to nostalgia, including for AES societies and ML parties that once confidently declared that they were fighting for communism. These forces seemed to have power that threatened capitalism and frightened its defenders.[86] But their power, to the extent that it was real, was not the democratic power of direct producers that points towards liberatory social revolution. People today who recognize the need to work towards an alternative to capitalism and are looking for ideas to inform their efforts should look elsewhere.

## CHAPTER 8

# AN ALTERNATIVE TRADITION

## SWIMMING AGAINST STRONG CURRENTS

**THE DREAM OF A SOCIETY** in which ordinary people would not be exploited is probably almost as old as class exploitation itself. Ngo Van, a communist who managed to avoid death at the hands of both French colonialism and Vietnamese Stalinism, notes that in China as much as in the West, "the same dreams and aspirations appear, the same uprisings full of the poetic fervour to reach heaven. The Chinese utopia … is the same utopia we encounter in the peasant revolts that shook the [W]estern world, whether that of Thomas Münzer in Germany or that of the [D]iggers and the [L]evellers in England, to mention only the most emblematic."[1] But the origins of communism as an identifiable political tradition are with the most radical organizers in the French Revolution at the end of the 1700s. Gracchus Babeuf and his cothinkers talked of fighting for a society of "common happiness," one based on a "community of labour" in which "sickening distinctions between rich and poor … between *rulers and ruled*" would be done away with.[2] In the 1820s in England, communism came together with feminism for the first time in the writing of William Thompson and Anna Wheeler.[3] Two decades later, Marx and Engels first fused communism and democracy; this marked the birth of a new communist tradition, which Draper calls "socialism from below" as opposed to the various forms of "socialism from above" including reformist parliamentary socialism and Marxism-Leninism.[4] Communism deepened its connections with opposition to patriarchy, racism, heterosexism, and cis supremacy in the twentieth and twenty-first centuries.[5]

If it were the case that Marxism-Leninism could be equated with communist politics altogether, if it simply were the communist tradition, then people who today see the need to work towards replacing capitalism with a better way of organizing society would have no reason to give communism any attention. However, there is a tradition of communism radically critical of AES and Marxism-Leninism that has existed as long as Stalinism itself. It may seem strange for anti-capitalists to think about tradition; after all, the defence of hallowed traditions is a hallmark of conservative thought. But the significance of tradition for radicals is different. In a loose sense, tradition can be about whichever people in the past are sources of inspiration in the present. In a more specific sense, a political tradition is a source of ideas about goals, strategies, and tactics for the struggle to transform society. When treated not dogmatically but critically, in the light of experience and the best analysis of the contemporary world, a tradition is an indispensable source of resources for radical organizers. For people who need ideas to guide their efforts to change society, building on a tradition is better than reinventing the wheel. This is true even when some of a tradition's ideas are flawed or no longer relevant.[6]

As previously mentioned in passing, the earliest counter-revolutionary signs within the CPSU were met with communist opposition, although at the time no one knew what lay ahead. The rise of the ruling group around Stalin and its taking control of the Comintern, replacing party leaders who did not support them with loyalists, changed and divided the communist movement around the world. It was these developments that forced the diverse tradition of anti-Stalinist communism into existence. This tradition only barely survived the violence of Stalinism, fascism, world war, and colonialism in the 1930s and 1940s, the dark time that one of its most eloquent writers, Victor Serge, called "Midnight in the Century."[7] But the survivors and those who later took up the tradition's banners have passed along precious resources for people who want to develop a new communist politics adequate to the terrifying challenges of our age.

To understand anti-Stalinist communism, one must appreciate just how strong the currents are against which it has had to swim. Like all anti-capitalist radicals, its supporters have often had to contend with employer punishment, state repression, harassment and violence from right-wing vigilantes, and hostility from the officials of unions and reformist parties. A case in point in the context of a capitalist democracy is the 1941 prosecution for sedition against the US government of members of the Socialist Workers' Party, a Trotskyist organization, which resulted in prison sentences for eighteen members.[8] The challenges have been worse in situations where radicals are denied the relatively greater space for legal political activity that is often afforded in capitalist democracies.

For example, in the years just before World War II in the British colony that later became Sri Lanka, the Lanka Equal Society Party faced "a systematic effort ... to disrupt ... meetings not only by shouting and beating of tom-toms, but by physical attacks by drunken hoodlums armed with clubs and knives. Very often, in those days, holding a public meeting involved elaborate organisation for the defence of the meeting against such attacks."[9] Yet such gangsterism pales in comparison with the deadly repression meted out by the Nazis where they held sway, and by the military forces that restored French colonial rule in Vietnam in 1945, killing over two hundred Trotskyists there.[10] Anti-Stalinist communists continue to face these obstacles from various foes today. The 2018 assassination of Rio de Janeiro municipal councillor Marielle Franco is a reminder that anti-communist murder is not just a historical matter.[11]

On top of the challenges faced by all anti-capitalist radicals, anti-Stalinist communists have also had to contend with particular difficulties caused by Stalinism. These were by far the most severe in the USSR. At the end of the 1920s, the CPSU expelled thousands of left oppositionists. Party-state authorities were soon rounding up communists who continued to dissent and sending them to distant carceral camps and settlements. In the late 1930s, the NKVD executed almost every single communist with oppositional views. Beyond the borders of the USSR, the NKVD assassinated Trotsky and a number of his supporters and other anti-Stalinist communists. They also infiltrated some anti-Stalinist communist groups in order to disrupt them.[12]

Outside AES countries, the most pervasive obstacles that Stalinism created for anti-Stalinist communists were the favourable reputation that AES societies enjoyed among many leftists and the respect that many had for CPs. This was both because of those parties' association with AES and because of their members' role in workplace and community struggles. For example, in the 1930s "there was great pro-Russian sentiment ... while to discuss and argue about the politics of the Spanish Civil War was most unpopular," recalled one British Trotskyist.[13] It was not until 1956 that the prestige of AES on the anti-capitalist left was dramatically tarnished: the combination of Khruschev's revelation of some of Stalin's murderous actions and the USSR's crushing of the Hungarian Revolution dealt the world Communist movement blows from which it never recovered.[14] Even when CPs were not mass parties, they were usually far larger than anti-Stalinist communist organizations, many of which were formed by people expelled from CP ranks and tarred by Communists with outrageous slanders that would have been laughable had they not been a licence for ostracism and worse. Trotskyism was accused of being an ally of fascism and "a menace to the world," in the words of a typical CP pamphlet.[15] The CPUSA supported the aforementioned 1941 prosecution of Trotskyists for sedition (although the same law would later be used against its members).[16] In 1942 the CPGB openly incited violence, calling on workers to treat Trotskyists "as you would treat an open Nazi"[17] (Communists were not precise, often dubbing all anti-Stalinist marxists "Trotskyites"). CP leaders were not shy about mobilizing their forces against their political opponents on the left. For example, during the May 1968 revolt in France, radical students, many of them anarchists and anti-Stalinist marxists, marched across Paris out to the massive Renault factory to support its striking workers, only to find their access blocked by rows of activists of the CP-led union federation.[18] For two decades after Comintern parties started to expel Trotsky's supporters in 1928, anti-Stalinist communists often had to deal with assaults by CP members. For example, Trotsky's supporters in the US faced attacks from the CPUSA in cities across the country after they launched as an independent organization at the end of 1928. Communists carried out assaults and attempted to break up their public activities. In New York City in 1932, CP members even dropped bricks and cobblestones from a rooftop above a Trotskyist street meeting, fatally injuring two of their own by mistake.[19] In 1947, when the CP had ministers in France's government, CP activists beat up workers during a Renault strike for higher pay in which Trotskyists were involved and which the CP leadership opposed.[20] Some Marxist-Leninists of the NCM occasionally engaged in violence against anti-Stalinists in the 1960s and 1970s.[21] The most extreme violence was the deliberate killing of anti-Stalinist revolutionaries by Communists. In the 1940s this happened to several people in France and more in Greece,[22] while in southern Vietnam, CP "squads systematically tracked down and detained Trotskyists, subsequently killing at least two dozen leaders ... This ... decision to wipe out an entire Marxist anticolonial cohort in the south shocked politically alert Vietnamese throughout the country."[23]

Every tradition of anti-capitalist radicalism has had to swim against the current in its efforts to fight for social transformation, but anti-Stalinist communism has faced the greatest difficulties. Its supporters have attempted to work towards human emancipation without the false hope that the future was being built by the leaders of one or more of the AES countries and that ML parties aligned with those countries could repeat that success elsewhere. When the prestige of AES societies and Marxism-Leninism was at its height, this political work took a tremendous amount of determination and commitment to principles. When anti-Stalinist communists have also had to contend with the threat of Stalinist violence on top of all other challenges, it has demanded even more courage. Since the collapse of most of the AES societies, doing this work has required political commitment without the consolation of believing that the history of AES vindicates the communist cause in the future. Bear this in mind as this chapter introduces the anti-Stalinist communist tradition and the political resources it bequeaths to people today who want to change the world.

## THREE ANCESTORS: MARX, ENGELS, MORRIS

Because Marx died in 1883, Engels in 1895, and William Morris in 1896, none of them lived to see AES.[24] But their thought contains nothing that lends support to ML ideas about communism and transition towards it. Once Marx and Engels had come to their new democratic communism, their central political principle was always that "the emancipation of the working class must be the act of the working class itself."[25] On the crucial issue of transition to communism:

> The period following a socialist revolution had several interchangeable labels in Marx's writings: "workers' state," the "political ascendency (or sway, *Herrschaft*) of the proletariat, "workers' political (or state) power," the "rule (*Herrschaft*) of the proletariat," and some others; and one of these, used in certain contexts, was the "dictatorship of the proletariat."[26]

This last term is perhaps the most misunderstood in Marx and Engels' thought. As Draper notes, at the time when they were writing, the word dictatorship had a different meaning than it came to have. At the time it "was not a synonym for despotism, tyranny, absolutism, or autocracy, and above all it was not counterposed to democracy." For Marx and Engels, "'dictatorship of the proletariat' meant nothing more and nothing less than 'rule of the proletariat.'"[27] For them, the process of transition to communism could only begin after social revolution had created working-class rule — not the rule of any minority acting on behalf of the working class. The transition would have to be driven by freely associating direct producers themselves. During this process, state power would weaken, not grow stronger. Their model of working-class rule was the highly democratic Paris Commune of 1871, which Marx celebrated as "the political form at last discovered under which to work out the economic emancipation of labour."[28] This and their conception of communism have been touched on earlier, as they inform this book's approach. We have also seen that while his collaborator Marx was still alive, Engels discussed the "modern state" taking control of productive forces and acting as a "collective capitalist"; this suggests that they believed state ownership could clothe capitalist exploitation, not transition beyond capitalism. Among the noteworthy late nineteenth-century communists who grasped the essence of their politics was cultural producer William Morris. He argued for the transformation of capitalism's alienated labour, for "the reduction of pain in labour to a minimum," and rejected the belief that

> the organization of life and necessary labour can be dealt with by a huge national centralization, working by a kind of magic for which no one feels himself responsible ... individual men [sic] cannot shuffle off the business of life on to the shoulders of an abstraction called the State, but must deal with it in conscious association with each other. That variety of life is as much an aim of true communism as equality of condition, and that nothing but a union of these two will bring about real freedom.[29]

All of this is a far cry from any kind of socialism from above.

## LUXEMBURG'S LIBERATORY POLITICS

Luxemburg did not live to see AES because she was murdered in 1919 by far-right paramilitaries acting at the orders of Social Democratic government ministers. Nevertheless, like Marx and Engels, the thought of this brilliant Polish-German revolutionary is antithetical to ML ideas about transition to communism (and much else). Chapter 1 introduced her liberatory understanding of what this process would have to be like, which has shaped this book's analysis.

Writing in 1918, Luxemburg, who supported the Russian Revolution and hailed the Bolsheviks for their revolutionary initiative, nonetheless recognized the dangers in the rapid decline of the new institutions of workers' democracy and of some of the ideas being expressed by Lenin and Trotsky. "Socialist democracy," she warned,

> is not something which begins only in the promised land after the foundations of socialist economy are created; it does not come as some sort of Christmas present for the worthy people who, in the interim, have loyally supported a handful of socialist dictators. Socialist democracy begins simultaneously with the beginnings of the destruction of class rule and of the construction of socialism ... It is the same thing as the dictatorship of the proletariat ... [which] consists in the *manner of applying democracy*, not in its *elimination* ... [It] must be the work of the *class* and not of a little leading minority in the name of the class.[30]

In the midst of the German Revolution of 1918, Luxemburg wrote of her organization, the Spartacus League, which was on the verge of uniting with other revolutionary socialists to form the new CP of Germany, that it was "not a party that wants to rise to power over the mass of workers or through them." It was "only the most conscious, purposeful part of the proletariat, which points the entire broad mass of the working class toward its historical tasks at every step, which represents in each particular stage of the Revolution the ultimate socialist goal, and in all national questions the interests of the proletarian world revolution." It would "never take over governmental power except in response to the clear, unambiguous will of the great majority of the proletarian mass of all of Germany, never except by the proletariat's conscious affirmation of the views, aims, and methods of struggle of the Spartacus League."[31]

While recognizing that the capitalist class would inevitably use violence to try to crush a social revolution, and that this resistance "must be broken step by step, with an iron fist and ruthless energy," Luxemburg also argued that "the proletarian revolution requires no terror for its aims; it hates and despises killing."[32] "Revolutionary activity and profound humanitarianism — they alone are the true breath of socialism. A world must be turned upside down. But each tear that flows, when it could have been spared, is an accusation, and he commits a crime who with brutal inadvertency crushes a poor earthworm."[33]

Luxemburg's thought is as different from Marxism-Leninism as oil and water and contains no basis for seeing AES as in transition to communism.

## PRO-BOLSHEVIK ANTI-STALINISTS

Opposition within the CPSU to undemocratic actions of the leadership began as early as 1919. The Democratic Centralists (DCs) and the short-lived Workers' Opposition argued for the party to change course. Smaller groups despaired of reforming the party from within and started to organize outside its ranks. Over time, as a new ruling class took shape, the DCs' outlook on the party-state and the society it ruled became more radical. They had some influence on a few dissident marxists outside the USSR, including philosopher Karl Korsch, author of the original and anti-dogmatic *Marxism and Philosophy*, who became an anti-Stalinist communist.[34] By the early 1930s, some of the DCs, by now incarcerated along with all other left-wing opponents of the state the NKVD was able to round up, concluded that the USSR had become a state capitalist society under a new ruling class. The same conclusion had also been reached by one of the smaller radical groupings, the Workers' Group. Almost every single one of these anti-Stalinist marxists in the USSR was executed in the late 1930s. They long remained largely unknown, even to most anti-Stalinist communists elsewhere.[35]

Less radical in its criticism of the USSR was the Left Opposition (LO), whose foremost leader was Trotsky. The LO came together against the emerging Stalinist leadership in 1923 and was quickly defeated, as mentioned in Chapter 2. In 1926 the LO joined with supporters of party leaders Grigory Zinoviev and Lev Kamenev in the United Opposition to the dominant group in the party-state leadership, only to be defeated the following year.[36] These oppositions were sharply critical of the path on which the group led by Stalin was steering the Comintern. Their criticism of its domestic policies was shallower, as their leaders still thought that it was possible to move in the direction of communism under a CPSU ruling undemocratically in the name of the working class if the party took a different course.[37] The Great Break led most of the LO to capitulate to the CPSU leadership. Those who did not go over to Stalin only recognized that it would take a revolution to remove the leadership after Hitler took power in Germany, an event which, as we have seen, the Comintern's Third Period line had facilitated.[38]

Trotsky, who was expelled from the CPSU in 1927 and deported from the USSR in 1929, rallied his supporters to form an international current. They were unsparing in their criticism of the Comintern's disastrous policies, first the Third Period and then the popular front.

However, as we saw in Chapter 6, Trotsky maintained that a transition towards communism was underway in the USSR but blocked by the bureaucratic rulers, whom he saw as a ruling layer, not a new class of exploiters. From this perspective, the revolution needed to unseat them would be a political revolution, not a full-fledged social revolution.[39]

Although this analysis was flawed, Trotsky and his supporters were attempting to build a communist current in opposition to Stalinism, one that preserved the politics that had made victory possible in Russia in 1917 and had then been promoted by the Comintern in its earliest years as they understood them. Their most important ideas included championing revolutionary socialism with the goal of establishing working-class rule in the form of multi-party council democracy; upholding a resolute working-class and anti-imperialist internationalism, in contrast to the Comintern's subordination of class and national liberation struggles to the foreign policy interests of the rulers of the USSR and anti-imperialist but pro-capitalist forces; refusing to postpone the fight for social revolution against capitalism to some future stage of history; aiming to win liberation from colonialism, imperialism, and pre-capitalist and capitalist exploitation in what we would now call the Global South by having the working class in alliance with the peasantry take power and at least open the door to a transition to communism, as had happened in Russia; recognizing that socialist revolution could not succeed in one country but had to spread if it was not to succumb; advocating united fronts against fascism and for winning reforms in the here and now; and rejecting the lies propagated by the rulers of the USSR about conditions in that country.[40] Unfortunately, Trotskyism was vastly overshadowed by the main forces on the left, social democratic reformism and Communism; as we have seen, the latter did its best to slander and demonize Trotsky and his supporters. Being marginalized fostered dogmatism, insularity, and sectarianism (mistaking what is good for one's group with what best advances the overall struggle) among anti-Stalinist communists. The Trotskyist current was also scarred from the beginning by the influence of undemocratic practices inherited from the Comintern in the mid-1920s, when it was headed by Zinoviev.[41]

There were also other marxists who opposed the politics of Stalinism from what they considered a pro-Bolshevik communist viewpoint. In 1935, one such group in Spain merged with Trotsky's supporters in that country to form the Workers' Party of Marxist Unification (Spanish initials: POUM). The following year a military coup touched off social revolution and civil war, and the POUM valiantly threw itself into the fight and grew rapidly. The POUM attempted to fight fascism and advance the revolution simultaneously, though not without making mistakes.[42] Ken Loach's fine 1995 film *Land and Freedom* tells a fictional tale based on this history. In contrast, the CP and its allies were committed to a popular front strategy and sought to limit the struggle to a defence of capitalist democracy. This led them to push "the proletarian revolution back within the bourgeois-democratic bounds from which it 'should' never have escaped."[43] This involved suppressing revolutionary workers and peasants, banning the POUM, and, as seen in Chapter 3, the murder by the NKVD of some of its members, including leader Andreu Nin. In Italy, Amadeo Bordiga maintained an intransigent anti-Stalinist communism that emphasized the revolutionary party in a way that ended up making the working class "disappear as the fundamental factor of the revolutionary process."[44] Later some other more or less pro-Bolshevik anti-Stalinist organizations emerged. These included the little group of courageous Jewish-Israelis and Palestinians known as Matzpen that formed in Israel in the 1960s. Matzpen proposed a regional revolutionary socialist strategy for the overthrow of Zionist settler colonialism and the other states in the region.[45]

The USSR's alliance with Nazi Germany in 1939 and the imposition of AES in Eastern Europe by its armies after World War II led some Trotskyists to reject Trotsky's analysis of the USSR. They analyzed it instead as a society in which a new ruling class ruled. Some saw AES as a non-capitalist class-divided society (bureaucratic collectivism), others as state capitalism.[46] From this analysis flowed a stance of "Neither Washington Nor Moscow" during the Cold War. This book draws in part on research by people educated in this tradition.[47] Such rethinking, which encouraged further reflection about the weaknesses of Trotskyism, was less common than an orthodox Trotskyism that saw the AES societies as in transition to communism but blocked by bureaucratic rulers.

The global radicalization of the mid-1960s through the mid-1970s bolstered Trotskyism's forces and led to engagement with new movements, including those for women's and lesbian and gay liberation. Experiences in those years and since have also highlighted Trotskyism's flaws. Some of these have been mentioned above, but another is the practice of organizing small, sometimes tiny, groups "as if" they were the parties rooted in the working class that they aspired to build, "only smaller," a practice that distorts groups that adopt it. More broadly, Trotskyism was defined at its origins by answers to political questions that are different than the burning questions facing communists in today's world.[48]

## JAMES, DUNAYEVSKAYA, AND CASTORIADIS

A current that grew out of Trotskyism is worth mentioning because, although it was tiny, some of its ideas resonated far beyond its ranks. In the 1940s, a tendency in the US Trotskyist group that had rejected Trotsky's analysis of the USSR formed around theorists CLR James, author of the pathbreaking history of the Haitian Revolution, *The Black Jacobins* (1938), and Raya Dunayevskaya. It later departed from Trotskyism altogether. Its distinguishing ideas were an emphasis on the importance of workers' self-organized efforts to make change both inside and outside the workplaces where they toiled for pay and also on the autonomous self-activity of women and Black people; affirmation of Marx's vision of communism and the transition to it as based on the free association of direct producers and the overcoming of alienated labour; analysis of AES societies as state capitalist; belief that the working class no longer needed revolutionary parties to make successful revolutions; and faith in inevitable revolutionary victory.[49] These US marxists converged with Socialism or Barbarism, a grouplet in France that had also broken with Trotskyism and whose leading theorist was Cornelius Castoriadis. Socialism or Barbarism emphasized workers' self-activity against the bureaucratic capitalist social order and viewed AES as capitalist.[50] The "unavoidable tensions and conflicts that arise within small political groups operating under unpromising circumstances"[51] and political disagreements led to a parting of the ways between James and his supporters and Dunayevskaya and hers. The experience of Socialism or Barbarism was similar.

These groups were miniscule. Their notions that revolution will inevitably triumph and that exploited and oppressed people need workers' councils but not also mass revolutionary political organizations in order to take power and begin the transition to communism are unhelpful. But their anti-bureaucratic ideas about self-activity ended up having a disproportionately large impact on some elements of the New Left of the 1960s and 1970s. These included radicals who took part in the explosive social revolt in France in 1968; Walter Rodney and, through him, the Working People's Alliance in Guyana; the Sojourner Truth Organization, which originated in the NCM in the US; and, perhaps most significantly, the marxist current in Italy known as *operaismo* ("workerism").[52]

## ANTI-BOLSHEVIK ANTI-STALINISTS

Soon after the formation of the Comintern in 1919, some communists broke away from it over disagreements with the Russian CP and with the majority decisions of the Comintern that communists should work within existing unions and participate in elections in capitalist democracies. Many of them then concluded that the Russian Revolution had not been a socialist revolution after all, but only a bourgeois revolution against feudalism. Having seen the state the Bolsheviks built after 1918 as already capitalist, they were opposed to AES from the start. Few such council communists, so-called because they stressed the importance of workers' councils as the basis for a transition towards communism and saw all parties as outmoded organizations, survived Midnight in the Century and the worst years of Cold War anti-communism. Those who did went on to connect with the New Left that took off from the mid-1960s. So too did a few like-minded marxists who differed with them in interpreting the Russian Revolution, as Korsch had, as a socialist revolution that had succumbed to capitalism in the late 1920s.[53]

This current's thought has some of the same weaknesses as those of the current previously discussed. Its greatest contribution is its clarity that

> workers' rule serves the purpose of introducing and carrying through the new system of production, accounting and regulation ... and in order to create the basis on which the free producers themselves may control production and administer it ... it functions so as to bring to life and to promote those very forces through which it itself as the function of rule progressively loses power, in order finally to make itself superfluous; workers' rule works so as to bring about its own demise at the earliest possible historical moment.[54]

This expresses a key idea of the kind of communist theory first developed by Marx and Engels. Some of this current's ideas also converge with those of the anarchist strand of the communist tradition.

## ANARCHIST COMMUNISM

Communism has never only been marxist; there have always been people committed to the goal of a classless and stateless society of freedom without property ownership of the Earth who have been guided by other theoretical approaches. In the second half of the nineteenth century, anarchists became distinguished from other socialists by their rejection of running candidates in elections and trying to use elected office for socialist ends. Anarchists affirmed the value of "local control, direct participation, small-scale community, and federative cooperation."[55] Many "caught the bug of adventurism and wild fantasy"[56] and endorsed insurrectionism. This involved carrying out assassinations and other terrorist attacks to try to spur the masses to revolt. Anarchist communism became influential among anarchists from the 1880s. Its supporters were divided between insurrectionists and supporters of mass struggle by workers and peasants. The latter were further divided between those who saw unions as vehicles for social revolution (syndicalists) and those who did not. Another disagreement existed between those who saw no need for revolutionary political organizations and those who believed that these were needed in addition to unions or other mass organizations of class struggle.[57]

Anarcho-communists differed in their responses to the Russian Revolution and what came after. Many of them joined the Comintern when it was founded and became marxists. Those who remained anarchists affirmed, in the words of writer Alexander Berkman, that "the meaning of Communist Anarchism is this: the abolition of government, of coercive authority and all its agencies, and joint ownership — which means free and equal participation in the general work and welfare."[58] They recognized that AES had nothing to do with evolution towards communism.

Anarcho-communist forces were strongest in Spain. When revolution and civil war erupted in 1936, the large National Confederation of Labour (Spanish initials: CNT) union body was officially pledged to anarchist communism. The Iberian Anarchist Federation (Spanish initials: FAI) also existed as a political organization dedicated to promoting that vision and opposing reformist tendencies within the CNT. Anarcho-communists did not hesitate to leap into action when faced with the military coup. They were involved in establishing workers' self-management and peasant collectivization of the land in some regions within the parts of the country where anti-fascists put down the coup. But their theory did not equip them for the challenge of figuring out how to unite with other forces to defend capitalist democracy against fascism and at the same time advance the revolutionary process that had begun. The CNT-FAI leadership accepted the idea that it was necessary to win the civil war before social revolution could proceed. To that end, they set aside anarchist principles and joined the Popular Front national government. From that position, in spite of conflicts with the Communists they did not oppose government moves to end collectivization. Anarchocommunist opposition to the CNT-FAI leadership existed but was too weak to affect events.[59]

Elsewhere, supporters of this marginalized current who physically and politically survived fascism, Stalinism, World War II, and the Cold War continued to uphold an internationalist anti-Stalinist revolutionary socialism. In spite of problems of dogmatism, sectarianism, and insularity that it shared with other currents, in some places anarchist communism influenced the radicalization that began in the mid-1960s and gained new adherents. The same happened with the brief radicalization at the end of the century. In most places, however, its forces remained smaller than those of anti-Stalinist marxism.

## RESOURCES FOR A NEW COMMUNISM

In spite of the mighty currents against which it has been forced to swim, anti-Stalinist communism has survived as a diverse living tradition. In response to ML taunts that it has never made a revolution, its supporters can note their ancestors' vital role in Russia in 1917 and their contributions to revolutions in Germany and Spain as well as to many other upsurges of working-class struggle. Many also point out that the revolutions made by ML forces in China, Cuba, and elsewhere have not been the kind of revolution that can begin a transition to communism. This tradition is a rich trove of ideas about communism, what would be required to initiate a transition towards such a society, the process of transition, and, crucially, strategy and tactics for getting to a break with capitalism. Such ideas are essential for people today who wish to fight for a better society. Importantly, these ideas are the product of serious efforts to analyze over a century of historical experiences, not wishful or dishonest thinking. In contrast to Marxism-Leninism, supporters of this tradition have insisted that party-state dictatorships cannot be the vehicle for transition towards communism, and that transition must be a highly democratic and liberatory process that over time dissolves class division, state power, alienation, and oppression. They have refused to follow most ML forces in adopting reformist popular front politics. Instead, they have argued for revolutionary socialist strategy, usually including militant struggle for reforms in the here and now. They have championed internationalist working-class solidarity and usually rejected campism. While far from perfect, their track record on democracy in movements is better than that of MLs. This does not mean that any current within the anti-Stalinist communist tradition possesses an adequate political program for the present, a coherent strategy for breaking with capitalism and initiating a transition in the world today. Developing such a strategy in any part of the world requires a sizeable political organization with sound theory and the ability to synthesize the experiences of many organizers across different fields of struggle in that context.[60] Nor is this tradition the sole repository of political resources useful for communists. Some thinkers and currents lacking a radical systematic critique of Stalinism also have ideas that can contribute to a communist politics for our time. These include, for example, Antonio Gramsci, author of stimulating reflections on how ruling classes rule, how the exploited and oppressed could come to rule, and much else; José Carlos Mariátegui, who analyzed aspects of South American reality; *operaismo*, whose best ideas can stimulate attention to how working classes are reshaped by capital and workers' own struggles; and a number of marxist writers on gender oppression, racism, and settler colonialism.[61] There are also non-communists from whom people who want to develop communist politics adequate for today can learn.[62] Nevertheless, it is the anti-Stalinist communist tradition that has best kept communism alive as a project for human emancipation.

# CHAPTER 9

# WHAT CAN WE HOPE FOR?

## CURRENT CONDITIONS FOR COMMUNISTS

**THE FALL OF AES IN EASTERN EUROPE AND THE USSR** from 1989–91 was widely interpreted as the end of communism and any other project of constructing an alternative to capitalism. The 1989 Tiananmen Square massacre of pro-democracy protestors by the Chinese military fed into the same view; if the CCP survived as a ruling party, unlike its counterparts in the USSR and Eastern Europe, it was only through bloody repression.[1] Around the world, parties that supported AES lost much of their support. Radical left forces that were highly critical of AES but considered it better than capitalism also suffered. Over time, the widespread perception that the alternative to capitalism had failed reduced the appeal even of radical politics that held that AES societies had not been in transition to communism at all. This belief in a historic failure fed into the mood expressed in the saying of unknown origins reported by cultural studies scholar Fredric Jameson: "it is easier to imagine the end of the world than the end of capitalism."[2]

Nevertheless, the realities of capitalism fuelled global surges of anti-capitalist sentiment and politics in the short-lived global justice movement that began in the late 1990s, in the wake of the Great Recession of 2007–09 and the austerity drive that followed, and more recently in response to climate change, how states handled the COVID-19 pandemic, and racism. This sentiment has often boosted support for reformist socialism: the left social democracy of Jeremy Corbyn in the UK, Jean-Luc Mélenchon in France, Bernie Sanders and the kind of politics dominant within the Democratic Socialists of America in the US, and the like. Today there are also many people who dream of freedom, of liberation, of a future more radically different from the present than what left social democracy seeks. However, they often think politically in terms of abolition, feminism, trans and queer liberation, degrowth, and/or anti-capitalism without also being communist (the point is not whether people use the term "communism" to name the society for which they wish to fight but what kind of society they wish to see established). The mood captured by Jameson is still very widespread.

All strands of communist politics have also been affected by how their political magnetism has been depleted by the ending of what we can call the classical workers' movement over the closing decades of the twentieth century, decades in which employers and states inflicted major defeats on the global working class. Of course, there are still unions and, in some places, other mass organizations of the working class. What no longer exists almost anywhere are "configurations of workers' organizations with a strong relationship to at least a small but significant minority of the class that affirm a commitment to the creation by workers of a fundamentally different society."[3] What is more, "infrastructures of dissent" — "the means through which activists develop political communities capable of learning, communicating and mobilizing together" — are much weaker than they once were.[4]

In part because of these developments, popular discontent arising from changes in society that have worsened life globally for many people since the Great Recession is being tapped and moulded by rising right-wing forces. These include both fascist and other far-right organizations, which aim to do away with capitalist democracy altogether, and a larger set of forces that want to weaken it further. Together they make up an "array of antidemocratic and reactionary forces seeking to reassert class rule and privilege, to exit the crises of our times on terms set by capital, to bring a specific kind of order to an increasingly unstable world," as theorists Todd Gordon and Jeffery R. Webber perceptively observe.[5] In these conditions, is communism a meaningful political project?

Before addressing that question, one objection needs to be discussed: even if socialist revolutions happen, the global ecological crisis will make transition to communism impossible. Upheavals stemming from climate change lie ahead, along with other dimensions of the crisis, including more pandemic outbreaks. Humanity needs to shift to non-fossil sources of energy as quickly as possible — an enormous undertaking. Doing this while at the same time allowing imperialized countries of the South to improve the lives of their inhabitants will require reducing energy use in imperialist countries. The use of many non-renewable resources must also be reduced, agriculture transformed, food systems changed, and many forms of pollution stopped.[6] According to some ecologists, people would not be able to both make such changes and also move towards communism, which they believe would involve ecocidal industrial growth. My response is that this is true for a transition towards "productivist" communism — one that would ignore or downplay the limits of our biosphere and retain most of capitalism's technological structure and the wasteful, consumer goods–fixated, car-dependent, jet-travelling way of life spawned in the imperialist countries during the post–World War II economic boom and then spread around the world.[7] But there is no reason to assume that people who had taken control of society and started to reconstruct it would take a productivist path. The extremely democratic institutions of self-government they would have created would provide an unparalleled framework for debating which priorities would shape the democratic planning of production and the reorganization of social life. Within that framework, and no longer shackled by capitalism's ecocidal drive, it would be far easier than in any capitalist society to argue for ecological concerns to be prioritized. "Private sufficiency, public luxury" could be a principle in the transition to an ecological communism, which is a goal worth fighting for no matter how severe the ecological crisis gets.[8] Without such a transition, capitalism will make it impossible to achieve all of the far-reaching changes that are urgently needed to address our dire ecological situation.

## IS THERE ANY HOPE FOR COMMUNISM?

Returning to the question of whether communism is a viable political project today, it is not hard to understand what capitalism is doing to humanity and the rest of nature. Some of this was touched on at the outset of this book, and much has been written about it.[9] Capitalism is doing what it is doing because of the essential character of its social metabolism. This is driven by its irrational logic: the competitive accumulation of capital on an ever-larger scale and at an ever-faster speed. Capitalism operates as it does not because of an imbalance that can be corrected but because of its inherent systemic imperatives. As the saying goes, "The system isn't broken. It was built this way." This is why it is *necessary* for humanity to move from capitalism to a better and entirely different way of organizing social life.

Whether communism is *possible* is where the major problem arises. Even many sympathizers are skeptical because we have not yet had a historical experience in which people have really begun to reconstruct society in the direction of communism, yet we do have a history of defeated revolutions and the disastrous experience of AES. Moreover, we are all affected by living in an age in which there is a sense that history is over, that we live in a world of the eternal present, that the future will be like the present, but probably worse.[10] This context clouds our ability to see that the world is not closed but "open, incomplete, unfinished."[11] We can better appreciate that openness if we understand that the present is just a moment of history. Over time humans have organized societies in a wide variety of ways, even if societies have been structured by a limited number of modes of production.[12]

The status quo that we often take for granted did not have to be as it is. It is the outcome of events and processes shaped by clashing class and other social forces in particular times and places. It is not the inevitable culmination of laws of history that could not have unfolded otherwise. Nor is it the product of random chance.[13] Consider just one counterfactual scenario: If the Russian CP's surplus-extracting state of proletarian origin had been overthrown in the early 1920s, it would have been replaced by a horrific counter-revolutionary military dictatorship: "the world would have had a Russian name for Fascism," as Trotsky once put it.[14] At the same time, communist politics would not have been distorted by Stalinism, and AES would never have existed. The history of the twentieth century would have been dramatically different.

Unpredictable novel happenings with far-reaching consequences are part of our history. Philosopher Ernst Bloch sees history as punctuated by such transformational happenings, those that are "radically new in history";[15] he calls one of these a novum. While Bloch generally sees the novum as good — the Russian Revolution is an outstanding example — theorist Alan Milchman argues that a novum can also be bad. He gives the example of the Holocaust.[16] The emergence in the USSR at the end of the 1920s of a new form of capitalism under rulers who used the language of marxism can also be seen as a bad novum. Recognizing that such happenings occur should reinforce the idea that the future will not be the present projected forward in a way that we can predict in detail, as a glance at forecasts made in the late twentieth century or earlier should remind us. There are many possible futures. Some would be *much* worse for humanity than the world as it exists today, others merely worse. In spite of the inescapable effects that capitalism's ecological crisis will have on all possible worlds, other futures would be better, even much better.

As well as insisting that history is still open, it is useful to think about two different kinds of possibility. Bloch distinguishes possibility in a passive sense — the "capability-of-becoming-other," which he calls "potentiality" — from possibility in an active sense — "active possibility" or "capacity." He illustrates the distinction with the example of a tree whose blossoms contain the potential to bear fruit but which needs favourable weather for that potentiality to be realized.[17] This distinction between passive and active possibility helps us to think about the prospect of a transition towards communism.

The potentiality for this kind of social reconstruction is vast. Under capitalism, people have raised the productive powers of labour to previously unimagined heights (the result of how corporations and capitalist states driven to generate higher profits and establish more control over people have developed productive forces, but also of people's creativity independent of firms and states) while shackling them to capital. Today's information technology and the semiconductors and other technologies that make it possible are just one example of this. The productivity of labour is so high that people could easily start to shorten their hours of work once the production of goods and services began to be democratically planned to meet human needs, including a non-ecocidal relationship with the rest of nature, instead of being driven by the limitless pursuit of profit. Simply redirecting the labour currently wasted on manufacturing goods that need to be replaced because of planned obsolescence, duplicate production of commodities by competing firms, advertising, luxury production, and military spending would have a big impact.[18] Shortening hours of work would give most people much more time for free life activities. Unlike in pre-capitalist societies, there is now "enough for all, with more left over"[19] to develop productive forces where necessary, such as electricity generation powered by renewable energy everywhere, and much else in the Global South. This does not mean, as some communists have thought, that enough must be "produced for everyone to have what they want."[20] That idea of abundance unknowingly reflects a capitalist ideology of unbounded acquisitiveness.

> Instead, abundance is a social relationship, based on the principle that the means of one's existence will never be at stake in any of one's relationships. The steadfast security that such a principle implies is what allows all people to ask "What am I

going to do with the time I am alive?" rather than "How am I going to keep living?"[21]

The foundation for such an "abundance of common wealth"[22] has existed for many decades.

Another aspect of the potentiality latent in today's productive forces is interconnectedness. Under capitalism today, labour is alienated and dominates the direct producers; we are atomized and pitted against each other by competition for jobs and housing, as well as in other ways. Yet labour is also interconnected to an extraordinary degree. Within workplaces, as theorist Ernest Mandel argues,

> jobs have become part of a *co-operative totality* which, potentially, once capitalism has been superseded by the reign of the associated producers, will open up undreamt-of possibilities for the development of individual talents and capacities too, precisely because the high level of objective cooperation of labour immensely widens the general scope of human endeavour and potential self-development.[23]

At the same time, across workplaces,

> branches of industry, countries, the more the centralization of capital advances, the more technical and economic integration advances also, creating closer and closer bonds of objective co-operation between producers who are still living hundreds if not thousands of miles apart. In this way too, capitalism prepares the ground for both the real unity of the human race and the real universality of the individual, made materially possible by this objective socialization of labour.[24]

That Mandel wrote those words almost half a century ago, long before the information technology we now take for granted, should bring home just how much potentiality for communism exists today. The interconnectedness that capitalism has generated would enable people who had begun to transition beyond capitalism to democratically plan what to produce, how to produce it, and how to reorganize society from top to bottom more easily than in the past. Today's computing power coupled with workplace self-management and new forms of democracy beyond the workplace would be potent ingredients for democratic planning.[25]

Another dimension of the potentiality for the start of a transition to communism is the existence of a growing global working class, a class with an interest in getting rid of capitalism and the power to do so. When this class engages in collective struggle against capital, it begins to "objectively [point] to a program, even when it consciously rejects it: namely the assumption of social responsibility by a democratically organized people, regardless of private interest — a program which, concretized, means the abolition of capitalism."[26] The logic of its class struggle is thus different from that of the peasantry, although peasants can certainly fight against capitalism.[27]

What is in short supply today is not potentiality but the active possibility needed to unlock it. What Bensaïd writes is important:

> Of course, we don't know how this crossing will be made or even if it ever will. We can confidently state, though, that such a crossing is indeed possible because this is a human matter, entirely of our own making. After all, economy, money, history, science, state and other such idols are our creations, not our almighty gods.[28]

The missing key is self-organized mass movements of direct producers that threaten to surge over the defensive barriers and diversionary channels erected by capitalist states and create dual power. Highly democratic mass organizations with the potential to replace the existing state are essential for the establishment of working-class rule and the start of transition. These have been mentioned in this book's discussions of Russia in 1917, the revolutionary wave across Europe in the years that followed, and Chile in 1972–73. They have also arisen in other times and places.[29] In recent years there have been many popular revolts. However, none has gone so far as to generate a situation of dual power.[30] That fact, along with our age's skepticism about an alternative to capitalism itself, is an important reason why "widespread and active resistance to the priorities imposed by neoliberal states ... has, to date, also been marked by the weakness of alternative projects based on enlarging emancipation and democratic control."[31] In recent years we have seen the desire for greater freedom and democracy bubbling up in brief protests and more sustained social movements, including those against racism and gender oppression and in solidarity with Palestinian liberation. Aspirations for truly radical social change are being expressed in languages of abolition, feminism, trans liberation, climate justice, and Palestinian freedom (which is not to say that people who talk in these terms always have radical aspirations[32]). In part because of the passing of the classical workers' movement and the weakness of infrastructures of dissent mentioned earlier, these yearnings have not yet helped to ignite mass movements in which working-class people have at least started to organize themselves in ways that point towards dual power, though they have potential to do so. But in the future, class struggle under capitalism could well give birth to dual power again.

Sociologist Neil Davidson argues that in the last century there were three periods he calls "revolutionary conjunctures": "1917–23, 1943–49, and 1968–76."[33] These are periods of years, on an international scale, that "can give rise to revolutionary situations" in specific places, "decisive turning points lasting days or weeks — perhaps months at most — in which the moment ('of truth') is either seized or allowed to pass."[34] Davidson suggests that economic crisis, catastrophic climate change, and mass migration, by themselves or in combination, are "plausible contenders" for "the triggers for a new revolutionary conjuncture" in the future.[35] War could also be a trigger. This is a rational basis for concluding that the active possibility of the start of a transition to communism could arise in the future. Just such a future and more are imagined by M.E. O'Brien and Eman Abdelhadi in their inspiring and frightening work of speculative fiction *Everything for Everyone*.[36] Even outside a revolutionary conjuncture, an isolated and short-lived revolutionary breakthrough, a Paris Commune of the twenty-first century, would have global reverberations. Seeing everyday people in our time taking control of society and at least opening the door to remaking the world would kindle a new communist movement. This would feed into the active possibility needed to go further.

## FROM POSSIBILITY TO POLITICS

There is enormous potentiality for at least real progress towards communism. If we accept that the active possibility for transition to begin could swell in the future, what follows? Our species is in dire need of replacing capitalism with a way of organizing our relationships with the rest of nature and each other that is liberatory and ecologically rational. That is precisely what a society in transition to communism would be. Thus, we ought to work to achieve what is possible. As theorist Terry Eagleton puts it, "It is irrational to hope for the impossible, but not for the vastly improbable." We cannot be certain about how much active possibility there will be of a breakthrough at some point in the future. Yet Eagleton is right: "there may be no hope; but unless we act as though there is, that possibility is likely to become a certainty."[37] What we can hope for we must also work for. The stakes are unfathomably high: to use writer Ian Angus's twist on a slogan made famous by Luxemburg: "ecosocialism or barbarism."[38] Therefore, we cannot sit this one out. We must place a bet. We must make the melancholy wager, to use the title of a fine book by Bensaïd.[39] We will never have the "quiet doctrinaire assurance of an absolute and definitive truth"[40] to give us certainty about the outcome we desire. We should act in the full knowledge of uncertainty. We should practise communist politics.

Providing such a politics is beyond the scope of this book. However, I will conclude with thoughts about a few essential elements of a viable communist politics for our time, drawing on what I see as some of the most important insights of the anti-Stalinist communist tradition. A social revolution that opens the way towards an ecological communism is a "regulatory horizon,"[41] the goal towards which communists should navigate, no matter how far it is from the political terrain on which we currently find ourselves, and one that has definite implications for what we do. The horizon influences the strategy to guide the political activity of people who want to contribute to attaining the goal. What such people do should not point in the opposite direction. For instance, communists in unions should work to foster militant, democratic, and solidaristic ways of organizing, including the ability and willingness to defy the law when necessary, rather than conforming with the routines of bureaucratic collective bargaining and grievance handling and accepting blinkered ideas about what "union issues" are.[42]

Simply proclaiming fidelity to communism achieves nothing; it is necessary to work towards the goal. Communist politics provide a compass with which to navigate, not a map. We must use them in the circumstances in which we find ourselves, avoiding "the main dilemmas that paralyze political reconstruction of the alternative today" insightfully noted by philosopher Isabelle Garo: "short-term pragmatism or preservation of an ultimate but inaccessible horizon; circumvention of the issue of the state or institutional integration; dispersion of struggles or unity decreed from above."[43] We must also understand that neither an international revolutionary conjuncture nor a revolutionary situation can be willed into existence, no matter how desperately anti-capitalists may desire them. They can only be brought on by crises in society. When such a crisis happens, "the task of revolutionaries is not to aid the bourgeoisie in restoring the *status quo ante* [the way things were previously] — which is usually impossible in any event — but to try to turn it to the advantage of the exploited and oppressed."[44]

If AES teaches us anything, it is that a transition towards communism will only get underway as the outcome of a revolutionary process that, to repeat Luxemburg's memorable words, "can be begun and carried out only by the masses of people themselves," one that "can be brought to victory only by the great majority of the working people themselves."[45] That is why there is such wisdom in the declaration by a cothinker of Castoriadis that

> *Meaningful action*, for revolutionaries, is whatever increases the confidence, the autonomy, the initiative, the participation, the solidarity, the equalitarian tendencies and the self-activity of the masses and whatever assists in their demystification. *Sterile and harmful action* is whatever reinforces the passivity of the masses, their apathy, their cynicism, their differentiation through hierarchy, their alienation, their reliance on others to do things for them and the degree to which they can therefore be manipulated by others — even by those allegedly acting on their behalf.[46]

Since the middle of the last century, such truths, which highlight the crucial importance of the kinds of collective action through which people change as they try to change society,[47] have been most consistently expressed by anti-Stalinist communists outside the pro-Bolshevik current within that tradition.

However, it is that current which has best understood another important truth: to work towards establishing working-class rule, the exploited and oppressed need to be guided by what Luxemburg calls "revolutionary Realpolitik." This is a politics with its feet on the ground, fully engaged with the messy complexity of reality. Its supporters work constructively with people who do not share their politics to help them take the next step together from where they are towards the revolutionary horizon. They strive to promote solidarity and the convergence of different movements and struggles, conscious that an injury to one is an injury to all. Supporters of such politics do this no matter how miserable their current context is from a communist perspective. Unlike "revolutionary-socialist utopianism," revolutionary Realpolitik is "a politics that only sets itself achievable goals that it pursues to obtain by the most effective means in the shortest time."[48] For this approach, "the daily struggle for reforms, for the amelioration of the condition of the workers within the framework of the existing social order, and for democratic institutions" where they do not exist is

> the only means of engaging in the proletarian class war and working in the direction of the final goal — the conquest of political power and the suppression of wage labour. Between social reforms and revolution there exists for the social democracy [in 1900, this term referred to marxian socialists] an indissoluble tie. The struggle for reforms is its means; the social revolution, its aim.[49]

People who wish to work towards that goal should be involved in workplace or community organizing, practising revolutionary Realpolitik in ways that are consistent with the ideas about "meaningful action, for revolutionaries" just presented. In so doing, they will benefit from cultivating such virtues as determined commitment to the long-term aim, patience in working towards it, and the audacity to take advantage of political opportunities when they arise.

# FURTHER READING

People wishing to learn more about particular topics discussed in this book will likely find works cited in relevant endnotes worth pursuing. More generally, here are a number of books I recommend for readers new to various topics.

**ON COMMUNISM:** Daniel Bensaïd's essay "The Powers of Communism" is excellent, as are two classic articles: Hal Draper's "The Two Souls of Socialism" and Franklin Rosemont's "Karl Marx and the Iroquois." David McNally's pamphlet *Socialist Politics in the Age of Trump* is well worth reading. Valuable though challenging for readers unfamiliar with their subjects are Peter Hudis, *Marx's Concept of the Alternative to Capitalism* and Isabelle Garo, *Communism and Strategy: Rethinking Political Mediations.*

**ON THE RUSSIAN REVOLUTION:** China Mieville, *October: The Story of the Russian Revolution.*

**ON THE USSR:** Mike Haynes, *Russia: Class and Power 1917–2000.*

**ON CHINA:** Ralf Ruckus, *The Communist Road to Capitalism: How Social Unrest and Containment Have Pushed China's (R)evolution since 1949* (though its understanding of the Maoist era is somewhat different than mine) and Eli Friedman, Kevin Lin, Rosa Liu, and Ashley Smith, *China in Global Capitalism: Building International Solidarity Against Imperial Rivalry.*

**ON CUBA:** Samuel Farber, *Cuba Since the Revolution of 1959: A Critical Assessment.*

**ON COMMUNIST PARTIES:** Duncan Hallas, *The Comintern.*

**THREE UNFORGETTABLE MEMOIRS:** Victor Serge, *Memoirs of a Revolutionary*; George Orwell, *Homage to Catalonia*; Ngo Van, *In the Crossfire: Adventures of a Vietnamese Revolutionary.*

# ENDNOTES

## CHAPTER 1

1. Jason Clemens and Steven Globerman, "Perspectives on Capitalism and Socialism: Polling Results from Canada, the United States, Australia and the United Kingdom," Fraser Institute, February 22, 2023, <fraserinstitute.org/studies/perspectives-on-capitalism-and-socialism>.
2. "Modest Declines in Positive Views of 'Socialism' and 'Capitalism' in the US," Pew Research Centre, September 19, 2022, <pewresearch.org/politics/2022/09/19/modest-declines-in-positive-views-of-socialism-and-capitalism-in-u-s/>.
3. See, for example, Johan Rockström et al., "Safe and Just Earth System Boundaries," *Nature* 619 (2023): 102–11, <doi.org/10.1038/s41586-023-06083-8>.
4. See the analysis in Todd Gordon and Jeffery R. Webber, "The Authoritarian Disposition: Capitalism, Liberalism, Fascism," *Spectre* 8 (Fall 2023): 42–55.
5. See Adam Hanieh, "Framing Palestine: Israel, the Gulf States, and American Power in the Middle East," Transnational Institute, June 13, 2024, <tni.org/en/article/framing-palestine>.
6. See Güney Işıkara, "Beating Around the Bush: Polycrisis, Overlapping Emergencies, and Capitalism," *Developing Economics*, November 22, 2022, <developingeconomics.org/2022/11/22/beating-around-the-bush-polycrisis-overlapping-emergencies-and-capitalism/>.
7. Vincent Bevins, *The Jakarta Method: Washington's Anticommunist Crusade and the Mass Murder Program That Shaped Our World* (New York: Public Affairs, 2020), 266. My figure of over one million is at the conservative end of Bevins' global estimate, including as it does a death toll in Indonesia in 1965–66 of 500,000, the lowest end of the range Bevins provides for that country.
8. See, for example, Ellen Schrecker, *Many Are the Crimes: McCarthyism in America* (Boston: Little, Brown and Co., 1998), but see also the comments about this book's shortcomings in Alan Wald, "The Costs of McCarthyism," *Against the Current* 85 (March–April 2000), <againstthecurrent.org/atc085/p1683/>.
9. US Congress, Senate, *Denouncing the Horrors of Socialism*, S Res. 9, 118th Congress, 1st sess., referred in Senate February 7, 2023, <congress.gov/bill/118th-congress/house-concurrent-resolution/9/text>.
10. Stéphane Courtois et al., *The Black Book of Communism: Crimes, Terror, Repression* (Cambridge: Cambridge University Press, 1999). For a good short review, see Paul Flewers, "Black Book of Communism," *Revolutionary History* 7, no. 4 (2000–2001), <marxists.org/history/etol/revhist/backiss/vol7/no4/flewers.html>.
11. Enzo Traverso, "The New Anti-Communism: Rereading the Twentieth Century," in *History and Revolution: Refuting Revisionism*, eds. Mike Haynes and Jim Wolfreys (London: Verso, 2007), 150, 151.

12  Douglas Greene, *Stalinism and the Dialectics of Saturn: Anticommunism, Marxism, and the Fate of the Soviet Union* (Lanham: Lexington Books, 2023), 76.
13  Máté Zombory, "The Anti-Communist Moment: Competitive Victimhood in European Politics," *Revue d'études comparatives Est-Ouest* 51, no. 2–3 (2020): 45–46, <doi: 10.3917/rece01.512.0021>.
14  Enzo Traverso, *Fire and Blood: The European Civil War 1914–1945*, trans. David Fernbach (London: Verso, 2016), 104.
15  Traverso, *Fire and Blood*, 111.
16  Kristen Ghodsee, "A Tale of 'Two Totalitarianisms': The Crisis of Capitalism and the Historical Memory of Communism," *History of the Present* 4, no. 2 (2014): 126; William Echikson, "Viktor Orbán's Anti-Semitism Problem," May 13, 2019, *Politico*, <politico.eu/article/viktor-orban-anti-semitism-problem-hungary-jews/>.
17  Greene, *Stalinism and the Dialectics*, 77. For example, according to Lithuania-based scholar Dovid Katz, there are many examples in the Baltic countries of local politicians making statements that depict Nazism as preferable to Stalinism. Dovid Katz, email message to author, May 31, 2024.
18  Liza Featherstone, "McCarthyite Laws Targeting Leftists are Still on the Books Across the Country," *Jacobin*, June 20, 2023, <jacobin.com/2023/06/mccarthyite-laws-targeting-leftists-are-still-on-the-books-across-the-country>.
19  Richard Seymour, "Trump Will Smite the Communists," Patreon.com, July 6, 2023, <patreon.com/posts/trump-will-smite-85572359>.
20  This book does not discuss these countries, though some of its analysis is relevant to understanding aspects of what they are and are not. On Latin American "socialist" governments other than Cuba (on which, see Chapter 5 of this book), see Jeffery R. Webber, *The Last Day of Oppression, and the First Day of the Same: The Politics and Economics of the New Latin American Left* (London: Pluto Press, 2017); Frank Gaudichaud, Massimo Modonesi, and Jeffery R. Webber, *The Impasse of the Latin American Left* (Durham: Duke University Press, 2022).
21  This line appears in the statement "As We See It" of the British libertarian socialist group Solidarity; despite my efforts I have been unable to discover whether it originated elsewhere, as it may have done. Maurice Brinton, "As We See It" (1967), <marxists.org/archive/brinton/1967/04/as-we-see-it.htm>.
22  Quoted in Hal Draper, "In Defence of the 'New Radicals,'" in *Socialism from Below*, ed. E. Haberkern (New Jersey: Humanities Press International, 1992), 126.
23  On the NCM in the US, see Max Elbaum, *Revolution in the Air: Sixties Radicals Turn to Lenin, Mao and Che* (New York: Verso, 2003) and reviews collected at <revolutionintheair.org>.
24  Kristin Ghodsee and Scott Sehon, "Anti-Anti-Communism," *Aeon*, March 22, 2018, <aeon.co/essays/the-merits-of-taking-an-anti-anti-communism-stance>.
25  Ghodsee and Sehon, "Anti-Anti-Communism."
26  Kristin Ghodsee, *Why Women Have Better Sex Under Socialism: And Other Arguments for Economic Independence* (New York: Nation Books, 2018), 3.
27  Ghodsee, *Why Women*, 177
28  Sophie Lewis, "For One Another," *The New Inquiry*, January 23, 2019, <thenewinquiry.com/for-one-another/>.

29  Lewis, "For One Another."
30  Lea Ypi, *Free: A Child and a Country at the End of History* (New York: WW Norton and Company, 2021), 260–62; Ondrej Belicek, "'People from Eastern Europe Could Teach Westerners a Thing or Two About the Failures of Liberalism in Our Societies,' says Lea Ypi," *LeftEast*, July 19, 2022, <lefteast.org/failures-of-liberalism-in-albania/>.
31  I prefer the term social industry to social media because it makes the point that what we are dealing with are capitalist enterprises. I take it from Richard Seymour, *The Twittering Machine* (London: Indigo, 2019).
32  Liza Featherstone, "Socialism Makes Summer Better," *Jacobin*, August 14, 2022, <jacobin.com/2022/08/socialism-summer-vacation-days-leisure-time-off>.
33  Madlen Nikolova, "Saving Bulgarian Communism's 'Concrete Spaceship,'" *Jacobin*, April 21, 2020, <jacobin.com/2020/04/buzludzha-bulgarian-communist-party-georgi-stoilov>.
34  Sheila Fitzpatrick, "What Was the Soviet Union?," interview by Owen Hatherly, *Tribune,* May 9, 2023, <tribunemag.co.uk/2023/05/what-was-the-soviet-union>.
35  Kristin Ghodsee and Julia Mead, "What Has Socialism Ever Done for Women?," *Catalyst* 2, no. 2 (2018): 109.
36  Barnaby Raine, "Left Fukuyamaism," *Salvage*, February 26, 2022, <salvage.zone/left-fukuyamaism-politics-in-tragic-times/>.
37  Salvatore Engel-Di Mauro, "Anti-Communism and the Hundreds of Millions of Victims of Capitalism," *Capitalism Nature Socialism* 32, no. 1 (2021): 2, <doi: 10.1080/10455752.2021.1875603>. Engel-Di Mauro subsequently co-translated Domenico Losurdo's defence of Stalin — on which, see note 40.
38  See Jodi Dean, *The Communist Horizon* (London: Verso, 2012) and Dean's posts on Twitter @Jodi7768.
39  Troy Vettese and Drew Pendergrass, *Half-Earth Socialism: A Plan to Save the Future from Extinction, Climate Change, and Pandemics* (London: Verso, 2022), 93, 130, 82.
40  For a short critique of one of the most notorious champions of Stalin on the left, see Douglas Greene, "On Grover Furr and the Moscow Trials," *The Blanquist*, May 3, 2017, <blanquist.blogspot.com/2017/05/on-grover-furr-and-moscow-trials.html>. On the defence of Stalin by Domenico Losurdo, the author of justly respected works on the history of political thought, see Greene, *Stalinism and the Dialectics*, 283–312.
41  For an introduction to this theoretical perspective, see my *We Can Do Better: Ideas for Changing Society* (Halifax: Fernwood Publishing, 2017), on which the following lines draw. For an academic journal article on my approach, see my "Theoretical Foundations of an Anti-Racist Queer Feminist Historical Materialism," *Critical Sociology* 42, no. 2 (2016): 289–306, <doi: 10.1177/0896920513507790>. I want to emphasize that in no way do I claim to have invented this theoretical perspective; I have merely sought to make it accessible to more people, argue for it, refine aspects of it, and use it to analyze aspects of society.
42  For introductions to the history of capitalism in North America north of Mexico, see James Parisot, *How America Became Capitalist: Imperial Expansion and the Conquest of the West* (London: Pluto Press, 2019) and

Bryan D. Palmer, *Colonialism and Capitalism: Canada's Origins 1500–1890* (Toronto: James Lorimer & Co., 2024). On capitalism, see Camfield, *We Can*, 55–67.

43 David McNally, *Against the Market: Political Economy, Market Socialism and the Marxist Critique* (London: Verso, 1993), 186.

44 Søren Mau, "Communism is Freedom," Verso Books, July 18, 2023, <versobooks.com/en-ca/blogs/news/communism-is-freedom>.

45 Hal Draper, "The Two Souls of Socialism," in *Socialism from Below*, 8–11. On Marx's theory about such a society, see Peter Hudis, *Marx's Concept of the Alternative to Capitalism* (Chicago: Haymarket Books, 2013).

46 For a thoughtful discussion of families, care, and beloved community in such a society, see M.E. O'Brien, *Family Abolition: Capitalism and the Communizing of Care* (London: Pluto Press, 2023).

47 Camfield, *We Can*, 123.

48 Paresh Chattopadhyay, *Marx's Associated Mode of Production: A Critique of Marxism* (New York: Palgrave Macmillan, 2016), 217.

49 J.V. Stalin, "Interview Between J. Stalin and Roy Howard," *Works*, vol. 14 (London: Red Star Press, 1978), <marxists.org/reference/archive/stalin/works/1936/03/01.htm>.

50 Alfred Evans Jr., "The Decline of Developed Socialism? Some Trends in Recent Soviet Ideology," *Soviet Studies*, 38, no. 1 (1986): 1–23, <http://www.jstor.org/stable/151988>.

51 Hudis, *Marx's Concept*, 190.

52 Thus I disagree with the strand of contemporary communist thought known as communization theory, which sees an immediate move through social revolution from capitalism to communism as possible and, moreover, holds that any recognition of the need for a period of transition to communism is counter-revolutionary (see Leon de Mattis, "What is Communization?," *Sic: International Journal for Communization*, accessed July 7, 2023, <sicjournal.org/what-is-communisation/index.html>). For a good discussion of Marx's thinking about communism and some misunderstandings of it, see Peter Hudis, "The Alternative to Capitalism in Marx's *Critique of the Gotha Program*," in Karl Marx, *Critique of the Gotha Program* (Oakland: PM Press, 2023), 1–40, and, at greater length, Hudis, *Marx's Concept*.

53 This is how William Morris and E. Belfort Bax defined the political power of the working class for which socialists were fighting, in their comments on a manifesto written not long after Marx's death. William Morris and E. Belford Bax, "The Manifesto of the Socialist League," cited in E.P. Thompson, *William Morris: Romantic to Revolutionary* (Oakland: PM Press, 2011), 740. On Marx's much-misunderstood ideas about a society in transition to communism, which were strongly influenced by the Paris Commune of 1871, see Hudis, *Marx's Concept*, 204–5.

54 For example, see William D. Haywood and Frank Bohn, *Industrial Socialism* (Chicago: Charles H. Kerr & Company, 1911), <marxists.org/archive/haywood-b/1911/industrial-socialism.pdf>.

55 Hudis, *Marx's Concept*, 205.

56 Rosa Luxemburg, "What Does the Spartakus League Want?," *Selected Political Writings*, ed. Dick Howard (New York: Monthly Review Press, 1971), <marxists.org/archive/luxemburg/1918/12/14.htm>.

57　Karl Marx, "The Eighteenth Brumaire of Louis Bonaparte," trans. Terrell Carver, in *Marx's "Eighteenth Brumaire": (Post)modern Interpretations*, eds. Mark Cowling and James Martin (London: Pluto Press, 2002), 43.
58　Leon Trotsky, *The History of the Russian Revolution* (New York: Pathfinder Press, 1987), xxi.
59　Michael Parenti, *Blackshirts and Reds: Rational Fascism and the Overthrow of Communism* (San Francisco: City Lights Books, 1997), 49.
60　Parenti, *Blackshirts and Reds*, 51.
61　Greene, *Stalinism and the Dialectics*, 76.
62　Greene, *Stalinism and the Dialectics*, 77.
63　Greene, *Stalinism and the Dialectics*, 27. There is a useful discussion of theorists of totalitarianism on pages 27–91.
64　J. Arch Getty and Oleg V. Naumov, *The Road to Terror: Stalin and the Self-Destruction of the Bolsheviks, 1932–1939* (New Haven: Yale University Press, 1999), 591–92.
65　Parenti, *Blackshirts and Reds*, 57.
66　For a refutation of the absurd claim made by Stalin apologist Grover Furr that Stalin and the CPSU leadership around him were not responsible for the mass executions of 1937–38, see Jean-Jacques Marie, "When Joseph Stalin Demolished Grover Furr," trans. David Fernbach, *historical materialism*, accessed June 5, 2024, <historicalmaterialism.org/book-review/when-joseph-stalin-demolished-grover-furr>. For a critique of Furr's defence of the claim made to justify the execution of "Old Bolsheviks" that they were part of a vast conspiracy to collaborate with Germany, Japan, Poland, and Britain against the USSR, see Greene, "On Grover Furr."
67　Edward Hallett Carr, *What is History?* (New York: Vintage Books, 1961), 32.
68　See Camfield, *We Can*.
69　Richard Seymour, "Fascism in the Age of Hyperreality," Patreon.com, June 21, 2023, <patreon.com/posts/fascism-in-age-84900683>.
70　Richard Seymour, "Who Do You Trust?," Patreon.com, May 2, 2023, <patreon.com/posts/who-do-you-trust-82399711>.
71　Naomi Klein, *Doppelganger: A Trip into the Mirror World* (Toronto: Alfred A. Knopf Canada, 2023), 243.

## CHAPTER 2

1　This chapter draws extensively on my "From Revolution to Modernizing Counter-Revolution in Russia, 1917–28," *Historical Materialism* 28, no. 2 (2020): 107–39, published by Brill.
2　Mike Haynes, *Russia: Class and Power 1917–2000* (London: Bookmarks Publishing, 2002), 22.
3　Neil Davidson, *How Revolutionary Were the Bourgeois Revolutions?* (Chicago: Haymarket Books, 2012), 297.
4　Steve A. Smith, *Russia in Revolution: An Empire in Crisis, 1890–1928* (Cambridge: Cambridge University Press, 2017), 88–98.
5　Smith, *Russia in Revolution*, 108.
6　Smith, *Russia in Revolution*, 117.
7　Smith, *Russia in Revolution*, 126, 140–42, 128–33.
8　China Mieville, *October: The Story of the Russian Revolution* (London: Verso, 2017).

9   Mieville, *October*, 164.
10  Steve A. Smith, "Petrograd in 1917: The View from Below" in *The Workers' Revolution in Russia, 1917: The View from Below*, ed. Donald H. Kaiser (Cambridge: Cambridge University Press, 1987), 77.
11  Smith, "Petrograd in 1917," 77.
12  Smith, *Russia in Revolution*, 151.
13  Steve A. Smith, *Red Petrograd: Revolution in the Factories 1917–1918* (Cambridge: Cambridge University Press, 1983), 24.
14  Trotsky, *History of the Russian*, 51.
15  Smith, *Russia in Revolution*, 158.
16  John Reed, "Soviets in Action," *The Liberator*, October 1918, <marxists.org/archive/reed/1918/soviets.htm>.
17  Kohei Saito, *Marx in the Anthropocene: Towards the Idea of Degrowth Communism* (Cambridge: Cambridge University Press, 2022), 226–36. I also discuss this issue in the final chapter of the present book.
18  John Marot, *The October Revolution in Prospect and Retrospect: Interventions in Russian and Soviet History* (Chicago: Haymarket Books, 2013), 35.
19  Alexander Rabinowitch, *The Bolsheviks in Power: The First Year of Soviet Rule in Petrograd* (Bloomington: Indiana University Press, 2007), 19–21.
20  Samuel Farber, *Before Stalinism: The Rise and Fall of Soviet Democracy* (London: Verso, 1990), 29.
21  Marcel Liebman, *Leninism Under Lenin* (London: Merlin, 1975), 230.
22  Liebman, *Leninism Under Lenin*, 230.
23  Diane P. Koenker, "Urbanization and Deurbanization in the Russian Revolution and Civil War," in *Party, State and Society in the Russian Civil War: Explorations in Social History*, eds. Diane P. Koenker, William Rosenberg, and Ronald Gregor Suny (Bloomington: Indiana University Press, 1989), 81; Rabinowitch, *Bolsheviks in Power*, 259, 224.
24  Smith, *Russia in Revolution*, 218.
25  Farber, *Before Stalinism*, 27; Rabinowitch, *Bolsheviks in Power*, 295, 301–2.
26  Liebman, *Leninism Under Lenin*, 230.
27  Smith, *Red Petrograd*, 206.
28  Smith, *Red Petrograd*, 241.
29  Franceso Benvenuti, "The Red Army," in *Critical Companion to the Russian Revolution 1914–1921*, eds. Edward Acton, Vladimir Iu Cherniaev, and William G. Rosenberg (Bloomington: Indiana University Press, 1997).
30  Wendy Z. Goldman, *Women, the State and Revolution: Soviet Family Policy and Social Life, 1917–1936* (Cambridge: Cambridge University Press, 1983), 57.
31  Smith, *Russia in Revolution*, 183.
32  Karl Marx, *The Civil War in France* (Peking: Foreign Languages Press, 1970), 78.
33  Marx, *The Civil War*, 69.
34  Hal Draper, *The "Dictatorship of the Proletariat" from Marx to Lenin* (New York: Monthly Review Press, 1987), 99.
35  Smith, *Russia in Revolution*, 209.
36  Thomas F. Remington, *Building Socialism in Bolshevik Russia: Ideology and Industrial Organization 1917–1921* (Pittsburgh: University of Pittsburgh Press, 1984), 163, 154.
37  David Mandel, *The Petrograd Workers and the Soviet Seizure of Power* (Basingstoke: Macmillan, 1984), 418.

38  Remington, *Building Socialism*, 83–86
39  Smith, *Russia in Revolution*, 224–28.
40  Simon Pirani, *The Russian Revolution in Retreat, 1920–24: Soviet Workers and the New Communist Elite* (Abingdon: Routledge, 2008), 56–57.
41  Koenker, "Urbanization and Deurbanization," 94.
42  Rabinowitch, *Bolsheviks in Power*, 391, 390.
43  "Programme of the Social-Democratic Workers' Party" (1903) <marxists.org/history/international/social-democracy/rsdlp/1903/program.htm>.
44  Vladimir Ilyich Lenin, *Two Tactics of Social-Democracy in the Democratic Revolution* (Peking: Foreign Languages Press, 1975).
45  Liebman, *Leninism Under Lenin*, 132.
46  Draper, "Dictatorship of the Proletariat," 26–41, 58–63.
47  Farber, *Before Stalinism*, 212.
48  Draper, "Dictatorship of the Proletariat," 136–42. For a very different contemporary marxist view, see Rosa Luxemburg, "The Russian Revolution," in *Rosa Luxemburg Speaks*, ed. Mary Alice Waters (New York: Pathfinder Press, 1970), 393–94.
49  Farber, *Before Stalinism*, 71–73.
50  Farber, *Before Stalinism*, 211.
51  Draper, "Dictatorship of the Proletariat," 100.
52  Vladimir Petrovich Sapon, "Kontseptsiya revolyutsionnogo osvobozhdeniya obshchestva v teoreticheskikh vozzreniyakh i politicheskoy praktike rossiyskikh levykh radikalov" (unpublished PhD dissertation, Universitet Lobachevskogo Nizhniy Novgorod, 2009), quoted in translation in Eric Blanc, "Was Stalinism Inevitable?," *SocialistWorker.org*, October 12, 2017, <socialistworker.org/2017/10/12/was-stalinism-inevitable>.
53  Oscar Sanchez-Sibony, *Red Globalization: The Political Economy of the Soviet Cold War from Stalin to Khruschev* (Cambridge: Cambridge University Press, 2014), 37.
54  Edward Hallett Carr, *Socialism in One Country, 1924–1926, vol. 1* (Harmondsworth: Penguin, 1970), 378.
55  Donald Filtzer, *Soviet Workers and Stalinist Industrialization: The Formation of Modern Soviet Production Relations, 1928–1941* (Armonk: M.E. Sharpe, 1986), 21, 160.
56  Carr, *Socialism in One*, 377–78.
57  Sanchez-Sibony, *Red Globalization*, 41.
58  Lynne Viola et al., eds., *The War Against the Peasantry, 1927–1930: The Tragedy of the Soviet Countryside* (New York: Yale University Press, 2005), 17.
59  Smith, *Russia in Revolution*, 370.
60  Viola et al., *The War*, 59.
61  Filtzer, *Soviet Workers*, 33.
62  Sanchez-Sabony, *Red Globalization*, 41-43.
63  Geoffrey E. Maurice Ste. Croix, *Class Struggle in the Ancient Greek World: From the Archaic Age to the Arab Conquests* (London: Duckworth, 1981), 43.
64  Smith, *Russia in Revolution*, 282; Pirani, *Russian Revolution*, 96–107
65  Pirani, *Russian Revolution*, 170.
66  Ibid, 215–25.
67  Smith, *Russia in Revolution*, 296.
68  Pirani, *Russian Revolution*, 225–32.

69 Thomas Henry Rigby, *Communist Party Membership in the ussr 1917–1967* (Princeton: Princeton University Press, 1968), 52, 352.
70 Smith, *Russia in Revolution*, 292.
71 Christopher S. Monty, "The Central Committee Secretariat, the Nomenklatura, and the Politics of Personnel Management in the Soviet Order, 1921–1927," *Soviet and Post-Soviet Review* 39 (2012): 166–91, <brill.com/view/journals/spsr/39/2/article-p166_3.xml>.
72 Stephen Sternheimer, "Administration for Development: The Emerging Bureaucratic Elite, 1920–1930," in *Russian Officialdom: The Bureaucratization of Russian Society from the Seventeenth to the Twentieth Century*, eds. Walter Pinter and Don Karl Rowney (Chapel Hill: University of North Carolina Press, 1980).
73 Jacek Kuron and Karol Modzelewski, *Solidarnosc: The Missing Link?* (London: Bookmarks, 1982), 24.
74 Gareth Dale, "After 1917: Civil War and 'Modernizing Counter-Revolution," *rs21*, October 26, 2017, <rs21.org.uk/2017/10/26/revolutonary-reflections-after-1917-civil-war-and-modernising-counter-revolution/>.
75 Marot, *October Revolution*, 45, 62.
76 Paresh Chattopadhyay, "Worlds Apart: Socialism in Marx and in Early Bolshevism: A Provisional Overview," *Economic and Political Weekly* 40, no. 53 (2005–06): 5629–34; Marot, *October Revolution*, 99–105.
77 This interpretation is supported by the critical examinations of the limited opposition to the Stalin-led majority of the ruling group mounted by Trotsky and the Left Opposition in Marot, *October Revolution*, 87–116 and John Molyneux, *Leon Trotsky's Theory of Revolution* (Brighton: Harvester Press, 1981), 102–4. Within the party, the most consistent opposition current was the Democratic Centralists — on whom, see Yurii Colombo, "Sapronov and the Russian Revolution," *International Socialist Review* 103 (2016–2017), <isreview.org/issue/103/sapronov-and-russian-revolution/>. There were also communist and other radical oppositionists outside the ranks of the CPSU, discussed in Pirani, *Russian Revolution*.
78 Greene, *Stalinism and the Dialectics*, 281.
79 For analysis of the possibility of a successful socialist revolution in Germany, see Chris Harman, *The Lost Revolution: Germany 1918 to 1923* (London: Bookmarks, 1982) and Sean Larson, "Germany 1923: Crucible of the World Revolution," *Spectre*, November 6, 2023, <spectrejournal.com/germany-1923/>. More broadly, see Donny Gluckstein, *The Western Soviets: Workers' Councils Versus Parliament 1915–1920* (London: Bookmarks, 1985).
80 This analysis is influenced by Michael Haynes, *Nikolai Bukharin and the Transition from Capitalism to Socialism* (London: Croom Helm, 1985). I believe that by 1923 (and possibly earlier) restoring working-class rule would have required a revolution against at least the dominant group in the party-state officialdom (see Camfield, "From Revolution," 126 n. 99).

# CHAPTER 3

1 Sheila Fitzpatrick, *The Shortest History of the Soviet Union* (New York: Columbia University Press, 2022), 79.
2 Sanchez-Sibony, *Red Globalization*, 47–56.

3   Fitzpatrick, *Shortest History*, 79.
4   J.D. Barber and R.W. Davies, "Employment and Industrial Labour," in *The Economic Transformation of the Soviet Union, 1913–1945*, eds. R.W. Davies, Mark Harrison, and S.G. Wheatcroft (Cambridge: Cambridge University Press, 1994), 103–4.
5   What follows draws on the close examination of what happened in workplaces in Filtzer, *Soviet Workers*. Filtzer demonstrates how severe shortages of labour power made it difficult for employers to discipline workers no matter what the law said. Filtzer also shows how state repression kept workers from resisting collectively but that they still responded as individuals by, for example, foot-dragging at work, leaving early, and changing jobs.
6   What follows draws above all on Moshe Lewin, *The Making of the Soviet System: Essays in the Social History of Interwar Russia* (New York: Pantheon Books, 1985), 91–177.
7   Fitzpatrick, *Shortest History*, 74. The term *kulak* was used as a political label to justify state policy rather than being a coherent concept referring to a distinct social layer of peasants. It is worth noting that "even the top 3.2 per cent of peasant households owned on average a mere 2.3 draught animals and 2.5 cows, as compared with the average of 1.0 and 1.1 for all households" (S.G. Wheatcroft and R.W. Davies, "Agriculture," in *The Economic Transformation of the Soviet Union, 1913–1945*, eds. R.W. Davies, Mark Harrison, and S.G. Wheatcroft (Cambridge: Cambridge University Press, 1994), 119).
8   Lewin, *Making of the Soviet*, 151.
9   Olena Lyubchenko, "Reassesssing Soviet Industrialization as Primitive *Soviet* Accumulation: Social Reproduction, Collectivization and Peasant Women's Revolts Under Stalin," *Journal of Agrarian Change* e12587 (2024), <doi.org/10.1111/joac.12587>.
10  Haynes, *Russia: Class*, 91.
11  Haynes, *Russia: Class*, 85.
12  Haynes, *Russia: Class*, 84, 85.
13  R.W. Davies, "Industry," in *The Economic Transformation of the Soviet Union, 1913–1945*, eds. R.W. Davies, Mark Harrison, and S.G. Wheatcroft (Cambridge: Cambridge University Press, 1994), 143–50.
14  Palgrave Macmillan, ed., "Volume 3 — International Historical Statistics 1750–2010: Europe," *International Historical Statistics*, last accessed July 11, 2023, 7–8, <link-springer-com.uml.idm.oclc.org/content/pdf/10.1057/978-1-137-30568-8_439.pdf?pdf=core>.
15  R.W. Davies, Mark Harrison, and S.G. Wheatcroft, eds., *The Economic Transformation of the Soviet Union, 1913–1945* (Cambridge: Cambridge University Press, 1994), 305–9, tables 33–40.
16  Davies, "Industry," 146–47; Haynes, *Russia: Class*, 99–104.
17  Haynes, *Russia: Class*, 87, 88, 167.
18  Fitzpatrick, *Shortest History*, 138. On the quality of the new housing, see Haynes, *Russia: Class*, 178–79.
19  Fitzpatrick, *Shortest History*, 137–38; Linda J. Cook, *The Soviet Social Contract and Why It Failed: Welfare Policy and Workers' Politics from Brezhnev to Yeltsin* (Cambridge: Harvard University Press, 1993), 48–52.
20  Moshe Lewin, *The Soviet Century* (London: Verso, 2005), 313.
21  Fitzpatrick, *Shortest History*, 154.

22 Lewin, *Soviet Century*, 314–15; Philip Hanson, *The Rise and Fall of the Soviet Economy: An Economic History of the ussr From 1945* (London: Longman, 2003), 247.
23 Haynes, *Russia: Class*, 91.
24 Kuron and Modzelewski, *Solidarnosc*, 23. The authors were writing about AES in Poland but this applies equally to the USSR.
25 Fitzpatrick, *Shortest History*, 89–90, 92–93, 188.
26 Goldman, *Women, the State*, 343.
27 Haynes, *Russia: Class*, 153–54.
28 Eric D. Weitz, "Racial Politics Without the Concept of Race: Reevaluating Soviet Ethnic and National Purges," *Slavic Review* 61, no. 1 (2002): 12.
29 Weitz, "Racial Politics," 18; Michael Haynes and Rumy Hasan, *A Century of State Murder? Death and Policy in Twentieth-Century Russia* (London: Pluto Press, 2003), 83.
30 Andrew Sloin, "Theorizing Soviet Antisemitism: Value, Crisis, and Stalinist 'Modernity,'" *Critical Historical Studies* 3, no. 2 (2016): 249–81, <doi: 10.1086/688349>.
31 Anika Walke, "Was Soviet Internationalism Anti-Racist? Toward a History of Foreign Others in the USSR," in *Ideologies of Race: Imperial Russia and the Soviet Union in Global Context*, ed. David Rainbow (Montreal: McGill-Queen's University Press, 2019), 302.
32 Haynes and Hasan, *A Century*, 69.
33 Haynes, *Russia: Class*, 116.
34 There is debate over whether the famine was an intentional genocidal attack on Ukraine. The interpretation I find most persuasive and on which I draw here is that of Terry Martin, *The Affirmative Action Empire: Nations and Nationalism in the Soviet Union, 1923–1939* (Ithaca: Cornell University Press, 2001), 273–308. On the death toll, see S.G. Wheatcroft and R.W. Davies, "Population," in *The Economic Transformation of the Soviet Union, 1913–1945*, eds. R.W. Davies, Mark Harrison, and S.G. Wheatcroft (Cambridge: Cambridge University Press, 1994), 68; Haynes and Hasan, *A Century*, 72–73.
35 Haynes and Hasan, *A Century*, 63–66; Wheatcroft and Davies, "Population," 77.
36 Haynes, *Russia: Class*, 121.
37 Haynes, *Russia: Class*, 126–34.
38 Paul Josephson et al., *An Environmental History of Russia* (Cambridge: Cambridge University Press, 2013), 75.
39 Josephson et al., *Environmental History*.
40 The discussion here and what follows draws on Duncan Hallas, *The Comintern* (London: Bookmarks, 1985); Fernando Claudin, *The Communist Movement: From Comintern to Cominform* (Harmondsworth: Penguin Books, 1975); Alexander Vatlin, "The Evolution of the Comintern, 1919-1943," trans. Stephen A. Smith, in *The Oxford Handbook of the History of Communism*, ed. Stephen A. Smith (Oxford: Oxford University Press, 2014), 187–94; Ian Birchall, *Workers Against the Monolith: The Communist Parties Since 1943* (London: Pluto Press, 1974); Alex de Jong, "Stalin Handed Hundreds of Communists Over to Hitler," *International Viewpoint*, September 2, 2021, <internationalviewpoint.org/spip.php?article7284>.
41 Andy Durgan, *The Spanish Civil War* (Basingstoke: Palgrave Macmillan, 2007), 66–70, 90–100. For a chilling detailed study of some of the NKVD's

murderous activities in Spain that also discusses other efforts of the state there, see Boris Volodarsky, *Stalin's Agent: The Life and Death of Alexander Orlov* (Oxford: Oxford University Press, 2015), 214–91.
42  For an account written by a British communist who was in Hungary at the time, see Peter Fryer, *Hungarian Tragedy* (n.p.: New Park, 1986), <marxists.org/archive/fryer/1956/dec/index.htm>.
43  Peter Robinson, "Portugal 1974–75: Popular Power," in *Revolutionary Rehearsals*, ed. Colin Barker (London: Bookmarks, 1987), 83–121; Phil Mailer, *Portugal: The Impossible Revolution* (London: Solidarity, 1987); Jonathan Haslam, *Russia's Cold War: From the October Revolution to the Fall of the Wall* (New Haven: Yale University Press, 2011), 279–90.
44  For theoretical discussion of the character of these revolutions, see Davidson, *How Revolutionary*, 459–65.
45  Odd Arne Westad, *The Global Cold War: Third World Interventions and the Making of Our Times* (Cambridge: Cambridge University Press, 2005), 64–65; Haslam, *Russia's Cold War*, 112–16.
46  Westad, *Global Cold War*, 253–79.
47  Sobhanlal Datta Gupta, *Comintern and the Destiny of Communism in India 1919–1943: Dialectics of Real and a Possible History* (Bakhrahat: Seribaan, 2006), 207–21.
48  Rashid Khalidi, *The Hundred Years' War on Palestine: A History of Settler Colonialism and Resistance, 1917–2017* (New York: Henry Holt and Company, 2020), 181.
49  Westad, *Global Cold War*, 127, 280–81.
50  Hanson, *Rise and Fall*, 42.
51  Jacques Sapir, *L'Économie Mobilisée* (Paris: Éditions la Découverte, 1990), 23–39.
52  Haynes, *Russia: Class*, 86.
53  Raya Dunayevskaya, *Marxism and Freedom: From 1776 Until Today* (New York: Columbia University Press, 1982), 239.
54  Haynes, *Russia: Class*, 86–87.
55  Hanson, *Rise and Fall*, 10–11.
56  Hanson, *Rise and Fall*, 27.
57  Lewin, *Soviet Century*, 358.
58  Lewin, *Soviet Century*, 359.
59  Sapir, *L'Économie Mobilisée*, 49.
60  On alienation, see James Rinehart, *The Tyranny of Work: Alienation and the Labour Process*, 5th ed. (Toronto: Thomson Nelson, 2005).
61  Donald Filtzer, "Labour Discipline, the Use of Work Time, and the Decline of the Soviet System, 1928–1991," *International Labour and Working-Class History* 50 (1996): 9.
62  Filtzer, "Labour Discipline."
63  Sanchez-Sibony, *Red Globalization*.
64  Haynes, *Russia: Class*, 104.
65  Haynes, *Russia: Class*, 194.
66  Sapir, *L'Économie Mobilisée*, 45–47.
67  John Molyneux, "Imperialism and Russia," *Irish Marxist Review* 7, no. 21 (2018), <marxists.org/history/etol/writers/molyneux/2018/07/imp-russia.htm>; Zbigniew Marcin Kowalewski, "Russian Imperialism: From the Tsar to Today, via Stalin, the Imperialist Will Marks the History of Russia," *New Politics*,

March 4, 2022, <newpol.org/russian-imperialism-from-the-tsar-to-today-via-stalin-the-imperialist-will-marks-the-history-of-russia/>; Haynes, *Russia: Class*, 101–2, 201–4.
68  Stephen Kotkin, *Magnetic Mountain: Stalinism as a Civilization* (Berkeley: University of California Press, 1995), 358.
69  Kuron and Modzelewski, *Solidarnosc*, 16.
70  Luxemburg, "What Does."
71  Lewin, *Soviet Century*, 379.

## CHAPTER 4

1  Maurice Meisner, *Mao's China and After: A History of the People's Republic*, 3rd ed. (New York: The Free Press, 1999), 7.
2  Meisner, *Mao's China*, 5–8; Mike Davis, *Late Victorian Holocausts: El Nino Famines and the Making of the Third World* (London: Verso, 2002), 341–75; Lucien Bianco, *Origins of the Chinese Revolution, 1915–1949*, trans. Muriel Bell (Stanford: Stanford University Press, 1971), 82–107.
3  Carl Riskin, *China's Political Economy: The Quest for Development Since 1949* (Oxford: Oxford University Press, 1991), 18.
4  Meisner, *Mao's China*, 6.
5  Meisner, *Mao's China*, 26.
6  Meisner, *Mao's China*, 27; Bianco, *Origins of the Chinese*, 55–60.
7  Meisner, *Mao's China*, 31–51; Bianco, *Origins of the Chinese*, 129–30, 143–66.
8  Meisner, *Mao's China*, 39.
9  Bianco, *Origins of the Chinese*, 150–51.
10  Bianco, *Origins of the Chinese*, 167–90.
11  Felix Wemheuer, *A Social History of Maoist China: Conflict and Change, 1949–1976* (Cambridge: Cambridge University Press, 2019), 20.
12  Elliott Liu, *Maoism and the Chinese Revolution: A Critical Introduction* (Oakland: PM Press, 2016), 8–43.
13  Meisner, *Mao's China*, 63.
14  Meisner, *Mao's China*, 117.
15  Bianco, *Origins of the Chinese*, 83–84.
16  Charlie Hore, *The Road to Tiananmen Square* (London: Bookmarks, 1991), 41.
17  Wemheuer, *Social History*, 55–65.
18  Riskin, *China's Political Economy*, 43–48.
19  Mark W. Frazier, *The Making of the Chinese Industrial Workplace: State, Revolution, and Labour Management* (Cambridge: Cambridge University Press, 2002), 106. See also Kim Yong-uk, "Workers in Mao's China: Labour and Capital under Chinese State Capitalism, 1949–62," in *State Capitalism and Development in East Asia Since 1945*, ed. Owen Miller (Leiden: Brill, 2023), 91–94.
20  Meisner, *Mao's China*, 108–14; Riskin, *China's Political Economy*, 54–65.
21  Meisner, *Mao's China*, 132.
22  Meisner, *Mao's China*, 134–47; Riskin, *China's Political Economy*, 85–90.
23  Meisner, *Mao's China*, 303.
24  For a good introduction to the period between the mid-1950s and the late 1970s, see Ralf Ruckus, *The Communist Road to Capitalism: How Social Unrest and Containment Have Pushed China's (R)evolution since 1949* (Oakland: PM

Press, 2021), 45–79, although my interpretation of Chinese society differs from Ruckus's in some respects.
25 Meisner, *Mao's China*, 463–64. On developments from 1978 to the end of the century, see *Mao's China*, 449–78 and for 1978 to 2020 see Ruckus, *Communist Road*, 81–163.
26 Tobias Ten Brink, *China's Capitalism: A Paradoxical Route to Economic Prosperity*, trans. Carla Welch (Philadelphia: University of Pennsylvania Press, 2019), 93.
27 Ten Brink, *China's Capitalism*, 147.
28 Au Loong Yu, *China's Rise: Strength and Fragility* (Pontypool: Merlin Press, 2012), 65–79.
29 Ten Brink, *China's Capitalism*, 169.
30 Isabella Weber and Hao Qi, "The State Constituted Market Economy: A Conceptual Framework for China's State-Market Relations," University of Amherst Political Economy Research Institute Working Paper Series 556, December 16, 2021, 2, < peri.umass.edu/?view=article&id=1547:the-state-constituted-market-economy-a-conceptual-framework-for-china-s-state-market-relations&catid=154>.
31 Weber and Qi, "The State," 6.
32 Weber and Qi, "The State," 16.
33 The phrase was likely coined, in another context, by Boris Kagarlitsky. See, for example, Boris Kagarlitsky, "Soviet Struggle: What is 'Left' and 'Right'?," *Against the Current* 27 (July–August 1990), <againstthecurrent.org/atc027/soviet-left-and-right/>.
34 Rebecca E. Karl, *China's Revolutions in the Modern World: A Brief Interpretive History* (London: Verso, 2020), 117.
35 Kim, "Workers in Mao's," 91.
36 Meisner, *Mao's China*, 415.
37 Westad, *Global Cold War*, 161.
38 Meisner, *Mao's China*, 235–36.
39 Kim, "Workers in Mao's," 136.
40 Wemheuer, *Social History*, 260–64, 71–73.
41 OECD, "Gross Domestic Product (GDP) (indicator)," accessed August 3, 2023, <data.oecd.org/gdp/gross-domestic-product-gdp.htm>.
42 Our World in Data, "Total Electricity Generation," updated December 12, 2023. <ourworldindata.org/grapher/electricity-generation?tab=table&country=~CHN>.
43 Our World in Data, "Median Income or Consumption Per Day, 1967 to 2021," updated October 3, 2022. <ourworldindata.org/grapher/daily-median-income?tab=table>.
44 OECD, "China, People's Republic of," accessed August 3, 2023, <data.oecd.org/china-people-s-republic-of.htm>.
45 Ruckus, *Communist Road*, 33.
46 Meisner, *Mao's China*, 148; Ruckus, *Communist Road*, 30, 37–38; Sally Sargeson, "The Demise of China's Peasantry as a Class," *Asia-Pacific Journal Japan Focus* 14, no. 13 (July 1, 2016), <apjjf.org/2016/13/Sargeson>.
47 Wemheuer, *Social History*, 20, 89. See also Kim, "Workers in Mao's," 96–100. On elections in the PRC, see Joshua Hill, *Voting as a Rite: A History of Elections in Modern China* (Cambridge: Harvard University Press, 2019).

48  Meisner, *Mao's China*, 117.
49  Ruckus, *Communist Road*, 32–33, 56.
50  Wemheuer, *Social History*, 73.
51  Wemheuer, *Social History*, 126–34, 270–71; Ruckus, *Communist Road*, 65–66.
52  Heather Worth et al., "'There Was No Mercy At All': Hooliganism, Homosexuality and the Opening-Up of China," *International Sociology* 34, no. 1 (2018), 38–57, <journals.sagepub.com/doi/10.1177/0268580918812265>.
53  Wemheuer, *Social History*, 38.
54  Wemheuer, *Social History*, 76–80, 152–57.
55  Wemheuer, *Social History*, 151. See also Felex Wemheuer, "Collectivization and Famine," in *The Oxford Handbook of the History of Communism*, ed. Stephen A. Smith (Oxford: Oxford University Press, 2014), 413–15.
56  Wemheuer, *Social History*, 67, 204–5. On the CR, see Ruckus, *Communist Road*, 60–71, or, for a book-length study, Yiching Wu, *The Cultural Revolution at the Margins: Chinese Socialism in Crisis* (Cambridge: Harvard University Press, 2014).
57  Wemheuer, *Social History*, 97–98. Percentage of the population incarcerated in camps calculated from the population figure for 1960 given in *Social History*, 269.
58  Robert Marks, *China: Its Environment and History* (Lanham: Roman and Littlefield Publishers, 2012), 270–71, 291; Judith Shapiro, *Mao's War Against Nature: Politics and the Environment in Revolutionary China* (Cambridge: Cambridge University Press, 2001), 13, 154–55.
59  Au Loong-Yu, "Depoliticizing the Debate on the Orwellian State," *Spectre* 6 (2022), 79, 84–85.
60  Sargeson, "Demise of China's."
61  Ruckus, *Communist Road*, 151, 152. The asterisks in the quotation are Ruckus's, used to refer "to the constructed character of gender," with "women*" used for "all who are described as women and all (trans*, inter*, or queer*) who intentionally choose a femme-like gender expression" (*Communist Road*, ix).
62  Eli Friedman, Kevin Lin, Rosa Liu, and Ashley Smith, *China in Global Capitalism: Building International Solidarity Against Imperial Rivalry* (Chicago: Haymarket Books, 2024), 66–67.
63  Ruckus, *Communist Road*, 152.
64  Worth et al., "'No Mercy.'"
65  Jiang Yaling, "China's 'Anti-Sissy' Campaign Unleashes a Wave of Online Transphobia," *Sixth Tone*, February 4, 2022, <sixthtone.com/news/1009746>.
66  Yueran Zhang, "What's Really Behind China's 'Common Prosperity' Program?," *New Labor Forum* 31, no. 2: 65.
67  Ruckus, *Communist Road*, 156, 176n. For a detailed study, see Darren Byler, *Terror Capitalism: Uyghur Dispossession and Masculinity in a Chinese City* (Durham: Duke University Press, 2022).
68  Ruckus, *Communist Road*, 176.
69  Ruckus, *Communist Road*, 176.
70  Zhang, "What's Really," 68.
71  Richard Smith, *China's Engine of Environmental Collapse* (London: Pluto Press, 2020), 49.
72  Simon Pirani, "China and the 'Left': What Planet Are These People On?," *People and Nature*, January 15, 2021, <peopleandnature.wordpress.com/2021/01/15/china-and-the-left-what-planet-are-these-people-on/>.

73  Climate Analytics, "China." Climate Action Tracker, updated June 6, 2023, <climateactiontracker.org/countries/china/>.
74  Nigel Harris, *The Mandate of Heaven: Marx and Mao in Modern China* (London: Quartet Books, 1978), 215.
75  Julia Lovell, *Maoism: A Global History* (New York: Alfred A. Knoph, 2019), 105.
76  Lovell, *Maoism*, 104–6.
77  Harris, *Mandate of Heaven*, 221.
78  Meisner, *Mao's China*, 388. The CPSU's outlook, though expressed differently, also defined the interests of revolutionaries globally as the same as those of the USSR and the "socialist bloc" it led.
79  Meisner, *Mao's China*, 379.
80  Harris, *Mandate of Heaven*, 232–33; Steven F. Jackson, "China's Third World Foreign Policy: The Case of Angola and Mozambique, 1961–93," *The China Quarterly* 142 (1995): 409.
81  Stuart Harris, *China's Foreign Policy* (Cambridge: Polity Press, 2014).
82  "Joint Statement between the People's Republic of China and Hungary on the Establishment of an All-Weather Comprehensive Strategic Partnership for the New Era," Ministry of Foreign Affairs of the People's Republic of China, May 9, 2024, <mfa.gov.cn/eng/zy/gb/202405/t20240531_11367513.html>.
83  Meisner, *Mao's China*, 120.
84  Riskin, *China's Political Economy*, 55.
85  Riskin, *China's Political Economy*, 119, 120.
86  The phrase is from Ten Brink, *China's Capitalism*, 69. On state direction of production under Mao, see Riskin, *China's Political Economy*, 161, 144–45, 202–4, 219, and Ten Brink, *China's Capitalism*, 69–72.
87  Michael Ellman, *Socialist Planning*, 3rd ed. (Cambridge: Cambridge University Press, 2014), 145.
88  Ten Brink, *China's Capitalism*, 81–142.
89  Ruckus, *Communist Road*, 74; Jackie Sheehan, *Chinese Workers: A New History* (London: Routledge, 1998), 87–88, 94–97, 140–41, 162–63; Andrew G. Walder, *Communist Neo-Traditionalism: Work and Authority in Chinese Industry* (Berkeley: University of California Press, 1986), 205–19.
90  Ruckus, *Communist Road*, 95–96, 113–14, 118–23.
91  Wu, *Cultural Revolution*, 23.
92  Yang Xiguang, "Whither China," quoted in Wu, *Cultural Revolution*, 182. On the Shengwulian current to which Yang belonged, see Wu, *Cultural Revolution*, 146–89. The "rusticated youth" were students ordered by the party-state during the CR to move to rural areas after graduation.
93  Meisner, *Mao's China*, 422.

# CHAPTER 5

1  Ada Ferrer, *Cuba: An American History* (New York: Scribner, 2021), 144–66, 91–94.
2  Ferrer, *Cuba*, 179.
3  Samuel Farber, *The Origins of the Cuban Revolution Reconsidered* (Chapel Hill: University of North Carolina Press, 2006), 9.
4  Ferrer, *Cuba*, 186–87, 191.

5   Farber, *Origins of the Cuban*, 8, 17–18.
6   Farber, *Origins of the Cuban*, 19.
7   Ferrer, *Cuba*, 225–26, 229.
8   Ferrer, *Cuba*, 230–43; Samuel Farber, *Revolution and Reform in Cuba, 1933–1960: A Political Sociology from Machado to Castro* (Middletown: Wesleyan University Press, 1976), 39.
9   Ferrer, *Cuba: An American*, 243.
10  Ibid, 244–47.
11  Ibid, 249–71; Farber, *Origins of the Cuban*, 22–26; Samuel Farber, "Cuba Before the Revolution," *Jacobin*, September 6, 2015, <jacobin.com/2015/09/cuban-revolution-fidel-castro-casinos-batista>.
12  Samuel Farber, *Cuba Since the Revolution of 1959: A Critical Assessment* (Chicago: Haymarket Books, 2011), 132.
13  Farber, *Origins of the Cuban*, 127–28, 38.
14  Farber, *Origins of the Cuban*, 117–19; Samuel Farber, *The Politics of Che Guevara: Theory and Practice* (Chicago: Haymarket Books, 2016), 27–34; Ferrer, *Cuba*, 299–311.
15  Farber, *Origins of the Cuban*, 219.
16  Farber, *Revolution and Reform*, 39.
17  Farber, *Revolution and Reform*, 116.
18  Ferrer, *Cuba*, 320.
19  Ferrer, *Cuba*, 324, 329–30; Farber, *Origins of the Cuban*, 121.
20  Ferrer, *Cuba*, 346–48.
21  Ferrer, *Cuba*, 349–67; Farber, *Origins of the Cuban*, 132-136; Farber, *Cuba Since*, 13–17.
22  Farber, *Origins of the Cuban*, 63.
23  Farber, *Origins of the Cuban*, 170.
24  Farber, *Origins of the Cuban*, 67–68.
25  Carmelo Mesa-Lago, *The Economy of Socialist Cuba: A Two-Decade Appraisal* (Albuquerque: University of New Mexico Press, 1981), 14–32; Farber, *Cuba Since*, 17–18.
26  Mesa-Lago, *Economy of Socialist*, 183–87.
27  Mesa-Lago, *Economy of Socialist*, 57–65.
28  Farber, *Cuba Since*, 73–81.
29  Farber, *Cuba Since*, 192.
30  Francisco J. Gonzalez, "'No Es Facil': Reflections on Cuba's New Family Code," *Parapraxis*, accessed June 5, 2024, <parapraxismagazine.com/articles/no-es-facil>.
31  Alejandro de la Fuente, *A Nation for All: Race, Inequality and Politics in Twentieth-Century Cuba* (Chapel Hill: University of North Carolina Press, 2001), 276.
32  Farber, *Cuba Since*, 52–56, 134–54; Samuel Farber, "Cuba's New Economic Turn," *New Politics*, October 18, 2020, <newpol.org/cubas-new-economic-turn/>.
33  Farber, *Cuba Since*, 192–21; Carla Colome Santiago, "'They Are Killing Us': Murders of Women in Cuba are Growing at an Alarming Rate," *Miami Herald*, September 17, 2023, <miamiherald.com/news/nation-world/world/americas/cuba/article278567939.html>.
34  Farber, *Cuba Since*, 168–83.

35  Armando Chaguaceda and Lennier Lopez, "Cuban Civil Society: Its Present Panorama," *New Politics* 16, no. 4 (2018), <newpol.org/issue_post/cuban-civil-society/>.
36  Raymar Aguado Hernandez, "The Cuban Left, More Critical and Decolonized," *New Politics* 19, no. 3 (2023), <newpol.org/issue_post/the-cuban-left-more-critical-and-decolonized/>.
37  Farber, *Cuba Since*, 105.
38  Farber, *Cuba Since*, 109.
39  Westad, *Global Cold War*, 213–14; Farber, *Cuba Since*, 109–11.
40  Westad, *Global Cold War*, 214; Farber, *Cuba Since*, 111–13.
41  Piero Gleijeses, *Conflicting Missions: Havana, Washington, and Africa, 1959-1976* (Chapel Hill: University of North Carolina Press, 2002), 300–46, 380.
42  Farber, *Cuba Since*, 114–16.
43  Farber, *Cuba Since*, 122, 118–19, 117; Leo Zeilig, *A Revolutionary for Our Time: The Walter Rodney Story* (Chicago: Haymarket Books, 2022), 325.
44  Evan Dyer, "Cornered in Ukraine and Isolated by the West, the Kremlin Returns to Cuba," CBC News, June 3, 2023, <cbc.ca/news/politics/russia-cuba-ukraine-putin-missiles-1.6863359>.
45  Farber, *Cuba Since*, 123.
46  John Lister, *Cuba: Radical Face of Stalinism* (n.p.: Left View Books, 1985), <marxists.org/history/etol/document/wsl/lister/cuba-lister85-ch5.htm>.
47  Mesa-Lago, *Economy of Socialist*, 15.
48  Carmelo Mesa-Lago, "Cuba's Centrally Planned Economy: An Equity Trade-Off for Growth," in *Latin American Political Economy: Financial Crisis and Political Change*, eds. Jonathan Hartlyn and Samuel A. Morley (New York: Routledge, 2019), 298.
49  Farber, *Cuba Since*, 53.
50  Farber, *Cuba Since*, 299; Mesa-Lago, *Economy of Socialist*, 51.
51  Samuel Farber, "The Future of Cuba — Part One," *New Politics*, February 13, 2023, <newpol.org/the-future-of-cuba-part-one/>.
52  Farber, *Cuba Since*, 55.
53  Alexander Hall Lujardo, "The Historical Burden of Actually Existing Socialism," *New Politics* 19, no. 3 (2023), <newpol.org/issue_post/the-historical-burden-of-actually-existing-socialism/>.
54  Lujardo, "The Historical Burden," 154.
55  Lisbeth Moya Gonzalez, "Cuba and the World," *New Politics* 19, no. 3 (2023), <newpol.org/issue_post/cuba-and-the-world/>.

# CHAPTER 6

1  Luxemburg, "What Does."
2  For example, Poland, analyzed in Kuron and Modzelewski, *Solidarnosc*; East Germany — on which, see Gareth Dale, *Between State Capitalism and Globalization: The Collapse of the East German Economy* (Bern: Peter Lang, 2004); Yugoslavia — on which, see Vladimir Unkovski-Korica, *The Economic Struggle for Power in Tito's Yugoslavia: From World War II to Non-Alignment* (London: I.B. Tauris, 2016); and Vietnam and Cambodia — on which, see Jonathan Neale, *The American War: Vietnam 1960–1975* (London: Bookmarks, 2001), 147–74.

3   Cornelius Castoriadis, "On the Content of Socialism," in *Political and Social Writings, vol. I, 1946–1955: From the Critique of Bureaucracy to the Positive Content of Socialism*, ed. David Ames Curtis (Minneapolis: University of Minnesota Press, 1988), 297.
4   Anton Ciliga, *The Russian Enigma* (Westport: Hyperion Press, 1973), 126. The fact that after Ciliga managed to leave the USSR (before the Great Purge, in which he would have almost certainly been executed along with other imprisoned communist oppositionists) he later became an anti-communist nationalist does not make his observation here or his account of his experiences in the USSR any less significant.
5   As noted in note 77 to Chapter 2, from 1919 on, there were communists inside and outside the CPSU who pushed to restore the extraordinary democracy that had existed in the first year of the Russian Revolution and who opposed the CPSU leadership on various policy issues.
6   See Gabriel Miasnikov, "The Latest Deception" (1930), <marxists.org/archive/miasnikov/1930/latest-deception/>. For a description of the ideas of various currents of marxist oppositionists in the USSR in the first half of the 1930s, see Ciliga, *Russian Enigma*, 209–37.
7   Carlos L. Garrido, "Book Launch Presentation: The Purity Fetish and the Crisis of Western Marxism," *Midwestern Marx*, June 13, 2023, <midwesternmarx.com/articles/book-launch-presentation-the-purity-fetish-and-the-crisis-of-western-marxism-by-carlos-l-garrido>. In vintage 1930s Stalinist style, Garrido hurls accusations at the amalgam of "Western Marxists" he constructs, including that they "endorse, directly or indirectly, capitalist-imperialism," see "bourgeois liberal democracy" as "the best of all possible worlds," are "tambourines enhancing the tune of mainstream media's war drums," and that their ideas are "an indispensable component of bourgeois hegemony."
8   Midwestern Marx (@MidwesternMarx), X, June 29, 2021, 8:34AM, <x.com/MidwesternMarx/status/1409867925427822605>.
9   For example, see *Fundamentals of Marxism-Leninism*, 2nd rev. ed. (Moscow: Foreign Languages Publishing House, 1963), 492–93, <marxists.org/reference/archive/stalin/works/fundamentals-marxism-leninism.pdf>.
10  Draper, "Two Souls," 9, 8.
11  Quoted in "Two Souls," 9.
12  Parenti, *Blackshirts and Reds*, 56.
13  Claudin, *Communist Movement*, 164.
14  I have encountered this charge in posts by supporters of AES on social industry platforms.
15  I discuss race in my "Elements of a Historical-Materialist Theory of Racism," *Historical Materialism* 24, no. 1 (2016), 31–70.
16  James Gilbert Ryan, *Earl Browder: The Failure of American Communism* (Tuscaloosa: University of Alabama Press, 1997), 246–61, EBSCOhost. In 1944, Browder had reconstituted the party as the Communist Political Association on the basis of projecting a continuation after the end of World War II of the alliance between the USSR, the US, and the other states then fighting the Axis powers.
17  Earl Browder, C. Wright Mills, and Max Shachtman, "Is Russia a Socialist Community? The Verbatim Text of a Debate," *New International* 16, no. 3 (May–June 1950): 145–76, <marxists.org/archive/shachtma/1950/03/russia.htm>.

18  See Michael Karadjis, "Is China Socialist Because It Reduced Poverty?," *New Politics* 19, no. 1 (2022), <newpol.org/issue_post/is-china-socialist-because-it-reduced-poverty/>.
19  Browder, Mills, and Shachtman, "Is Russia." At the time, Shachtman had started to shift rightward, away from revolutionary socialist opposition to both Western capitalism and the USSR, but had not yet sided with the former against AES; his regrettable drift is irrelevant to this particular issue. See Peter Drucker, *Max Shachtman and His Left: A Socialist's Odyssey Through the "American Century"* (Atlantic Highlands: Humanities Press International, 1994).
20  Albert Szymanski, *Is the Red Flag Flying? The Political Economy of the Soviet Union Today* (London: Zed Press, 1979), 221, 201.
21  Szymanski, *Is the Red Flag Flying?*, 199.
22  Szymanski, *Is the Red Flag Flying?*, 199.
23  Fitzpatrick, *Shortest History*, 155, 175–77.
24  Kuron and Modzelewski, *Solidarnosc*, 24.
25  See Leon Trotsky, *The Revolution Betrayed: What is the Soviet Union and Where Is It Going?* (New York: Pathfinder, 1970); Isaac Deutscher, *Stalin: A Political Biography* (New York: Oxford University Press, 1967), 621–29; Ernest Mandel, *Power and Money: A Marxist Theory of Bureaucracy* (London: Verso, 1992).
26  Friedrich Engels, *Anti-Duhring*, trans. modified by Hal Draper, quoted in Hal Draper, *Karl Marx's Theory of Revolution, vol. 4, Critique of Other Socialisms* (New York: Monthly Review Press, 1990), 88.
27  James Connolly, "The New Evangel," *Workers' Republic*, June 10, 1899, <marxists.org/archive/connolly/1901/evangel/stmonsoc.htm>.
28  Karl Marx, *The Poverty of Philosophy* (Moscow: Progress Publishers, 1955), 134.
29  Trotsky, *Revolution Betrayed*, 8.
30  For a detailed assessment of Trotsky's analysis of the USSR, see John Molyneux, *Leon Trotsky's*, 115–34. On Deutscher's adaptation of Trotsky's analysis, which has a lot in common with how many anti-anti-communists today understand AES, see Julius Jacobson, "Isaac Deutscher: The Anatomy of an Apologist," November 1965, <marxists.org/history/etol/writers/jacobson/1965/10/deutscher.htm>.
31  I take the formulation about "good things" from Farber, *Cuba Since*, 272.
32  Hal Draper, *Karl Marx's Theory of Revolution, vol. 1, State and Bureaucracy* (New York: Monthly Review Press, 1977), 436.
33  Gareth Dale and Vladimir Unkovski-Korica, "Varieties of Capitalism or Variegated State Capitalism? East Germany and Yugoslavia in Comparative Perspective," *Business History* (November 14, 2022): 12, <tandfonline.com/doi/full/10.1080/00076791.2022.2134348>.
34  Exceptions include small numbers of self-employed people, including small farmers in Cuba (Mesa-Lago, *Economy of Socialist*, 112, 130–31).
35  Even when in the PRC the state provided the most extensive support for the social reproduction of those workers who had permanent positions in state enterprises, including food in canteens, housing, and medical care provided through workers' work units, workers were still dependent on wage-labour to survive because their access to those goods and services was tied to their status as employees. The party-state did not provide this level of support to all urban wage-workers, let alone all citizens.

36  Alan S. Milward, *War, Economy and Society 1939–1945* (Berkeley: University of California Press, 1980) is a dated but still useful introduction.
37  AES in Yugoslavia was different in that it involved a constrained form of workers' self-management within enterprises, significant market regulation of production, and deeper integration into global capitalism (see Unkovski-Korica, *The Economic*).
38  Vladimir Kontorovich and Alexander Wein, "What Did the Soviet Rulers Maximize?," *Europe-Asia Studies*, 61, no. 9 (2009): 1594, <tandfonline.com/doi/full/10.1080/09668130903209145>.
39  Kim, "Workers in Mao's," 141.
40  Kim, "Workers in Mao's," 142–43. On 143, Kim quotes Marx: "Accumulation for accumulation's sake, production for production's sake."
41  Dale and Unkovski-Korica, "Varieties of Capitalism": 7.
42  Colin Barker, "States in Capitalism: Reflections on Value, Force, Many States and Other Problems," *rs21*, May 10, 2019, <rs21.org.uk/wp-content/uploads/2019/06/Value_Force-Colin_Barker.pdf>.
43  Aufheben, "What Was the USSR? Part IV: Towards a Theory of the Deformation of Value," *libcom.org*, April 9, 2005, <libcom.org/article/what-was-ussr-part-iv-towards-theory-deformation-value>.
44  Even in the PRC after the GLF and before the turn to market Stalinism, probably the AES society where labour market discipline was weakest, it was possible, though rare, for workers in permanent positions in state enterprises to be dismissed for unsatisfactory work performance. Firings for political reasons or because of criminal conviction and a prison sentence were less uncommon. See Andrew G. Waldner, *Communist Neo-Traditionalism: Work and Authority in Chinese Industry* (Berkeley: University of California Press, 1986), 69–73.
45  It is important to know that the term *state capitalism* has also been used in senses that are different than my use here. A truly adequate account of AES societies as a particular kind of capitalism remains to be written, but see Aufheben, "What Was the USSR?"; Owen Miller and Gareth Dale, "The Emergence and Development of Capitalism in East Asia: The State Capitalist Approach," in *State Capitalism and Development in East Asia Since 1945*, ed. Owen Miller (Leiden: Brill, 2023), 1–43; Dale and Unkovski-Korica, "Varieties of Capitalism." There has long been debate among marxists about the character of AES. For a lengthy review, see Marcel van der Linden, *Western Marxism and the Soviet Union*, trans. Jurriaan Bendien (Chicago: Haymarket Books, 2009), but for a short, insightful analysis from a perspective similar to mine, see Martin Thomas, "Three Traditions? Marxism and the USSR," *Historical Materialism*, 14, no. 3 (2006): 207–43. In my view, recognition that AES involves class exploitation, is not in transition to communism, and is neither qualitatively superior to nor worse than capitalism matters more than understanding it as capitalist.
46  For the latter, see, for example, Fitzpatrick, *Shortest History*.
47  The term *Stalinism* can also be used to refer to the ML ideology developed in AES societies, with variations including Maoism and Castroism, as discussed in the next chapter.
48  Fryer, *Hungarian Tragedy*.
49  Bini Adamczak, *Yesterday's Tomorrow: On the Loneliness of Communist Specters and the Reconstruction of the Future*, trans. Adrian Nathan West (Cambridge: MIT Press, 2021), 107.

# CHAPTER 7

1. On the Derg's killing of tens of thousands of people in the 1970s, see Jacob Wiebel, "The Ethiopian Red Terror," in *Oxford Research Encyclopedia of African History*, ed. Thomas Spear (Oxford: Oxford University Press, 2017), <doi.org/10.1093/acrefore/9780190277734.013.188>.
2. Vladimir Tikhonov, "'The Soviet Problem' in Post-Soviet Russian Marxism, or the Afterlife of the USSR," *Historical Materialism*, 29, no. 4 (2021): 180.
3. Draper, "Two Souls," 19.
4. Morris and Belfort Bax, "Manifesto of the Socialist," 740.
5. Draper, *"Dictatorship of the Proletariat,"* 129.
6. Ellen Meiksins Wood, *Democracy Against Capitalism: Renewing Historical Materialism* (Cambridge: Cambridge University Press, 1995), 234.
7. "Marxism" took shape in the 1880s, drawing on some of Marx's ideas, with Friedrich Engels and Karl Kautsky playing key roles. An adequate study of this remains to be written, but for a taste, see Georges Haupt, "Marx and Marxism," in *The History of Marxism, vol. 1, Marxism in Marx's Day*, ed. Eric J. Hobsbawm (Bloomington: Indiana University Press, 1982), 265–89.
8. Daniel Bensaïd, *Marx for Our Times: Adventures and Misadventures of a Critique*, trans. Gregory Elliott (London: Verso, 2002), 2, 3, 4. On Marx's thought, the best introduction is still Alex Callinicos, *The Revolutionary Ideas of Karl Marx* (London: Bookmarks, 1983), although this is tinged with a certain orthodoxy. On Marx's theory of capitalist society, see Simon Clarke, *Marx, Marginalism and Modern Sociology: From Adam Smith to Max Weber*, 2nd ed. (Basingstoke: Macmillan, 1991), 49–143, which captures how Marx's theory differs radically from the thinkers who influenced it and from most versions of marxism. On Marx's politics, see Hal Draper, *Karl Marx's Theory of Revolution*, 5 vols. (New York: Monthly Review Press, 1977–1990). Other important studies include Hudis, *Marx's Concept*; Kohei Saito, *Marx's Ecosocialism: Capital, Nature, and the Unfinished Critique of Political Economy* (New York: Monthly Review Press, 2017); Kevin B. Anderson, *Marx at the Margins: On Nationalism, Ethnicity, and Non-Western Societies*, expanded ed. (Chicago: University of Chicago Press, 2016); Bensaïd, *Marx for Our Times*.
9. On the marxism of the Second International, see Lucio Colletti, "Bernstein and the Marxism of the Second International," in *From Rousseau to Lenin: Studies in Ideology and Society*, trans. John Merrington and Judith White (New York: Monthly Review Press, 1974), 45–108. On Lenin's thought, see Neil Harding, *Lenin's Political Thought: Theory and Practice in the Democratic and Socialist Revolutions* (Humanities Press: Atlantic Highlands, 1983); Anders Molander, "Monopoly and Socialism in Lenin's Analysis of Imperialism," trans. anon., 1977, accessed October 3, 2023, <scribd.com/document/370042555/Monopoly-and-Socialism-in-Lenin-s-Analysis-of-Imperialism>.
10. Farber, *Before Stalinism*, 195–205.
11. Georges Labica, *Le Marxisme-Leninisme (Eléments Pour Une Critique)* (Paris: Bruno Huisman, 1984), 28, <marxists.org/francais/labica/works/1984/LE-MARXISME-LENINISME.pdf>. My translation here.
12. Nigel Harris, *Beliefs in Society: The Problem of Ideology* (London: C.A. Watts and Co., 1968), 172.
13. Herbert Marcuse, *Soviet Marxism: A Critical Analysis* (New York: Columbia University Press, 1958), 149–50.

14  Marcuse, *Soviet Marxism*, 101–2, 179–81.
15  Liu, *Maoism and the Chinese*, 3.
16  Farber, *Politics of Che Guevara*.
17  Two of the producers profiled here, Hakim and Midwestern Marx, are ML: see Armand D. Jackson, Ivonne Ortiz, and Xuandi Wang, "Meet the Left YouTubers Blowing Up the Alt-Right Pipeline," *In These Times*, August 21, 2023, <inthesetimes.com/article/breadtube-lefttube-youtube-olayemi-olurin-contra points-fabsocialism-hakim-midwestern-marx-natalie-wynn-altright-pipeline>.
18  For example, Kai Heron and Jodi Dean, "Climate Leninism and Revolutionary Transition: Organization and Anti-Imperialism in Catastrophic Times," *Spectre*, June 26, 2022, <spectrejournal.com/climate-leninism-and-revolutionary-transition/>. "Climate Leninism" is not a coherent body of thought since ecosocialists who use this term do not have a common understanding of what Leninism means. For an excellent discussion of Leninism, see Charlie Post, "Leninism?," *rs21*, March 8, 2015, <rs21.org.uk/2015/03/08/leninism-2/>.
19  Sidney Hook, *Towards the Understanding of Karl Marx: A Revolutionary Interpretation* (Amherst: Prometheus Books, 2002), 218.
20  For an introductory discussion of these issues, see my *We Can Do*, 45–54. For deeper exploration, see Alex Callinicos, *Making History: Agency, Structure and Change in Social Theory* (Cambridge: Polity Press, 1987).
21  The Paris Commune was an important influence on Marx's thinking about this. See Paul Thomas, *Karl Marx and the Anarchists* (London: Routledge and Kegan Paul, 1980), 56–122; Derek Sayer and Philip Corrigan, "Late Marx: Continuity, Contradiction and Learning," in *Late Marx and the Russian Road: Marx and the "Peripheries of Capitalism,"* ed. Teodor Shanin (New York: Monthly Review Press, 1983), 82–89.
22  Draper, "Two Souls" (although this does not do justice to the best elements of the anarchist-communist tradition). Lenin and Trotsky were less consistent in this than the others mentioned. The debate here between most of the communists mentioned and Marxism-Leninism is not about whether political organizations of revolutionaries are needed, but about what they should be like and what their relationship to the struggles of the exploited and oppressed should be (though some anarcho-communists reject them altogether).
23  Claudin, *Communist Movement*, 307–644; Birchall, *Workers Against*; Ernest Mandel, *From Stalinism to Eurocommunism: The Bitter Fruits of "Socialism in One Country,"* trans. Jon Rothschild (London: New Left Books, 1978), 188–90.
24  For a discussion of Eurocommunism from a sympathetic perspective, see Geoff Eley, *Forging Democracy: The History of the Left in Europe, 1850–2000* (Oxford: Oxford University Press, 2002), 408–16. For a detailed critical engagement, see Mandel, *From Stalinism*.
25  Communist Party of Canada, "Chapter 6: For a People's Government," accessed October 4, 2023, <communist-party.ca/chapter-6-for-a-peoples-government/>.
26  Praful Bidwai, *The Phoenix Moment: Challenges Confronting the Indian Left* (Noida: HarperCollins Publishers India, 2015), 204.
27  Bidwai, *The Phoenix Moment*, 209–11.
28  Bidwai, *The Phoenix Moment*, 213–14.
29  Bidwai, *The Phoenix Moment*, 260.
30  Bidwai, *The Phoenix Moment*, 161.

31 William Shoki, "Where Will Neoliberalism End," *Africa is a Country*, January 1, 2020, <africasacountry.com/2020/01/where-will-neoliberalism-end>.
32 David P. Thomas, "The South African Communist Party (SACP) in the Post-Apartheid Period," *Review of African Political Economy* 34, no. 111 (2007): 135. <jstor.org/stable/20406366>.
33 Benjamin Fogel, "South Africa Could Use a Communist Party," *Mail and Guardian*, January 27, 2020, <mg.co.za/thoughtleader/analysis/2020-01-27-south-africa-could-use-a-communist-party/>.
34 Tom Lodge, *Red Road to Freedom: A History of the South African Communist Party 1921–2021* (Woodbridge: James Currey, 2022), 465.
35 Fogel, "South Africa."
36 Lodge, *Red Road*, 479–80.
37 Mike Gonzalez, "Chile 1972–73: The Workers United," in *Revolutionary Rehearsals*, ed. Colin Barker (London: Bookmarks, 1987), 46.
38 Gonzalez, "Chile 1972–73," 49, 51, 53, 63, 75–77, 79.
39 Peter Winn, *Weavers of Revolution: The Yarur Workers and Chile's Road to Socialism* (Oxford: Oxford University Press, 1986), 241).
40 On ML reformism, see Claudin, *Communist Movement*, 622–24; Mandel, *From Stalinism*, 188–208.
41 Mandel, *From Stalinism*, 194.
42 For the case supporting this claim, see Charlie Post, "The Capitalist State and Socialist Strategy," *Rampant*, April 2, 2020, <rampantmag.com/2020/04/the-capitalist-state-and-socialist-strategy/>.
43 Rosa Luxemburg, *Reform or Revolution* (London: Bookmarks, 1989), 75.
44 Ian Birchall, "France 1968: 'All Power to the Imagination,'" in *Revolutionary Rehearsals*, ed. Colin Barker (London: Bookmarks, 1987), 31.
45 Daniel Singer, *Prelude to Revolution: France in May 1968*, 2nd ed. (Cambridge: South End Press, 2002), 276.
46 Communist Party of Canada, "Chapter 5: The Working Class and People's Struggle," accessed October 5, 2023, <communist-party.ca/chapter-5-the-working-class-and-peoples-struggle/>.
47 CrazyColin16, "'Communism is Americanism of the 20th Century' Card Issued by the American Comminist [sic] Party During the 1936 Campaign," r/Propaganda Posters, Reddit, posted March 15, 2021, <reddit.com/r/PropagandaPosters/comments/m5kle7/communism_is_americanism_of_the_20th_century_card/>.
48 See image included in David Camfield, "The History and Politics of the Communist Party of Canada: An Overview," *Briarpatch*, July 29, 2020, <briarpatchmagazine.com/articles/view/the-history-and-politics-communist-party-of-canada>.
49 Claudin, *Communist Movement*, 241.
50 Birchall, *Workers Against*, 163–66; Bevins, *Jakarta Method*.
51 Vijay Prashad, *The Darker Nations: A People's History of the Third World* (New York: The New Press, 2007), 160–61; Abdelwahab Himmat, "A History of the Sudanese Communist Party" (unpublished doctoral dissertation, University of South Wales, 2019), 107–8, <pure.southwales.ac.uk/ws/portalfiles/portal/5206971/Himmat_last_Version_7march.pdf>.
52 David Camfield, "Class Politics for Times of Deepening Global Crises," *Midnight Sun*, February 10, 2024, <midnightsunmag.ca/class-politics-for-times-of-deepening-global-crisis/>.

53 On alliances, see Mandel, *From Stalinism*, 210–14.
54 David Camfield, "The Rationality and Limitations of Labour Union Bureaucracy," in *The Handbook of the Past, Present and Future of Labour Unions*, ed. Gregor Gall (Newcastle upon Tyne: Agenda Publishing, 2024), 295–314.
55 John McIlroy, "Notes on the Communist Party and Industrial Politics," in *British Trade Unions and Industrial Politics, vol. 2, The High Tide of Trade Unionism*, eds. John McIlroy, Nina Fishman, and Alan Campbell (Aldershot: Ashgate, 1999), 219.
56 Stephen Sherlock, *The Indian Railways Strike of 1974: A Study of Power and Organized Labour* (New Delhi: Rupa & Co, 2001), 437.
57 Sherlock, *The Indian Railways Strike*, 425–29.
58 Bryan D. Palmer, *Solidarity: The Rise and Fall of an Opposition in British Columbia* (Vancouver: New Star Books, 1987), 36.
59 Mick Armstrong, "The NSW BLF: The Battle to Tame the Concrete Jungle," *Marxist Left Review* 20 (2020), <marxistleftreview.org/articles/the-nsw-blf-the-battle-to-tame-the-concrete-jungle/>.
60 Tom O'Lincoln, *Into the Mainstream: The Decline of Australian Communism* (n.p.: Stained Wattle Press, 1985), <marxists.org/subject/stalinism/into-mainstream/ch07.htm>.
61 Armstrong, "The NSW BLF."
62 See Birchall, *Workers Against*.
63 Stathis Kouvelakis, "Syriza's Electoral Quagmire Reflects Its Crushing of Greeks' Hopes," *Jacobin*, June 9, 2023, <jacobin.com/2023/06/greece-general-election-syriza-new-democracy>.
64 Jairus Banaji, "The Ironies of Indian Maoism," *International Socialism* 128 (2010), <isj.org.uk/the-ironies-of-indian-maoism/>.
65 Alex de Jong, "The Philippine Left in a Changing Land," *New Politics* 17, no. 2 (2019), <newpol.org/issue_post/the-philippine-left-in-a-changing-land/>.
66 Francesco Saverio Leopardi, "The Left Has Played a Key Role in the Palestinian Struggle," *Jacobin*, July 2, 2024, <jacobin.com/2024/07/palestine-left-pflp-habash-fatah-plo-hamas>; Mostafa Omar, "The National Liberation Struggle: A Socialist Analysis," in *Palestine: A Socialist Introduction*, eds. Sumaya Awad and brian bean (Chicago: Haymarket Books, 2020), 63–66.
67 In the US, the highest-profile such group is the Party of Socialism and Liberation.
68 Claudin, *Communist Movement*, 301.
69 Claudin, *Communist Movement*, 390.
70 ML supporters of the China-led camp and the Russian invasion of Ukraine are criticized by the KKE. See "On the Termination of the Activity of the European Communist Initiative," Communist Party of Greece, September 11, 2023, <inter.kke.gr/en/articles/ON-THE-TERMINATION-OF-THE-ACTIVITY-OF-THE-EUROPEAN-COMMUNIST-INITIATIVE/>. For an example of views about Ukraine that overlap in some ways with those offered by the Russian state, see "On the Current Stage of the War in Ukraine and the Path to Peace," Communist Party of Canada, February 24, 2023, <communist-party.ca/on-the-current-stage-of-the-war-in-ukraine-and-the-path-to-peace/>.
71 Gilbert Achcar, "The Left and Ukraine: Two Pitfalls to Avoid," *Labour Hub*, June 28, 2023, <labourhub.org.uk/2023/06/28/the-left-and-ukraine-two-pitfalls-to-avoid/>.

72  Todd Gordon and Jeffery R. Webber, "Complex Stratification in the World System: Capitalist Totality and Geopolitical Fragmentation," *Science and Society* 84, no. 1 (2020): 117, <guilfordjournals.com/doi/10.1521/siso.2020.84.1.95>.
73  Friedman, Lin, Liu, and Smith, *China in Global Capitalism*.
74  John Clarke, "When My Enemy's Enemy is Not My Friend: Campism in Dangerous Times," *Spectre* 5 (Spring 2022): 46–61; Ashley Smith, "Imperialism and Anti-Imperialism Today," *Tempest*, May 24, 2024, <tempestmag.org/2024/05/imperialism-and-anti-imperialism-today/>.
75  Typical is the description of Ukraine as "a fascistic regime" and "a den of neo-Nazis and fascists who occupy key positions in the highest spheres of public administration and the state" in "Act Now to Stop the US-NATO War Drive to War With Russia!" Communist Party of Canada, January 24, 2022, <communist-party.ca/act-now-to-stop-the-us-nato-drive-to-war-with-russia/>. For analysis of fascism in Ukraine by a Ukrainian socialist, see Taras Bilous, "The Far Right in Ukraine," *New Politics*, February 8, 2023, <newpol.org/the-far-right-in-ukraine/>.
76  On ideas about China among pro-China leftists, see Brian Hioe, "Manichaeism with Chinese Characteristics: A Look Back on the 'China and the Left' Conference," *New Bloom*, September 30, 2021, <newbloommag.net/2021/09/30/china-and-the-left-conference/>. On the oppression of the Uyghurs, see Byler, *Terror Capitalism*.
77  I interviewed Dalton, who was a CPC member from 1975 to 1991 and who was fired in 1996, in 2003.
78  Liu, *Maoism and the Chinese*; Farber, *Politics of Che Guevara*. On Stalin, see Erik van Ree, *The Political Thought of Joseph Stalin: A Study in Twentieth Century Revolutionary Patriotism* (London: Routledge, 2002), although the author's perspective is very different from mine.
79  For example, on the CPUSA in unions, see Kim Moody, *An Injury to One is An Injury to All: The Decline of American Unionism* (London: Verso, 1988), 49–50, and, for Canada, see Benjamin Isitt, *Militant Minority: British Columbia Workers and the Birth of a New Left, 1948–1972* (Toronto: University of Toronto Press, 2011), 53.
80  See Ngo Van, *Viêt-nam 1920–1945: Révolution et Contre-Révolution Sous La Domination Coloniale* (Paris: Nautilus, 2000) and the memoir by Ngo Van, *In the Crossfire: Adventures of a Vietnamese Revolutionary*, trans. Hélène Fleury, Hilary Horrocks, Ken Knabb, and Naomi Sager (Oakland: AK Press, 2010).
81  Kenneth M. Roberts, *Deepening Democracy: The Modern Left and Social Movements in Chile and Peru* (Stanford: Stanford University Press, 1998), 259–60.
82  Alex de Jong, "Muddying the Revolution," *Jacobin*, September 2, 2018, <jacobin.com/2018/09/community-party-philippines-sison-ndf-murder>.
83  For example, on the CPC from 1957 into the 1980s, see Norman Penner, *Canadian Communism: The Stalin Years and Beyond* (Toronto: Methuen, 1988), 250–66; on the CPUSA, see Michael Goldfield, "100 Years of American Communism," *Jacobin*, December 10, 2019, <jacobin.com/2019/12/communist-party-usa-history>; on the NCM in the US, see Elbaum, *Revolution in the Air*.
84  Draper, "Two Souls," 33.
85  For a good critical overview of the CPUSA, see Goldfield, "100 Years." As this

article shows, the early contributions made by CPs, while uneven, were generally less flawed than they became after the Stalinist leadership of the CPSU imposed tight control on all Comintern affiliates from the late 1920s on.
86  See Raine, "Left Fukuyamaism."

## CHAPTER 8

1   Ngo Van Xuyet, "Ancient Utopia and Peasant Revolts in China" (2004), *libcom.org*, published September 12, 2012, <libcom.org/article/ancient-utopia-and-peasant-revolts-china-ngo-van-xuyet>.
2   Ian Birchall, *The Spectre of Babeuf*, 2nd ed. (Chicago: Haymarket Books, 2016), 151, 156, 194.
3   Barbara Taylor, *Eve and the New Jerusalem: Socialism and Feminism in the Nineteenth Century* (London: Virago Press, 1983), 17. On the significance of Thompson and Wheeler's ideas, see Susan Ferguson, *Women and Work: Feminism, Labour and Social Reproduction* (London and Toronto: Pluto Press and Between the Lines, 2020), 43–47.
4   Draper, "Two Souls."
5   Cinzia Arruzza, *Dangerous Liaisons: The Marriages and Divorces of Marxism and Feminism* (Pontypool: Merlin Press in association with Resistance Books and the IIRE, 2013); Tithi Bhattacharya, ed., *Social Reproduction Theory: Remapping Class, Recentring Oppression* (London: Pluto Press, 2017); Arun Kundnani, *What is Antiracism? And Why It Means Anticapitalism* (London: Verso, 2023); Peter Drucker, *Warped: Gay Normality and Queer Anticapitalism* (Chicago: Haymarket Press, 2014); Jules Joanne Gleeson and Elle O'Rourke, eds., *Transgender Marxism* (London: Pluto Press, 2021).
6   David Camfield, "How Should Socialists Think About Tradition?," *Tempest*, April 9, 2024, <tempestmag.org/2024/04/how-should-socialists-think-about-political-tradition/>.
7   The phrase forms the title of Victor Serge, *Midnight in the Century*, trans. Richard Greeman (New York: New York Review of Books, 2014).
8   Donna T. Haverty-Stacke, *Trotskyists on Trial: Free Speech and Political Persecution Since the Age of FDR* (New York: New York University Press, 2015).
9   Leslie Goonewardene, "A Short History of the Lanka Sama Samaja Party" (1960), <marxists.org/history/etol/writers/goonewardene/1960/lssp.htm>. At this time the LSSP was led by Trotskyists but contained a Stalinist minority. In 1940, the former expelled the latter.
10  Alex de Jong, "Being Brave Because It is Right," *Jacobin*, April 13, 2017, <jacobin.com/2017/04/henk-sneevliet-marx-lenin-luxemburg-front-indonesia-communists-internationalism>; Nathaniel Flakin, *Martin Monath: A Jewish Resistance Fighter Among Nazi Soldiers* (London: Pluto Press, 2019); Van, *In the Crossfire*, 131.
11  "Marielle Presente!," *International Viewpoint*, July 30, 2018, <internationalviewpoint.org/spip.php?article5630>.
12  Aleksei Gusev, "The 'Bolshevik Leninist' Opposition and the Working Class, 1928–1929," in *A Dream Deferred: New Studies in Russian and Soviet Labour History*, eds. Donald Filtzer et al. (Bern: Peter Lang, 2008), 153–69; Aleksei Gusev, "The Left of the Left: The Democratic Centralists in the Anti-Stalinist

Opposition" (unpublished manuscript, n.d.); Susan Weissman, *Victor Serge: The Course is Set on Hope* (London: Verso, 2001), 210–23; Volodarsky, *Stalin's Agent*, 214–91.

13 *Harry Wicks: A Memorial* (London: Socialist Platform, 1989), 14, 15.
14 See Birchall, *Workers Against*, 79–97; Eley, *Forging Democracy*, 329–36.
15 Alexander Bittelman, *Trotsky the Traitor* (New York: Workers Library Publishers, 1937). <stars.library.ucf.edu/cgi/viewcontent.cgi?article=1495&context=prism>.
16 Haverty-Stacke, *Trotskyists on Trial*, 79.
17 W. Wainwright, "Clear Out Hitler's Agents! An Exposure of Trotskyist Disruption Being Organized in Britain" (1942), <marxists.org/history/international/comintern/sections/britain/clear-them-out/index.htm>.
18 Chris Harman, *The Fire Last Time: 1968 and After* (London: Bookmarks, 1988), 107.
19 Bryan D. Palmer, *James P. Cannon and the Emergence of Trotskyism in the United States, 1928–38* (Leiden: Brill, 2022), 72–96.
20 See the dossier of articles on this strike in *Revolutionary History* 2, no. 1 (Spring 1989), <marxists.org/history/etol/revhist/backissu.htm>.
21 Some examples in the US are mentioned in *Against Violence in the Workers Movement*, Education for Socialists (New York: Socialist Workers Party National Education Department, 1974).
22 Pierre Broué and Raymond Vacheron, *Meurtres au Maquis* (Paris: Grasset, 1997); Loukas Karliaftis, "Stalinism and Trotskyism in Greece (1924–1949)," *Revolutionary History* 3, no. 3 (Spring 1991), <marxists.org/history/etol/revhist/backiss/vol3/no3/staltrot.html>.
23 David G. Marr, *Vietnam: State, War, and Revolution (1945–1946)* (Berkeley: University of California Press, 2013), 409.
24 On Engels, see Darren Roso, "Engels After Marx: A (Critical) Defence," *Marxist Left Review* 26 (2023), <marxistleftreview.org/articles/engels-after-marx-a-critical-defence/>.
25 This is Engels' slight rephrasing of Marx's classic formulation. See Hal Draper, "The Principle of Self-Emancipation in Marx and Engels," *Socialist Register* (1971): 81–109, <marxists.org/archive/draper/1971/xx/emancipation.html>.
26 Hal Draper, *Karl Marx's Theory of Revolution, vol. 3, The "Dictatorship of the Proletariat"* (New York: Monthly Review Press, 1986), 1.
27 Draper, *"Dictatorship of the Proletariat,"* 11, 26.
28 Marx, *Civil War*, 72.
29 William Morris, "Looking Backward," *Commonweal* 5, no. 180 (June 22, 1889), <marxists.org/archive/morris/works/1889/commonweal/06-bellamy.htm>.
30 Rosa Luxemburg, "The Russian Revolution," in *Rosa Luxemburg Speaks*, ed. Mary-Alice Waters (New York: Pathfinder Press, 1970), 393–94.
31 Luxemburg, "What Does."
32 Luxemburg, "What Does."
33 Rosa Luxemburg, "Against Capital Punishment," in *Rosa Luxemburg Speaks*, ed. Mary-Alice Waters (New York: Pathfinder Press, 1970), 399.
34 On Korsch, see Darren Roso, "Weimar's Marxist Heretic: Reading Karl Korsch Today," *Spectre*, January 14, 2022, <spectrejournal.com/weimars-marxist-heretic/>.
35 Colombo, "Sapronov and the Russian"; Gusev, "Left of the Left"; Pirani, *Russian Revolution*; Simon Pirani, ed., *Communist Dissidents in Early Soviet*

36 See Marot, *October Revolution*, 90–98.
37 Marot, *October Revolution*, 89.
38 Marot, *October Revolution*, 98–105.
39 Linden, *Western Marxism*, 63–69.
40 See Molyneux, *Leon Trotsky's*, 40–46, 144–63.
41 Joel Geier, "Zinovievism and the Degeneration of World Communism," *International Socialist Review* 93 (2014), <isreview.org/issue/93/zinovievism-and-degeneration-world-communism/index.html>.
42 Andy Durgan, "Marxism, War and Revolution: Trotsky and the POUM," *Revolutionary History* 9, no. 2 (2006), <marxists.org/history/etol/document/spain/Durgan-Trotsky-and-POUM.pdf>.
43 Claudin, *Communist Movement*, 224.
44 Pietro Basso, "Introduction: Yesterday's Battles and Today's World," in *The Science and Passion of Communism: Selected Writings of Amadeo Bordiga (1912–1965)*, ed. Pietro Basso (Chicago: Haymarket Books, 2021), 71.
45 See the material available at matzpen.org.
46 Joel Geier, "Trotskyism Confronts World War II: The Origins of the International Socialists," *Marxist Left Review*, February 15, 2022, <marxistleftreview.org/articles/trotskyism-confronts-world-war-ii-the-origins-of-the-international-socialists/>; Duncan Hallas, "Introduction to *Origins of the International Socialists*" (London: Pluto Press, 1971), <marxists.org/archive/hallas/works/1971/xx/introis.htm>.
47 These authors include Colin Barker, Hal Draper, Samuel Farber, and Mike Haynes.
48 On the limits of Trotskyism, see David Camfield, "A Letter About Trotskyism," June 6, 2011, *Prairie Red*, <prairiered.ca/archive/a-letter-about-trotskyism>; David Camfield et al., "A Letter from Canadian Comrades," March 21, 2019, *SocialistWorker.org*, <socialistworker.org/2019/03/21/a-letter-from-canadian-comrades>.
49 David Camfield, "The Two Souls of CLR James's Socialism," *Critique* 29, no. 1 (2001), 159–78; Kent Worcester, *CLR James: A Political Biography* (New York: State University of New York Press, 1996), 83–99.
50 Marcel van der Linden, "*Socialisme Ou Barbarie*: A French Revolutionary Group (1949–65)," *Left History* 5, no. 1 (1998): 7–37.
51 Worcester, *CLR James*, 126.
52 Zeilig, *A Revolutionary*, 33–36; Sojourner Truth Organization: 1969–1986, <sojournertruth.net/>; Steve Wright, *Storming Heaven: Class Composition and Struggle in Italian Autonomist Marxism* (London: Pluto Press, 2002).
53 Linden, *Western Marxism*, 36–43.
54 Group of International Communists, *Fundamental Principles of Communist Production and Distribution* (1930). <marxists.org/subject/left-wing/gik/1930/01.htm>.
55 Eley, *Forging Democracy,*, 95.
56 Daniel Guérin, *Anarchism: From Theory to Practice*, trans. Mary Klopper (New York: Monthly Review Press, 1970), 74.
57 Michael Schmidt and Lucien van der Welt, *Black Flame: The Revolutionary Class Politics of Anarchism and Syndicalism* (Oakland: AK Press, 2009), 89, 91, 128–38.

58 Alexander Berkman, *What is Anarchism?* (Edinburgh: AK Press, 2003), 156.
59 Stuart Christie, *We, the Anarchists! A Study of the Iberian Anarchist Federation (fai), 1927–1937* (Hastings and Petersham North: The Meltzer Press and Jura Media, 2000); Agustin Guillamon, *The Friends of Durruti Group: 1937–1939*, trans. Paul Sharkey (Edinburgh: AK Press, 1996).
60 Charlie Post and Kit Adam Wainer, *Socialist Organization Today* (2006), <solidarity-us.org/sot/>.
61 Antonio Gramsci, *Selections from the Prison Notebooks*, trans. Quintin Hoare and Geoffrey Nowell Smith (New York: International Publishers, 1971); José Carlos Mariatégui, *Seven Interpretive Essays on Peruvian Reality* (1928), trans. Marjory Urquidi, <marxists.org/archive/mariateg/works/7-interpretive-essays/index.htm>; Salar Mohandesi, "Class Consciousness or Class Composition?," *Science & Society*, 77, no. 1 (2013): 72–97. <jstor.org/stable/41714416>; and Wright, *Storming Heaven*; Lise Vogel, *Marxism and the Oppression of Women: Toward a Unitary Theory* (Chicago: Haymarket Books, 2014); Asad Haider, *Mistaken Identity: Race and Class in the Age of Trump* (London: Verso, 2018); Kevin Ochieng Okoth, *Red Africa: Reclaiming Revolutionary Black Politics* (London: Verso, 2023); The Red Nation, *The Red Deal: Indigenous Action to Save Our Earth* (Brooklyn: Common Notions, 2021).
62 These include some anti-capitalist anti-racist feminists, for example Emma Dabiri, *What White People Can Do Next: From Allyship to Coalition* (n.p.: Penguin Books, 2021), and supporters of internationalism from below such as those involved with The Peoples Want (thepeopleswant.org), only some of whom are communists.

# CHAPTER 9

1 On an introduction to events in China in 1989, see Ruckus, *Communist Road*, 103–9.
2 Colin Cremin, *Totalled: Salvaging the Future from the Wreckage of Capitalism* (London: Pluto Press, 2015), 28.
3 David Camfield, "What Happened to the Workers' Movement?," *Salvage*, January 9, 2018, <salvage.zone/what-happened-to-the-workers-movement/>.
4 Alan Sears, *The Next New Left: A History of the Future* (Halifax: Fernwood Publishing, 2014), 2.
5 Gordon and Webber, "The Authoritarian Disposition," 43.
6 These are all widely reported conclusions of ecological research. I touch on the issues in David Camfield, *Future on Fire: Capitalism and the Politics of Climate Change* (Oakland: PM Press, 2022).
7 See Simon Pirani, "Social and Ecological Crisis: It's About Living Differently," *People and Nature* (blog), September 20, 2021, <peopleandnature.wordpress.com/2021/09/21/social-and-ecological-crisis-its-about-living-differently/>.
8 George Monbiot, "Private Sufficiency, Public Luxury," ISEE-ESEE-Degrowth Joint Conference 2021, streamed live on July 17, 2021, YouTube video, <youtube.com/watch?v=KWRRPed4Ds0>. On ecological communism, see Camfield, *Future on Fire*, 69–75.
9 For example, on capitalism and the world today, see Alex Callinicos, *The New Age of Catastrophe* (Cambridge: Polity Press, 2023).

10   Ed Rooksby, "Review of Mark Fisher's *Capitalist Realism: Is There No Alternative?*," Ed Rooksby, June 6, 2012, <edrooksby.wordpress.com/2012/06/10/review-of-mark-fishers-capitalist-realism-is-there-no-alternative/>.
11   Alan Milchman, "Marxism and the Holocaust," *Historical Materialism* 11, no. 3 (2003): 104.
12   One book that emphasizes this variation is David Graeber and David Wengrow, *The Dawn of Everything: A New History of Humanity* (London: Penguin Books, 2022), although from the perspective of reconstructed historical materialism it can certainly be criticized — see, for example, Nancy Lindisfarne and Jonathan Neale, "All Things Being Equal," *The Ecologist*, December 17, 2021, <theecologist.org/2021/dec/17/all-things-being-equal>; Peter Kulchyski, "Everything Goes: Three Problems With *The Dawn of Everything*. A Review of *The Dawn of Everything* by David Graeber and David Wengrow," *Historical Materialism*, accessed October 31, 2023, <historicalmaterialism.org/book-review/everything-goes-three-problems-with-dawn-everything-review-dawn-everything-david>.
13   See Callinicos, *Making History*.
14   Leon Trotsky, *Stalin: An Appraisal of the Man and His Influence*, 2nd ed. (London: MacGibbon and Kee, 1968), 412. Although Trotsky was referring to what he thought would have happened if the Bolsheviks had not taken power in 1917, I think his suggestion applies to this scenario, too.
15   Milchman, "Marxism and the Holocaust," 99.
16   Milchman, "Marxism and the Holocaust," 99.
17   Ernst Bloch, *The Principle of Hope*, trans. Neville Plaice, Stephen Plaice, and Paul Knight (Oxford: Basil Blackwell, 1986), 232, 231.
18   Benjamin Selwyn, *The Global Development Crisis* (Cambridge: Polity Press, 2014), 204.
19   Friedrich Engels, "The Principles of Communism," *Selected Works, Volume One*, trans. Paul Sweezy (Moscow: Progress Publishers, 1969), 81–97, <marxists.org/archive/marx/works/1847/11/prin-com.htm>.
20   Martin Thomas, "Stalinism and State Capitalism," *Workers' Liberty*, February 22, 2005, <workersliberty.org/story/2005-02-22/stalinism-and-state-capitalism>.
21   Aaron Benanav, *Automation and the Future of Work* (London: Verso, 2020), 89.
22   Kohei Saito, *Marx in the Anthropocene: Towards the Idea of Degrowth Communism* (Cambridge: Cambridge University Press, 2022), 231.
23   Ernest Mandel, Introduction to "Results of the Immediate Process of Production," in Karl Marx, *Capital: A Critique of Political Economy, vol. 1*, trans. Ben Fowkes (New York: Vintage Books, 1977), 946.
24   Mandel, Introduction.
25   One of the more accessible recent discussions of democratic planning is Aaron Benanav, "How to Make a Pencil," *Logic* 12 (December 20, 2020), <logicmag.io/commons/how-to-make-a-pencil/>.
26   Hal Draper, *Karl Marx's Theory of Revolution, vol. 2, The Politics of Social Classes* (New York: Monthly Review Press, 1978), 47–48.
27   Draper, *The Politics of Social Classes*, 40–48. On the working class today, see Camfield, *We Can*, 57, 59–62, 100–8. See also Michael A. Lebowitz, *Beyond Capital: Marx's Political Economy of the Working Class*, 2nd ed. (Basingstoke: Palgrave Macmillan, 2003).

28  Daniel Bensaïd, *Le Pari Mélancolique* (Paris: Fayard, 1997), 291. Translation of this line by Raghu Krishnan.
29  See Barker, *Revolutionary Rehearsals*.
30  See Colin Barker, Gareth Dale, and Neil Davidson, eds., *Revolutionary Rehearsals in the Neoliberal Age* (Chicago: Haymarket Books, 2021).
31  Colin Barker, "Social Movements and the Possibility of Socialist Revolution," in *Revolutionary Rehearsals in the Neoliberal Age*, eds. Colin Barker, Gareth Dale, and Neil Davidson (Chicago: Haymarket Books, 2021), 64.
32  For critiques of some such non-radical politics, see Haider, *Mistaken Identity*; Cinzia Arruzza, Tithi Bhattacharya, and Nancy Fraser, *Feminism for the 99%: A Manifesto* (London: Verso, 2019); Camfield, *Future on Fire*.
33  Neil Davidson, "The Actuality of the Revolution," in *Revolutionary Rehearsals in the Neoliberal Age*, eds. Colin Barker, Gareth Dale, and Neil Davidson (Chicago: Haymarket Books, 2021), 345.
34  Davidson, "The Actuality of the Revolution" (with italics removed).
35  Davidson, "The Actuality of the Revolution," 357–62. On global heating and revolution, see Andreas Malm, "Revolution in a Warming World: Lessons from the Russian to the Syrian Revolutions," *The Bullet*, April 23, 2018, <socialistproject.ca/2018/04/revolution-in-a-warming-world/>.
36  M.E. O'Brien and Eman Abdelhadi, *Everything for Everyone: An Oral History of the New York Commune, 2052–2072* (Brooklyn: Common Notions, 2022). I recommend this thoughtful and original piece of speculative fiction, which I find plausible in many ways, although I do not share the communization theory that informs it (see note 52 to Chapter 1) and see the minimal role of workplace struggle in its imagined revolutionary future as a flaw.
37  Terry Eagleton, *Hope Without Optimism* (Charlottesville: University of Virgina Press, 2015), 48, 43.
38  Ian Angus, "The Origin of Rosa Luxemburg's Slogan 'Socialism or Barbarism,'" *Climate and Capitalism*, October 22, 2014, <climateandcapitalism.com/2014/10/22/origin-rosa-luxemburgs-slogan-socialism-barbarism/>.
39  Bensaïd, *Le Pari*.
40  Bensaïd, *Le Pari*, 294 (my translation).
41  Bensaïd, *Le Pari*, 287.
42  See Tim Goulet, "Unions and the Rank and File Strategy: Socialists in the Labor Movement," *Tempest*, July 18, 2023, <tempestmag.org/2023/07/unions-and-the-rank-and-file-strategy/>.
43  Isabelle Garo, *Communism and Strategy: Rethinking Political Mediations*, trans. Gregory Elliott (London: Verso, 2023), 256.
44  Davidson, "The Actuality," 357.
45  Luxemburg, "What Does."
46  Brinton, "As We See It."
47  See Barker, "Social Movements," 29–31.
48  Rosa Luxemburg, "Marxist Theory and the Proletariat," *Vorwarts*, no. 64 (March 14, 1903), trans. Christian Fuchs, <marxists.org/archive/luxemburg/1903/03/14-abs.htm>.
49  Luxemburg, *Reform or Revolution*, 21.

# INDEX

abortion, 27, 43, 65
actually existing socialism (AES),
  critiques of, 17–18, 80, 93, 96–7, 133
  depictions of, 6–7, 17–18, 52, 81, 84, 99
  marxist narratives and, 45, 87, 92, 115, 123–4, 136
  skepticism about sources on, 3, 17, 19
  uncritical supporters of, 9–10, 16–18, 73, 81, 93
  use of term, 5–6
AES societies, 47, 49, 68
  alienation in, 85, 94, 103–5
  analyses of, 10, 52–4, 59–61, 69–72, 82–6
  bureaucracy/Stalinism and, 91, 97–100, 120–2, 127, 165n47
  capitalism in, 29, 54–5, 61, 94–8, 128, 164n44, 165n45
  conceptions of socialism/communism in, 14–18, 91
  conflict between, 48, 54–7, 60, 67–9, 94, 102
  costs of, 42–5, 62–6, 79–80, 84
  dubious portrayals of, 18, 54, 77–8, 86–9
  exploitation as integral to, 35, 42, 52–3, 66, 69–71, 79–80, 84–5
  features of, 7–8, 26, 41–3, 51, 59, 80, 85, 96–9
  industrialization in, 42–5, 49–52, 69–72, 85–8, 95–6
  Marxism-Leninism and, 67–8, 99, 102–8, 116–17, 122–4
  objections defending, 86–93
  repression in, 35, 39–44, 49–53, 64–6, 77, 90–6, 99
  restructuring of, 52, 57–60, 66–7, 69–71, 97
  social relations in, 15–16, 25, 32, 52–3, 82–5, 93–7
  transitions to communism (or not), 36, 87–91, 93–4, 99–100, 127, 133

USSR involvement with, 45–8, 113, 119, 126
African National Congress (ANC), 105–6
agriculture, 22, 73, 83, 134
  collectivization of, *see* collectivization
  environmental damage from, 44–5, 55, 64
  industrial impacts of slow growth in, 42, 58, 64
  state control over, 32, 39–40, 58
  workers, 42, 55, 62–5, 70
  *see also* farming; peasants
Aguado Hernandez, Raymar, 80, 84
alienation,
  AES social relations of, 85, 94, 103–5
  in China, 59, 70–2
  societal transcendence of capitalist, 13–14, 123, 128, 132, 142
  in USSR, 31, 34, 49–52
  workers', 31, 34, 49–52, 70, 84, 138
Allende, Salvador, 106
anarchist communists, 100, 130–1, 167n22
anarchists, 30, 47, 103–4, 121
Angola, 68
anti-anti-communism, 164n30
  growth of, 6, 8–9
  perspective of, 5–7, 9
anti-Bolshevik anti-Stalinists, 129;
  *see also* pro-Bolshevik anti-Stalinists
anti-capitalism,
  critiques of AES, 17, 82
  Marxism-Leninism and, 99–100, 115–17
  visioning societal, 7–8, 10, 114–15, 141–2
anti-capitalist sentiments, 133
  adulteration by AES, 99–100, 120
  as anti-anti-communist, 5
  challenges to, 7, 119–22
anti-communist arguments, 77, 162n4
  criticisms of AES and, 17, 20–1, 86, 97–9

dubious, 2–5, 17–19, 36, 39
  questioning, 5; *see also* anti-anti-communism
  responding to, 10, 86–9, 96–7
anti-communist measures, 2, 4, 120, 129
anti-imperialist struggles, 104, 108, 113, 126
  CPSU versus CCP/Cuban, 55, 67–8, 81–2, 103
anti-racist feminist marxism, 10–11, 174n62
anti-Stalinism, 19
  anti-Bolshevik, 129
  communist, 119–22, 125–7 131–2, 141–2
  marxist, 20, 47, 83, 91, 121, 125
  pro-Bolshevik, *see* pro-Bolshevik anti-Stalinists
Australia, 1, 3, 110–11; *see also* New South Wales Building Labourers Federation (NSW BLF)
authoritarianism, 9
  party-state, 47, 51, 70–1, 84, 87
autocracy, 23, 29, 122

Banaji, Jairus, 112–13
Batista, Fulgencio, 74–6
Beleaguered Fortress, 28, 30, 102
Bensaïd, Daniel, 101–2, 139, 141, 144
Berkman, Alexander, 130
biodiversity loss, 2, 45
*Black Book of Communism*, 3, 17–18
Bloch, Ernst, 136–7
Bolsheviks, 57, 129
  amid Civil War, 26–31, 33–6
  governance beliefs, 29–30, 102
  revolutionary role, 23–5, 45, 123
  Stalin's killing of, 18, 43
  *see also* pro-Bolshevik anti-Stalinists
bourgeoisie, 63, 92
  governance by, 105, 109, 162n7
  revolutions by, 29–30, 89, 127, 129, 142
Britain, 8, 100, 146n21
  colonial capitalism of, 12, 54, 120
  Soviet Union, relations with, 26, 31, 46–8, 149n66
  *see also* Communist Party of Great Britain; United Kingdom
Browder, Earl, 89

campism, 9, 114, 132
camps, 8, 39
  forced labour, 18, 44, 64–5, 80, 120, 158n57
Canada, 1, 3, 12, 26, 100;
  *see also* Communist Party of Canada
capitalism, 144
  AES as better than, 86, 91, 93–4, 133
  AES integration of, 29, 46–7, 54–5, 61, 68, 94–8, 128
  anti-anti-communism and, 6–10
  Comintern integration of, 46–7, 55–6, 104, 108, 126, 129
  destructiveness of, 1, 5, 8, 20, 91–2, 99, 133–5
  dubious portrayals of, 9–10, 19–20, 100, 114
  features of, 12–13, 94–6, 106–7, 114, 133–8
  lack of public support for, 1–2, 133–6
  Marxism-Leninism and, 101, 103–4, 107–8, 116–17
  possibility of breaking from, 7–8, 13–17, 91, 98–9, 118, 131–41
  productive forces of, 11–13, 89, 91–2, 95–6, 137
  reformism and, 105–9, 111–13
  state, 96, 101, 104, 123–9, 137, 139
  supporter demonization of communism, 2, 5
  *see also* anti-capitalist sentiments
capitalist democracies, 29, 47, 106, 119, 127–31, 134
capitalists,
  Chinese, 54–6, 61, 68, 72, 112–14
  collective, 91–2, 123
  Cuban control by US/sugar, 73–7, 83
  progressive, 104, 108–9, 111
  Tsarist Russian/USSR and, 22–4, 29, 34–5, 47, 90
  working class versus, 22–3, 55, 83, 90, 101, 124, 140
Carr, E.H., 18–19, 31
Castoriadis, Cornelius, 85, 128, 142
Castro, Fidel, 3, 76–7, 79, 81
Chattopadhyay, Paresh, 14
child care, 11, 35
  socialist approach to, 7, 41, 52, 63
Chile, 104, 106, 139

China,
  AES development in, 54, 56–64
  capitalist development in, 54–6, 59–61, 64–6, 68, 72, 112–14
  differences since Mao, 3, 6, 59, 69
  ecological destruction in, 64, 66
  foreign investment in, 54, 59
  geopolitical interests, 41, 56–7, 67–8
  industrialization of, 57–61, 63–4, 69–72
  leftist inspiration from, 6, 20, 54, 112, 118
  market Stalinism in, 59, 61, 64, 84–5, 164n44
  Nationalist Party, 48, 55–7, 60
  restructuring of, 57–60, 66–7, 69–71
  US tensions with, 2–3, 54, 56, 60, 68
  see also People's Republic of China (PRC)
Chinese Communist Party (CCP),
  collectivization, 58–9, 62–4
  Comintern relations with, 55, 67–8
  formation and achievements of, 55–6, 59–61, 66
  Great Leap Forward (GLF), 63, 69, 78, 164n44
  oppressive tactics of, 62–6, 69–72, 133
  party-state leadership, 58–71, 92, 95, 99, 114, 164n35
  People's Liberation Army (PLA), 56–7, 60, 64, 70
  USSR relations with, 46, 48, 54–7, 60, 67–9
  Uyghurs, oppression of, 65, 114
Chinese Revolution, 69–71, 76
Ciliga, Ante/Anton, 85, 162n4
class,
  concept of social, 32, 91–2
  divisions, 11, 15, 87, 92, 127
  exploitation, *see* class exploitation
  landlord, 22–3, 55, 57
  middle, 75–6, 106, 108
  peasant, 25, 34, 42, 139
  relations, 11, 42, 67, 85–6
  ruling, *see* ruling class
  struggle, 27, 55, 67–8, 93–4, 111–12, 131–4
  working, *see* working class
class exploitation,
  AES core structure of, 35, 42, 52–3, 66, 69–71
  communist vision of ending, 14–15, 118
  inability to recognize, 27–8, 34, 37, 87, 89–91
  (re)development of, 11, 19, 28, 32, 42, 124–5
  working-class rule versus, 24–30, 115–16, 122–4, 134, 139–43
class society, 101
  AES upholding, 23, 27–30, 85–6, 92, 124–8
  costs of, 42–5, 61–5, 79–80
  (lack of) transition to communism, 13–15, 88–90, 93, 122–3
Claudin, Fernando, 88, 109
climate change, 66
  capitalism and, 1–2, 99
  need for responses to, 1–2, 133–4, 140
climate Leninism, 103, 166n18
CNT-FAI (National Confederation of Labour-Iberian Anarchist Federation, Spain), 130–1
Cold War, 6–7, 105, 127, 129, 131
collectivization, 70–2, 130–1
  forced farm, 32, 39–42, 58–9, 62–4
colonialism, 4, 46, 97
  capitalist, 12, 73–4
  Chinese freedom from semi-, 59, 69, 71
  European, 12, 59, 69, 71
  leftist struggle against, 97, 119, 126–7
  settler, 12, 49, 108, 127, 132
  Trotskyist deaths amid French, 116, 120–1
Comintern, the, 121, 129–30
  CCP versus, 55–6, 67
  CPSU control of, 45–6, 48, 113, 119, 126
  creation and mobilizing of, 45, 47, 55–6, 103
  policies/tactics of, 88, 104, 108, 115
  Third Period of, 45–6, 111, 125–6
communism,
  AES breeding aversion to, 99–101
  anti-Stalinist, 119–22, 125–7 131–2, 141–2
  concepts of, 13–15
  democracy and, 3, 10, 13–15, 83, 108, 116–18, 131–2
  desirability of, 13–15, 53, 107, 118, 123–5, 142
  ecological, 135–6, 140–1
  leftist portrayals of, 13, 16–18, 84–6, 110, 121

relations of production in, 13, 15, 25, 92, 129, 135–7
societal transformation to, 13–17, 20, 87–90, 93, 122–3, 134
Stalinism, critques of, 5, 96–8, 99–100, 119
see also anti-anti-communism; anti-communist arguments
Communist Party of Australia (CPA), 110–11, 115
Communist Party of Canada, 104, 108, 110
Communist Party of Great Britain (CPGB), 48, 97, 110, 121
Communist Party of Greece (KKE), 111–12, 169n70
Communist Party of India (CPI), 48
  Maoist, 112–13
  Marxist split from, 105, 110
Communist Party of the Philippines (CPP), 113, 116
Communist Party of the Soviet Union (CPSU), 8
  CCP policies versus, 48, 55–7, 67–9, 94, 102
  claims of achieving communism, 14
  Comintern control, 45–8, 113, 119, 126
  critiques of, 3, 103–4
  industrialization of, 8, 25, 31–40, 52, 78, 83, 92
  lack of support for global revolutions, 45–9, 53, 55, 67–8, 81
  party-state leadership, 31–6, 38–45, 51, 85–6, 99
  as ruling layer, 36, 45, 102, 119–20, 125–6
  worker exploitation/repression by, 35, 40–2, 44, 149n66
Communist Party of the United States of America (CPUSA), 89, 108, 121
Connolly, James, 92
conspiracy theories, anti-communist, 3, 20, 77, 149n66
Council of People's Commissars (CPC), 25–6
counter-revolution, 15, 47, 136, 148n52
  modernizing, 35, 44, 47, 54
  in USSR, 26, 34–6, 43–4, 54, 63, 119
Cuba, 20
  Afro-Cubans' treatment in, 73, 79–80
  anti-anti-communism and, 6, 10

capitalists, 73–7, 83
class exploitation in, 77, 79–80, 84–5
colonial/US capitalist control of, 73–5, 77–9
global struggle involvement, 48, 81–2
July 26th Movement, 76, 78
mobilization economy, 83
nationalist populism in, 75–7
Platt Amendment, 73–5
Popular Socialist Party (PSP), 76–8, 82
private sector activity in, 79, 83–5
sugar production in, 73–8, 83
uncritical leftist support for, 93, 114, 131
USSR involvement with, 76–8, 80–2
women's treatment in, 75, 79–80
Cuban Revolution, 73–6
  party-state leadership, 77–83
Cultural Revolution (China), 58, 63–4, 67

Dale, Gareth, 35
Davidson, Neil, 140
democracy,
  assessment of AES society, 10, 15, 87–8
  capitalist, 29, 47, 106, 119, 127–31, 134
  communism and, 3, 83, 108, 116–18, 131–2
  concepts of, 101, 112–13, 115, 122
  economic, 15, 49–50, 100
  lack of, 10, 30–4, 57, 62, 83, 116
  "national," 104, 106
  organizing and, 115–17, 122–4, 131–2, 139–41
  participatory, 15, 26, 29, 123–4
  party leadership weakening, 22–8, 36, 69, 92, 106, 125
  political, 15, 29, 76, 100
  protests for, 47, 69, 76, 107–8, 114, 133
  social, 17, 45–6, 88, 100, 123, 126, 133
democratic control,
  in planning, 10, 15, 28, 49, 69–70, 135–9, 143
  radical, 77, 106–7, 111, 115–16
  soviet, 23–5, 27–9, 47, 107
  suspension/lack of, 30–4, 42, 57, 70–1, 83
  visions of communist, 10, 13–15, 101, 103–4
  workers'/peasants', 23–7, 29–32, 47, 94, 126
Deng Xiaoping, 58, 67–8

de Ste. Croix, G.E.M., 32
Deutscher, Isaac, 91, 164n30
dictatorships, 2, 62
   Cuba, 74–6, 82
   military, 24, 106, 136
   party-state, 24, 30, 42, 97, 131–2
   of the proletariat, 122, 124
divorce, 27, 43, 61, 65
Draper, Hal, 116, 118, 122, 144
Dunayevskaya, Raya, 49, 128

Eagleton, Terry, 140–1
Eastern Europe, 6, 58, 81
   anti-communism in, 4
   collapse of Communism/AES in, 2–3, 73, 78, 133
   USSR control of, 4, 46, 52, 127
ecological communism, 135–6, 140–1
ecological crisis/destruction,
   building AES and, 41, 44–5, 64, 66
   capitalism causing, 20, 99, 134–5
   lack of action on, 1–2, 14, 114–15
ecosocialism, 9–10, 103, 141, 166n18
education, 67, 93, 116
   AES access to, 38, 41, 52, 103
   in Cuba, 78–9
   women's, 7, 105
emancipation, human, 93
   global struggles for, 45, 121–3, 139
   self-, 103–4, 116, 122–3
   transformative goal of, 14, 21, 132
   women's, 42
Engel-Di Mauro, Salvatore, 9
Engels, Friedrich, 129
   AES versus, 87–8, 100, 122–3
   societal understandings, 10, 30, 89, 91–3, 103, 118
Ethiopia, 48–9, 82, 99
*Everything for Everyone* (O'Brien and Abdelhadi), 140
exploitation, 165n45
   AES built on, 35–6, 52–3, 66, 69–71, 79–80, 88
   class, 25, 52, 55, 64–6, 71
   concept of, 11, 49, 123
   gendered, 42–3, 79
   intensification of, 35–6, 40–2, 84–5
   struggles to end, 14, 22, 62, 93, 118, 126
   unions versus, 62, 64

famine/starvation, 2, 18, 26, 43–4, 63, 154n34
farming, 12
   collectivized, 32, 39, 58
   cooperative, 58, 164n34
   environmental impacts of, 44–5, 63, 64–6
   landlord exploitation in, 11, 55, 59, 64–5
   state control over, 22, 42–5, 58–9, 62–4
   *see also* agriculture
Farber, Samuel, 77, 81, 144
far-right forces, 2, 5, 20, 68, 123, 134; *see also* right-wing forces
fascism, 114, 121, 136, 169n75
   anti-communist critiques and, 3–4
   downplaying of, 45–6
   rising, 2, 4, 109, 134
   "social," 45, 88
   struggles against, 45–7, 119, 126–7, 131
Featherstone, Liza, 8
feudalism, 10–12, 28, 48, 54, 63, 129
Fitzpatrick, Sheila, 8, 38
food, 55, 134
   (lack of) access to, 1, 23, 63, 164n35
   shortages/rationing, 22–3, 26, 38
France, 26, 31, 46–7, 133
   colonialism, 12, 118, 120
   communist organizing in, 107–8, 120–1, 128–9
Fryer, Peter, 97–8

Garo, Isabelle, 141, 144
Garrido, Carlos, 86–8, 162n7
Geertz, Clifford, 7
gender, 14, 158n61
   equality/emancipation, 27, 61
   oppression, 42–3, 65, 79–80, 109, 132, 139
   relations, 11, 63, 79
   *see also* same-gender relations
geopolitical interests, 48, 68, 78, 115
   competition/ military defence and, 12, 40–1, 50–2, 94–5
Germany, 43, 96, 149n66
   Comintern policies toward, 46, 48, 88, 111, 125
   communist/revolutionary organizing in, 36, 46, 118, 123–4, 131
   struggles against Nazi, 4, 41, 46, 88, 125
   USSR alliance with, 46, 113, 127

USSR self-defence against, 4, 26, 41, 46–8, 51
Ghodsee, Kristen (*Why Women Have Better Sex under Socialism*), 6–9
Gonzalez, Lisbeth Moya, 84
Gordon, Todd, 134
Gramsci, Antonio, 132
Grau, Ramon, 74–5
Great Break (USSR), 86, 125
    AES/industrialization following, 35–6, 39–40, 57, 88, 92, 96–8
    development/process of, 20, 35–6, 38–40, 94
    harm caused by, 38–40, 43–4, 51–2
Great Depression, 38, 74
Great Leap Forward (GLF), 63, 69, 78, 164n44
Great Purge (USSR), 19, 43, 63, 162n4
Great Recession (2007–09): 2, 133–4
Greene, Douglas, 3, 17–18, 36
Gorbachev, Mikhail, 52
Guevara, Che, 77, 102, 115
Guyana, 82, 129

Hall Lujardo, Alexander, 84
Haynes, Mike, 49, 144
health care, access to, 3, 38, 41, 52, 61–2, 78
heterosexism, 63, 65, 79–80, 118
historical materialism, 16–17, 91; *see also* reconstructed historical materialism
House of Terror Museum (Budapest), 4
housing, 164n35
    accessible/building of, 3, 7, 41
    loss of/poor, 38–9, 138
Hudis, Peter, 14, 144
Hungary, 68
    revolution in, 47, 67, 97–8, 120

imperialism,
    AES and radical mobilizing against, 88–9, 98, 103–4, 108, 135
    British, 48
    Chinese, 52, 54–5, 114
    Cuba and, 75, 80–4
    opposition to Western/US, 9, 48–9, 58–60, 67–8, 113–14, 126
    *see also* anti-imperialist struggles
imperialized countries, 20, 75, 93, 134

India,
    Communist government in, *see* Communist Party of India (CPI)
    independence movements in, 48–9
Indigenous societies, 12
Indonesia, 4, 109, 145n7
industrialization, 15, 105, 135, 138
    analysis of AES, 42–5, 49–52, 69–72, 85–8, 95–6
    capitalist, 19, 22, 59
    Chinese, 57–8, 60–1, 63–4, 83
    USSR, 8, 25, 31–40, 52, 78, 83, 92
inflation, 1, 22, 56
internationalism, 126, 131–2, 174n62
Iran, 82, 114
Israel, 2, 49, 127

James, CLR (*Black Jacobins*), 128
Jameson, Fredric, 133–4
Japan, 26, 41, 54, 56, 59, 95–6
Jiang Jieshi, 55–7

Khruschev, Nikita, 14, 41, 120
Kim Yong-uk, 60, 95
Korsch, Karl, 125, 129
Kouvelakis, Stathis 111–12
Kuron, Jacek, 42, 90

labour, 101
    alienated, 49–52, 70, 84, 94, 123, 128
    capitalist relations of, 12, 22, 38–40, 69–70, 118
    dead/living, 50, 95
    exploitation, 11–12, 38–40, 84–5, 143
    forced, 18, 32, 44, 64–5, 80
    productivity, 12, 51–2, 61, 94–6, 137
    reproductive/unpaid, 11, 42–3, 62–3, 80; *see also* social reproduction
    revolutionary struggles of, 16, 25, 28, 78–9, 123, 138
    surplus, *see* surplus labour
land,
    dispossession, 12, 32–5, 40–3, 52, 62, 83, 92
    redistribution, 23, 57, 77, 105, 109
    rights, 23
    seizure of, 23, 28, 77
landlords,
    in AES, 57, 69

exploitation by, 11, 55
government support for, 23–4, 34, 57
peasant antagonism with, 22–3, 55
Tsarist Russian, 22–4
leftists, 23, 126
on AES, 54, 84–6, 91, 96–7, 103–4, 120
anti-anti-communism and, 6–9
on communism, 13, 16–18, 84–6, 110, 121
on Cuba, 73–6, 81, 84, 86
repression/limitations of, 2, 90, 100, 110–12, 116, 125
Lenin, Vladimir, 3
Bolshevik leadership, 23–4, 167n22
theoretical contributions of, 30, 101–4, 114, 124
Lewin Moshe, 39, 41, 50–1, 53
Lewis, Sophie, 7–8
liberation struggles,
Chinese support for, 41, 56–7, 67–8
lack of USSR support for, 45–9, 53, 55, 67–8, 81
organizing for, 45–9, 67, 97, 108–9, 112–13
Liebman, Marcel, 26
life expectancy, 41, 61, 78, 90
Loach, Ken (*Land and Freedom*), 127
Luxemburg, Rosa, 87, 100, 141
on democracy, 30, 101, 103
on socialist/communist revolution, 15–16, 53, 107, 123–5, 142

Machado, Gerardo, 74
Malaysia, 67
Mandel, Ernest, 138
Mao Zedong, 90, 115
China today versus under, 3, 6, 59
governance of China, 48, 56–7, 61, 67–8, 95, 102
harmful policies of, 58, 60–4, 70–2, 99
Mariátegui, José Carlos, 132
markets, capitalist, 101
AES openness to, 31, 54, 58–61, 69–70
communist/socialist challenges to, 3, 7, 13–15, 87
Cuban sugar production and, 74–5
government control versus, 49, 51–2, 65–6, 94
market Stalinism, 59, 61, 64, 84–5

Marx, Karl, 100
analysis of social realities, 10, 13–17, 101–3, 122–3
on relations of production, 50, 27–30, 91–2, 95
on working-class rule/democracy, 27–9, 87–9, 93, 101, 115–18, 128–9
marxism, 105, 121
AES narratives and, 45, 87, 92, 115, 123–4, 136
anti-anti-communism and, 6
anti-racist feminist, 10–11, 174n62
Bolsheviks', 30, 102, 125–6
"cultural," 5
Stalinism versus, 14, 20, 47, 83, 86, 91, 102
threads of, 125–6, 128–31, 132
Marxism-Leninism (ML), 18, 131
AES and, 67–8, 99, 102–8, 116–17, 122–4
democracy and, 113, 115–16, 118, 131–2
ideologies/critiques of, 73, 78, 100–3, 118–19
threads of, 102–8, 110–13
violence and, 48–9, 99, 113–16, 121
maternity leave, 39, 41
Mau, Søren, 13
McCarthyism, 3, 17
means of production, 35, 42, 90–2, 100
Meisner, Maurice, 60, 71–2
Menshevik Party, 23, 26
Mieville, China, 23, 144
military, 67, 102, 114, 120
conflicts, 2, 28, 35, 54–6, 74, 97
coups, 47–8, 75, 106, 109, 127, 130
dictatorship, 23–4, 106, 136
governance representation by, 23, 57, 62, 71, 107
industrial production for, 22–3, 40–1, 50–2, 60
resources directed to, 28–9, 33–6, 70, 81–3, 94, 137
violence, 75, 106, 109, 120, 133
mobilization economies, 49–52, 69–70, 83, 94
mode(s) of production, 30, 136
AES, 16, 40–2, 51, 58, 95
capitalist, 11–13, 95–6
egalitarian-communal, 12

feudal, 11–12
*see also* means of production; productive forces; relations of production
Modzelewski, Karol, 42, 90
Morris, William, 122–3, 148n53
Muslims, targeting of, 65

nationalism, 44
  Communist party, 108–9
  Cuban left-wing, 73, 75–7, 81
  fascist, 47–8, 68
  protests, 52, 55
  right-wing, 4
Nationalists, Chinese, 47–8, 55–60
nationalization, economic, 27–8, 77, 100, 107, 112
  Chinese, 58, 72
nature, rest of, 101
  AES building costs to, 41, 44–5, 64, 66, 114
  capitalist harm to, 12, 14, 99, 135, 140
  human conscious transformation of, 11, 140–1
  Indigenous vs. Euro-colonial relations with, 12
  repairing capitalist harm to, 14, 137, 140–1
  social metabolism with, 11, 135
  *see also* ecological crisis/destruction; ecosocialism
Nazis (Germany), 4, 41, 46, 88, 125
Nazism, 4, 146n17
New Communist Movement (NCM), 6, 121, 129
New Economic Policy (NEP), USSR, 31–2, 34–6
New Left, 6, 128–9
New South Wales Building Labourers Federation (NSW BLF), 111, 112
NKVD (People's Commissariat of Internal Affairs, USSR), 18–19, 47, 120, 125–7

*operaismo*, 129, 132

Palestine, 2, 49, 113, 127, 139–40
Parenti, Michael, 17–18, 86–8
Paris Commune, 27, 123, 140, 148n53
party-state leadership, 91–2, 96, 120, 152n80

Chinese Communist, 58–71, 92, 95, 99, 114, 164n35
Cuban, 79–83
Soviet, 31–6, 38–45, 51, 85–6, 99, 125
peasants, 76, 109
  appropriation of goods/labour from, 11, 28, 31–2, 34–7, 62, 69–71
  collectivization and, *see* collectivization
  deaths of, 18, 60–1
  dispossession of land, 32–5, 39–43, 52, 62, 83, 92
  landlord exploitation of, 11, 22–3, 55, 57–8, 65–6
  revolutionary movements, 47–8, 54–7, 79, 118, 126–7, 139
  soviets/democratic organizing of, 23–5, 35–6, 47–8, 57, 74, 103–5
  state/political interests versus, 23, 27–9, 39–40, 44, 55–6
People's Commissariat of Internal Affairs, USSR, *see* NKVD
People's Republic of China (PRC), 63
  analysis of AES in, 85, 92, 94–5
  bureaucratic rule of, 20, 69–70, 89, 95
  creation/achievements of, 57, 61, 164n35
  exploitation/violence by, 69–70, 79, 83, 92, 99
  global struggles, support for, 66–8
  mobilization economy, 69–70
Pirani, Simon, 33
planned economies,
  democratic, 10, 15, 28, 83, 69–70, 135–9, 143
  myths of AES, 49–50
Poland, 4, 46, 149n66, 154n24
popular front(s),
  Comintern policy of, 46, 104, 108, 125
  communist/ML strategy of, 47, 104, 108–10, 127, 132
Popular Front (Spanish government), 47, 108–9, 131
Portugal, revolution in, 47–8, 108
POUM (Workers' Party of Marxist Unification, Spain), 126–7
poverty, 87, 105, 118
  rural, 25–6, 55, 58
pre-capitalist societies, 13, 22, 126, 137
pro-Bolshevik anti-Stalinists, 125–8, 142
productive forces, 11, 25

analysis of AES, 85–7, 89, 91–2
Chinese development of, 61, 63, 66, 71
communism and, 12–13, 103
Cuban development of, 79, 83
potentialities of, 123, 137–8
USSR development of, 30–1, 35–6, 40–1
*see also* means of production; mode(s) of production; relations of production
proletariat, the,
AES organizing narratives of, 50, 85
dictatorships of the, 92, 124
revolutionary organizing, 16, 24, 122, 124, 127, 143
surplus-extracting states originating from, 28–9, 32, 136
purity fetishism, 17, 86–7

Qing dynasty, 54–5, 60, 71s
queer people, 5, 27, 65, 79–80, 133, 158n61; *see also* trans people

Rabinowitch, Alexander, 29
race, relations of, 11, 14, 43, 80, 109
racism, 88
experiences of, 43, 63, 65, 80
official state opposition to, 43, 79, 118, 133
struggles against, 63, 97, 132, 139
radical left, 6, 23, 133
Raine, Barnaby, 9
reconstructed historical materialism, 10–11, 13, 21, 84
relations of production,
AES, 25, 32, 52, 57, 78, 89–94
communist, 13, 15, 25, 92, 129, 135–7
exploitation in, 32, 34–5, 42–4, 62, 71
vertical vs. horizontal, 11, 94
*see also* means of production; mode(s) of production; productive forces
revolution, 118
Chinese Communist Party, 56–7, 61–2, 67–71, 76
counter-, *see* counter-revolution
CPSU resistance to further, 45–9, 53, 55, 67
Cuban, *see* Cuban Revolution
debates about AES, 87–8, 99–104, 107–8, 130–1, 136
German, 124, 131
Hungarian, 47, 67, 97–8, 120

international organizing for, 45–9, 67, 97, 108–9, 112–13
leftist/communist notions of, 13–16, 91–3, 126–8
Luxemburg's theorizing on, 15–16, 53–4, 107, 123–5, 142
Marx's theorizing on, 13–15, 101–4, 121–4
Russian, *see* Russian Revolution
social, 22, 46–8, 93, 117, 125–7, 130–1, 141–3
Stalinism versus, 99–100, 130–1
*see also* Cultural Revolution (China)
revolutionary conjunctures, 139–42
revolutionary Realpolitik, 142–3
right-wing forces, 1–2, 99, 119
attempted overthrows by, 47, 77
on communism, 4–6
revolutionary, 23, 25–6
*see also* far-right forces
Rodney, Walter, 82, 129
ruling class, 12, 132
leftist allying with, 102, 108–9, 114–15
loss of power/replacement of, 24, 61–2, 84, 125–7
industrialization policies, 30–1, 34–6, 40, 42–4, 49, 51
repression by, 42–4, 49, 65–6, 77, 90–4, 96
rise of Communist, 32–6, 40, 59, 86
ruling layer becoming, 32, 91, 102, 126
state bureaucracy of, 45, 59, 85–6, 90–4
rural communities, 94, 160
life expectancy/mortality rates, 41, 78
loss of land in, 62, 74
peasant organizing in, 23, 74–5
revolutionary rulers and, 56–8, 112
state exploitation of, 22–3, 35, 49, 54–5, 63, 70, 74
transformation of, 58–9
Russia, 2, 6, 82, 99
Bolsheviks in, *see* Bolsheviks
Great Break in, *see* Great Break (USSR)
leftist/communist support for, 89, 114, 120, 136
revolution in, *see* Russian Revolution
social reforms in, 27, 39, 89, 114
soviets in, *see* soviets
Tsarist, 22, 52
Ukraine invasion by, 44, 82, 114

Russian Revolution, 55, 123, 136, 144
    Civil War, 26–31, 33–6, 101–2, 126
    critiques of, 3, 8, 45, 89, 97, 129–31
    development of, 22–3, 43, 54, 73, 101, 139
    Provisional Government, 23–5

same-gender relations, 27, 63, 79–80
Sapir, Jacques, 49, 51
Sehon, Scott, 6–7
Seymour, Richard, 19
Shachtman, Max, 89, 92, 163n19
Singer, Daniel, 108
Smith, Steve, 23–4, 26
social democrats, 143
    denouncing of, 17, 45–6, 88
    governance (failures) by, 46, 88, 123
    reformism of, 100, 126, 133
socialism,
    from above/below, 118, 123
    actually existing, *see* actually existing socialism (AES)
    country claims of, 5, 31, 53–4, 58, 73
    denouncing of, 2–3
    eco-, *see* ecosocialism
    as ideal/beneficial economic system, 1, 6
    in one country, 31, 33, 45–6, 68, 126
    leftist debates on categorizing state, 7–10, 31, 84–7, 91–2, 97–8, 129
    party, 23, 25, 42, 76, 101, 119
    revolutionary, 24, 55, 77, 107, 122–7, 131–2
    societal, *see* AES societies
    state, 6–7, 9, 87, 90–1, 100–1
    struggle for, 29, 35, 87–8, 104–6, 116, 118
    as transition to communism, 14–17, 20, 87–9, 134
    women's rights under, 7–9
Socialism or Barbarism, 128, 141
socialist construction, industry as, 36–8, 42, 57–8, 69
socialist market economy, Chinese, 54, 58, 65
Socialist Revolutionaries (SRs, Russia), 23, 25–6, 30
social metabolism, 11, 135
social reproduction, 68, 80, 89, 164n35
soldiers, 73, 76, 81
    Chinese, 56, 67
    Russian Revolution, 22–4

sources on AES, skepticism about, 3, 17, 19
South African Communist Party (SACP), 105–6
Soviet Congress, 25–6
soviets, 36, 47, 107
    changes demanded by, 23, 25, 30
    creation of, 23–4
    power of, 24–9
    suppression/dissolution of, 26, 28–9, 32
Spain, 10, 12, 88, 126
    Cuba and, 73, 82
    revolutionary movements in, 47, 130–1
Spanish Civil War, 47, 108–9, 120, 126–7, 130–1
Sri Lanka, 68, 120
Stalin, Joseph, 51
    communist critiques of, 47, 85–7, 136
    lack of democracy, 33–4, 115
    leftist support for, 10, 31, 36, 88, 112–13
    policies of, 47–8, 88–9, 115
    socialism, development of, 14, 36, 52, 68, 97–8
Stalinism, 6, 118
    anti-communist critiques of, 3, 96–7
    communist critiques of, 5, 96–8, 99–100, 119
    harms committed in the name of, 19, 39, 43–4, 56, 119–22
    market, 57, 59–61, 64, 84–5, 164n44
    Marxism-Leninism and, 102–4, 115, 119
    transition to socialism/communism, 14, 19, 36, 52
    *see also* anti-Stalinism
state, the,
    agricultural control by, 32, 39–40, 42–5, 58–9, 62–4
    bureaucracy of, 45, 59, 85–6, 90–4
    exploitation by, 22–3, 35, 49, 54–5, 63, 70, 74
    peasants versus, 23, 27–9, 39–40, 44, 55–6
    promoting security of, 49, 51–2, 65–6, 94
    repression by, 35, 39–44, 49–53, 64–6, 77, 90–4, 96
state-owned enterprises, 28, 40, 57–9, 69, 90–2, 96
state power,
    AES society, 16, 18, 40, 49–53, 71, 100
    authoritarian, 9, 47, 51, 70–1, 84, 87
    capitalist, 96, 101, 103–4, 123–9, 137, 139

command-administrative, 28
surplus-extracting, 28–9, 31–2, 35, 136
transcendence of, 13–15, 87, 92, 116, 122–3, 132
state property objection, 91–2
state socialism, 6–7, 9, 87, 90–1, 100–1
strikes, 57, 106, 121
  general, 74, 76, 107–8
  suppression of, 51, 59, 79
students, 78
  living accommodations of, 41, 160n92
  protests by, 48, 55, 107–8
  support for striking workers, 108, 121
Sudan, 109
surplus labour,
  AES built from, 42, 62, 69, 79
  concept of, 11, 96
  lack of worker control over, 31, 90–1, 94–6
  state extraction of, 28–9, 32–4, 64, 136
  *see also* labour
Szymanski, Albert, 90, 92

Third World, 51, 88, 96, 103
  AES (lack of) support for liberation in, 48–8, 67, 81
Tibet, 63
totalitarianism, 2–4, 6, 17–18
trans people, 5, 65, 133, 140; *see also* queer people
Traverso, Enzo, 3–4
Trotsky, Leon,
  Bolshevik leadership, 23, 125, 152n77
  theorizing of, 36, 91, 103, 124–7, 136
Trotskyism, 119
  groups rejecting, 127–8
  orthodox, 91, 127–8
  theorizing of on AES, 91–2, 126
  suppression of, 116, 120–1, 126
Trump, Donald, 5–6

Ukraine,
  Russian invasion of, 82, 114
  Stalinist oppression of, 43–4, 154n34
unionized workers, 92
  Cuban, 75–6
  lack of, 112
  mobilizing by communist, 115–16, 119, 121, 129–30, 141

support for, 7, 106, 110–12
unions, 9, 134
  attempts to influence officials from, 110, 119
  formation of, 23, 59
  state control of, 27, 39, 44–5, 59, 62, 77–80, 83
United Kingdom, 1, 40, 133; *see also* Britain; Communist Party of Great Britain (CPGB)
United States, 128–9
  AES animosity toward, 56, 81–2, 113–15
  anti-capitalist sentiment in, 1, 103, 133
  anti-communist stance of, 2–4, 6–7, 105–6, 119
  Chinese relations with, 54–6, 60, 67–8, 95, 99, 114
  Communist Party of, *see* Communist Party of the United States of America (CPUSA)
  Cuba tension with, 73–7, 84
  imperialism of, 20, 48–9, 58–60, 67–8, 113–14, 126
  (neo)colonialism of, 12, 73–4
  USSR versus, 26, 41
urban areas,
  movement to, 39, 41, 44–5, 62, 74–5
  peasant exploitation to feed, 26, 28, 35, 40, 63–4
  revolutionary ruler policies and, 35, 40–4, 49, 57–9, 77
  standard of living in, 26, 38, 41
  state exploitation of, 22, 35, 42, 49, 55
  women in, 62–3
  workplace democracy in, 26–9, 94
USSR (Union of Soviet Socialist Republics),
  alienated labour in, 31, 34, 49–52
  capitalists in, 22–4, 29, 34–5, 47, 90
  CCP relations with, 46, 48, 54–7, 60, 67–9
  Central Committee (CC), 26, 33–4
  Civil War, 26–31, 33–6, 101–2
  counter-revolution in, 26, 34–6, 43–4, 54, 63, 119
  Cuba, involvement in, 76–8, 80–2
  Democratic Centralists (DCs), 125
  Gosplan/Gossnab, 50–1
  Eastern European control, 4, 46, 52, 127
  Germany, relations with, 4, 26, 41, 46–8, 51, 113, 127

industrialization of, 8, 25, 31–40, 52, 78, 83, 92
Left Opposition (LO), 33, 120, 125, 152n77
mobilization economy, 49–52
New Economic Policy (NEP), 31–2, 34–6
*nomenklatura* system, 34
United States versus, 26, 41
see also Great Break; Great Purge; NKVD; Russian Revolution
Uyghurs, oppression of, 65, 114
Venezuela, 5, 114
Vietnam, 6, 67, 118
  murder of Trotskyists/non-Communists in, 116, 120–1
violence, 124
  AES achievements and, 43–4, 119
  gendered, 65, 80–1
  Marxist-Leninist, 48–9, 99, 113–16, 121–2
  military/police, 75, 106–9, 120, 133
  party-state, 40, 47, 75, 79, 83, 92, 99
  settler colonial, 2, 12

wages, 31, 57, 74, 76–7, 143
  dependence on, 28, 62, 65, 70, 109, 164n35
  inflation versus, 1, 22, 38
  minimum, 75, 107
wage-workers, 11–12, 83, 92, 112
  rural/urban, 22, 55, 164n35
  women, 39, 79
Webber, Jeffery R., 134
women, 127
  education, 7, 41, 105
  independent mobilizing of, 40, 47–8, 80, 128
  labour force participation, 7, 35, 39, 42–3, 65, 79
  oppression of, 23, 42–3, 62–5, 79–80
  state socialist support for, 7, 9, 42–3, 61, 65, 75
Wood, Ellen Meiksins, 101
workers' councils, 36, 45, 128–9
  Russian Revolution, *see* soviets
working class,
  alienated labour of, 31, 34, 49–52, 70, 84, 138
  barriers to improved conditions for, 4, 9, 75, 108–9, 112
  capitalists versus, 22–3, 55, 83, 90, 101, 124, 140
  communist/democratic mobilizing and, 13, 36, 93, 101–2, 131–2
  exploitation of, 22–3, 32–5, 40–4, 49, 62–4, 70–1, 77–80
  lack of control by, 12, 28, 32, 42, 61–2
  parties (supposedly) representing, 29–30, 34–6, 76, 90, 108, 125–8
  power, 23, 25, 52–3, 104
  rule, 23–30, 115–16, 122–4, 134, 139–43
  Russian Tsarist, 22, 29
  societal reorganization, 25, 29, 40, 46, 57, 90–1
workplaces, 28, 41, 138
  Communist participation in, 111, 115, 120
  democratic self-management of, 23, 26–7, 30, 47, 106–8, 128, 143
  dual power, 23–5, 27
  lack of worker control in, 51, 70, 79, 84, 94, 101
World War I: 22, 38
World War II: 52, 56, 120, 131
  Comintern actions amid, 46, 113
  military equipment production in, 41, 94

Xi Jinping, 65, 89

Yiching Wu, 71
Ypi, Lea, 8

Zinoviev, Grigory, 125–6